HALF and HALF

HALF and HALF

Writers on Growing Up Biracial and Bicultural

Edited and with an introduction by

Claudine Chiawei O'Hearn

Pantheon Books | New York

FOR DAVID

All rights reserved under International and Pan-American Copyright
Conventions. Published in the United States by Pantheon Books,
a division of Random House, Inc., New York, and simultaneously in
Canada by Random House of Canada Limited, Toronto.

"Lost In Place" by Garrett Hongo was originally published in
L.A. Weekly in 1996.

"What Color Is Jesus?" by James McBride was originally published in
somewhat different form in *Washington Post Magazine* in 1988.

Library of Congress Cataloging-in-Publication Data

Half and half : writers on growing up biracial and bicultural / edited and
with an introduction by Claudine Chiawei O'Hearn.
p. cm.
ISBN 0-375-40031-1 (hardcover). — ISBN 0-375-70011-0 (paperback)
1. Children of interracial marriage—United States—Juvenile literature.
2. Racially mixed people—United States.
3. Multiculturalism—United States.   I. O'Hearn, Claudine Chiawei
HQ777.9.M65 1998
306.84'6—dc21   97-49597

Random House Web Address: http://www.randomhouse.com

Book design by Chris Welch

Printed in the United States of America
First Edition
2 4 6 8 9 7 5 3 1

CONTENTS

v

CONTENTS

INTRODUCTION

Claudine Chiawei O'Hearn

I was walking down the street the other day, on my way home from the gym, when a large woman with wiry hair run amok approached me, mumbling to herself and looking somewhat deranged, as only New Yorkers can look. As she neared me, she looked me in the eye and barked, "Half-breed bitch." I had already passed her by the time I figured out what she had said. Shocked, my first reaction was a mix of surprise and even pleasure: "How'd she know? What gave it away?" It wasn't until a block later that I became enraged and thought of a witty retort.

I stopped being American when I first came to the States to live eight years ago. Growing up in Asia, I knew being mixed set me apart, but I didn't have to name it until people began to ask, Where are you from? My father was raised in a working-class Irish American family in Fall River, Massachusetts. My mother was born near Shanghai, China, but when she was seven, on the eve of the communist revolution, she and her family fled to Taiwan. They met, romantically, and I think aptly, on an airplane (my mother was a flight attendant) and soon married—though not without first encountering resistance. My father's family were familiar with only stereotypes of Asian women, and so were not eager to invite China into the O'Hearn fold. My mother's family felt the same and took it a step further by hiring a private detective, who fortunately was unable to dig up anything incriminating about my father. Both sides eventually got over it, so we can laugh about it now, and frequently do. Following my mother's example, both of her sisters married Caucasians, creating a whole generation of hapas (Hawaiian for half) in our family.

My parents settled in Hong Kong, where I was born, and moved to Singapore, Belgium, and Ohio and finally settled in Taiwan. I consider these all to be home, with the exception of Akron, Ohio, where I experienced my first sting of racism when preschool classmates pushed me off playground slides, pulled tight their eyes, and idiotically chanted, "Ching, Chang, Chong, Chinese." Early learners. As coached by my mother, I retorted, "Chinese are better." But since these places are all home, they forfeit their definition as a single place I can come from. Suspended, I can go anywhere but home.

I don't look especially Chinese—my eyes are wide and lidded, and my hair has a Caucasian texture and color. When my mother and I walked together, people would stare, often rudely. I could see questions in their curious looks: "Is this your daughter?" We looked incongruous. It never occurred to me that my mother and I looked any more different than any other mother and daughter; and even if we did, that it would affect how we related to each other. I don't think I minded so much because I assumed that I would find a home in the States when I went there for college. To me, America was summer vacations; getting up at six in the morning to watch *Scooby Doo* and the rest of the Saturday morning cartoons; eating Pop Rocks and macaroni and cheese (which I would inhale in large amounts); and best of all, shopping at the mall. Coupled with what I saw in the movies, this was my small window into American life.

Because most people didn't know where to place me, I made up stories about myself. In bars, cabs, and restaurants I would try on identities with strangers I knew I would never meet again. I faked accents as I pretended to be a Hawaiian dancer, an Italian tourist, and even once a Russian student. It always amazed me what I could get away with. Being mixed inspired and gave me license to test new characters, but it also cast me as a foreigner in every setting I found myself in.

My brother looks Chinese—70 percent to my 30 percent. And though he might dispute this, I have always felt that he was more readily accepted as being Chinese. I resented him for the ease with which he could slip into the culture, whereas I had to constantly prove and explain myself. I remember how during Chinese New Year, as tradition, we would go from house to house, eating large meals, playing mah jong, and collecting red envelopes containing untold amounts of cash that would later be gambled away. I dreaded these occasions because I felt excluded, whereas my brother, it seemed, was welcomed. Questions about what he planned to do with his life, when was he going to find a girlfriend, etc., were asked of him, while I was mostly treated with polite comments about the style of my dress and carted off to watch TV. I'd sit in the corner, grumbling as I snacked on M&Ms and watermelon seeds and watched badly dubbed American movies. My parents were exasperated by my long face and didn't understand why I was bothered even as they had me pegged as the American one. My mother accused me of not dating Chinese guys as proof of my being Americanized. Of course when I did eventually date one, she didn't approve of him because he wore an earring, dressed all in black, and was known to smoke cigarettes. My decision to study in Ireland on a semester abroad rather than in China, a country I have yet to visit, seemed to further confirm my predilection. I defended my choice because it conveniently fit my English major and why wouldn't I want to explore my Irish heritage. Truthfully, I was afraid to go to China because it was foreign to me. This may seem absurd considering that I had been living in Taiwan for over ten years, but I knew it would require something of me that I was not prepared to give. I wasn't ready to take that journey yet. During the time I lived in Taiwan, China had seemed forbidding—I remember hearing stories about people we knew going and being detained for long periods of time. It wasn't until after I left for college that government restrictions preventing travel between the two countries were relaxed.

But then I would also benefit from the privileges of being an American. I remember how I would bypass long lines and the price of admission at nightclubs that welcomed foreigners, while my brother had to present a passport as proof of his citizenship. Even though I attended an international school, my friends fell into two groups—the Asians and the foreigners. The biracials blended in both directions, moving between the groups, though always somewhat outside each. Looking back, I think the distinctions came more into focus as we grew older. I remember once one of my American friends let slip a racial slur, something about irreputable, gold-digging Chinese women trying to trap Western men. Appalled, I pointed to my face—the product of such "unholy" joinings. She responded, "Oh, you're not *really* Chinese"—as though this were a plus.

When I came to the States for college, I became another sort of expatriate. Since I lacked the cultural tools necessary to roam undetected (knowledge of key television shows, important cultural references, even the subtle nuances of American English that you miss out on when you grow up abroad), I had to fake it and laugh at jokes I didn't get. Luckily I was familiar with *The Simpsons,* had seen almost every episode of *The Love Boat* on videotape, and vaguely knew who Howard Stern was. I got tired of hearing, "Oh, you wouldn't understand, you're not from here."

Toward the end of my first year, I went to hear Angela Davis speak. In making a point about the racism and inequality of the American educational system, she asked the white students to raise their hands if they had taken a course in black/Asian/etc. studies. A few proud students lifted their arms, and I was one of them. Then she asked the students of color to raise their hands if they had taken a course that focused on white/Western studies. Every one of them raised their hands, and the point was made. One was made for me as well, for I had hesitated, unsure whether to join them, although I wasn't sure why I assumed I belonged to the first group any more than the second. I ended up raising my hand for both, looking around to see if anyone noticed. I realized that although I had been making a point all year of letting people know that I was Chinese and enjoyed surprising them, I had learned to believe that I was American/white—I didn't differentiate. Could I be both, or did one trump the other?

It's easier to be white. To be Chinese, to be half Chinese, is work. I often find myself cataloguing my emotions, manners, and philosophies into Chinese and American, wary if the latter starts to outweigh the former. Three points Asia. How can I be Chinese if I prefer David Bowie to Chinese pop, if I can more easily pass as an American, if I choose to live in New York and not return to Asia where my family still lives, if English is my first language and Chinese remains a distant second? How can I be Chinese when I struggle to communicate with my grandparents? I am unable to tell them about friends, boyfriends, life-altering experiences, beliefs, new jobs—to tell them about my life and who I have become—and the result is they don't really know me. I'm ashamed to admit that there have been times I dreaded visiting them because of the humiliation of having to resort to hand gestures and second-grade Chinese.

And yet I play the part of a foreigner here all the time. I insist on not being American and tell people about the various customs that are foreign to me—Thanksgiving Day turkey and football, milk shakes, *It's a Wonderful Life* at Christmas, and fireworks on the Fourth of July. I remember once I got carded when I was an underage summer school student at Tufts University trying to get a drink at a T.G.I. Fridays in Boston. Undaunted, I decided to try a different tactic and responded, in exchange-student-accented English, "Ah, we do not have IDs in China. I do not understand your strange customs." The waitress looked baffled, but I still didn't get any rum in my Coke. When I visit my American cousins, though they are welcoming, I can't help but notice that familial ties don't wash over cultural differences. Sometimes, when I would visit for more than a couple days, I would start speaking with a grossly exaggerated Boston accent, in an attempt to get whitified and bridge the gap. By sharing an accent, perhaps I could be more a part of the family and share their history. Very rarely do the two families come together, and when they do, it is a jarring family portrait.

I think back to what my mother replied when I asked her if it bothered her that I looked so Western, so *not*-Chinese. What did she think when she looked at me? With seemingly uncomplicated conviction, she told me that she didn't care because she didn't break me down into Chinese and American. "I see my daughter, finish your dinner." Ultimately, I think she is right, for racial and cultural identity becomes an inherent sum of who you are and what your experiences have been. But I question how much she really believes what she says. My parents' difficulty with my recent choices of partners has exposed their belief that I will marry a Caucasian and that my brother will marry a Chinese, an assumption based on some vague and undefinable notion of what we look like and how they see us. My brother, it happens, is dating a Chinese woman, whose parents, ironically, don't approve of him because he isn't Chinese enough. "Why make life harder for yourself than it has to be? Different cultures will make marriage difficult," is what my father says when he sees me getting angry. Exasperated, I point to his own marriage as a sign of his illogic. "Have you forgotten that you're married to a Chinese woman?" But more important, I wonder whose racial and cultural background will match my own. I get silence for an answer.

For those of us who fall between the cracks, being "black," being "white," being "Chinese," being "Latino," is complicated. These essays, exemplary of the legion meanings of race and culture, are about inconstant categories and shifting skins. Skin color and place of birth aren't accurate signifiers of identity. One and one don't necessarily add up to two. Cultural and racial amalgams create a third, wholly indistinguishable category where origin and home are indeterminate. And yet, I am also reminded of a comment made by a notable mixed-race fiction writer in response to Tiger Woods's declaration of his Asian and black heritage (and I paraphrase): "When the black truck comes around, they're gonna haul his ass on it."

What name do you give to someone who is a quarter, an eighth, a half? What kind of measuring stick might give an accurate estimation? If our understanding of race and culture can ripen and evolve, then new and immeasurable measurements about the uniqueness of our identities become possible.

LOST IN PLACE

Garrett Hongo

One Labor Day some years ago, I was sitting at the dining table at my place in Eugene, Oregon, gazing out of the picture window over the front lawn at my two boys, Hudson and Alex, as they took turns splashing around in a wading pool with a small group of their friends. It was Alex's seventh birthday party, and his mother had arranged for about a dozen other boys to come over and celebrate with him. It was hot in Oregon, and the children would queue up in the most well-behaved manner and then yell like rioters as they took long jumps, triple jumps, and belly flops into the tiny pool I'd filled with a garden hose earlier that morning. Alex was loudest of all, improvising a variety of whoops, giggles, and *Ohh, mannnnn!*'s as he took his sailing dives into the grass-specked water.

"Watch, Dad! Watch!" he'd yell, and then take a sprint toward the inflated skirts of the pool, leaping and splashing down, showering that summery water on his brother and their playmates.

This might have been happiness itself, but, from inside the house, gazing up from the book of poems I was trying to read, I had the acute feeling that much of this was wrong. Except for my two sons, the hair on all the other boys was blond. Shiny yellow blond, strawberry blond, dirty-dishwater blond, or towheaded straw blond—but blond. No one else seemed bothered by this or even to notice—not my wife, who is brunette, not my in-laws, who are also brown-haired. But it drove me into an instant panic. And I began to feel angry.

I grew up among a mix of peoples both in Hawai'i and in Los Angeles. Born in Hawai'i, I spent my childhood among Hawaiians and Filipinos and Samoans on the North Shore of O'ahu before my family settled in Los Angeles in the late fifties. I went to primary school in midtown L.A., to fifth and sixth grades in Woodland Hills, and to junior high school and high school in Gardena.

We moved first to a neighborhood of apartment houses and old bungalows that housed a mix of peoples who arrived there from Jalisco or Hattiesburg, Honolulu or Hong Kong. I heard jump-rope rhymes in Japanese and the English of Southern blacks, I heard hopscotch songs from Sonora and Seoul, and I played cat's cradle with my cousins, who gave me elaborate instructions in Hawaiian pidgin English. In Woodland Hills, my family had moved on up, and that meant most of the other families in our neighborhood were white, and I felt racially isolated and socially quite lonely for a couple of years. We moved to Gardena, therefore, where there are a ton of Japanese Americans and their grocery stores, nurseries, auto-body and transmission-repair shops, and teriyaki taco stands. I was home, Jim, and, in junior high, I had a ball learning the boogaloo and the Philly dog from the black kids bused in from Compton.

By high school, I dressed and talked "blackJap" while beginning to read deeply in the literature books our white teachers assigned to us. But only the Jewish kids would talk about books, so on Friday nights, rather than rumble with recidivist car-club boys or take a date to a Chicano dance hall, I drove over to the Fairfax district with my new friends, who introduced me to their cousins who went to Hollywood High and University High. Rather than chase the waves for good surf in Hermosa Beach, I started feeling comfortable hanging out at kosher delis, the Samuel French Bookstore, all-night diners and art-movie theaters, talking Salinger and LeRoi Jones and Buñuel with kids who reminisced about Hebrew school and their bar and bat mitzvahs.

When I got bored, I went to hear jazz at Spanky's on Washington with my black friends. Or I went to the Lighthouse down in Hermosa with a white saxophone player I knew. At home, my family still did things Hawaiian- and Japanese-style—no shoes in the house, gas-station calendars from Kahuku Plantation, rice with every meal, chopsticks instead of forks, and vacations in Vegas that I avoided. And, within myself, none of this seemed especially strange. Yet I was aware I was crossing borders, that I couldn't carry with me too many signs as I traveled from one neighborhood or group of folks to another. A cultural slip could cancel my ticket-of-transit. I had become a magpie, an ethnic chameleon, a junior-league multi-culti before the fact.

My own children, though, were growing up in a very different kind of world. It was all white, and, I began to think, I'd made a big mistake. How would they know about others? And how would they relate to me?

Last month, my son Alex asked for some photographs of himself as a baby. He needed them for a bulletin-board project his fifth-grade class was doing. The idea was to scramble up a bunch of baby pictures with current ones and make everyone try to match the baby with the fifth-grader.

I rummaged around in the family albums and came up with a set of snapshots of Alex in Hawai'i, Houston, and Missouri. He swam with other kids in small *keiki* ("sprout") ponds by the ocean in Hawai'i, sat alone in a fire engine and wore a fireman's hat in Houston, and waved a tiny American flag at his younger brother by the forsythia bush in Missouri.

"Oh, no," Alex groaned. "This isn't going to work."

"Why not?" I asked.

"Because no one else in my class is Asian American," Alex said. "All people have to do is choose the baby with the black hair, and they know it's me. There's no mystery and there's no fun."

"Well," I said, improvising, "you're just unique, man. That's all."

"I'm tired of being unique, Dad," Alex answered. "I'm tired of being easy to pick out." I had to admit I could understand his feelings. Being different wears you down.

Eugene had been a choice of ours, my wife's and mine. She is from here and grew up feeling supported and secure. We came because we knew the schools would be good, because it was a way to give our children grandparents and an extended family, provide the base of familial and geographic stability she'd enjoyed as a child, as opposed to all the shifting around that I had done. It was safe, cheap, and manageable for the middle-class people we were becoming.

We'd met in college, at Pomona near Los Angeles, and fell in love sharing our family histories. On her father's side, my wife is descended from Mennonite farmers who moved to Oregon from Manitoba, where they had lived on a commune like the ones they'd been forced from in Ukraine and in Holland before that. The Mennonites are both a religious sect and an ethnic group. On her mother's side, my wife is descended from North Dakota Quakers who moved to Oregon after the Depression. My people are southern Japanese peasants and samurai who, dispossessed of their farms and swords, immigrated to Hawai'i at the end of the nineteenth century to work as laborers, union organizers, and storekeepers in the sugarcane fields and pineapple plantations. We recognized each other as children of a world diaspora.

She played the violin and studied music, while I set about trying to build a career as a poet, writing largely about the Japanese American past. I found work in universities far-flung from L.A.—in Texas, Missouri, and Orange County—with colleagues schooled in literature but ignorant and, I thought, scornful of the kinds of histories my wife and I had sprung from. We lived in Hawai'i for a while, then I was offered a job at the University of Oregon. It seemed an end to our wanderings.

But eventually I realized that, as an academic inducted into what Caribbean poet Derek Walcott once called "white fellowships," I had become too far removed from the world of urban ethnic and cultural diversity from which I had sprung. Living in Eugene had been happy enough for my family, and, mostly, for me in it, but some years ago I began to have problems with the town.

I grew bored with the two of three "good" restaurants, the commercial cineplexes in the shopping malls, and the company of blandness that characterizes the generally suburban life I'd fallen into. I lamented that there were hardly any black people, Latinos, or Asian Americans—no brothers and sisters at all.

At faculty mixers hosted by the dean, I zoned out. I faked my way through neighborhood get-togethers and receptions at my kids' elementary school. I was getting angry and depressed. Everyone around me talked mainly about fly-fishing, pasta salads, and summer classical-music festivals. Even the style and rhythm of their speech wore me down. It was all so complacent, untroubled, so blandly innocent of woe, that I resorted to moviegoing for my dose of the real. I shouted in celebration at Sam Jackson's soliloquy in *Pulp Fiction.*

"We need that man in Eugene!" I yelled. The good people in the dark theater, stunned and embarrassed for me, stayed politely silent.

Failing to stand guard over myself at backyard lawn and sundeck parties, I'd kid the sweet neighbors, the colleagues and their wives dressed in cottons from L. L. Bean, try switching subjects, and even risk putting them down. When things like the L.A. riots, Spike Lee's *Malcolm X,* or the Million Man March made the news, acquaintances in India Import skirts would start saying something mildly disparaging and then stop, realizing my sympathies were different.

Recently, a woman I recognized from the PTA stopped me in the popcorn line at the movies.

"Oh, Mr. Hongo," she said, "I'm so glad I ran into you. I've been meaning to ask if you'd come and speak about your native culture to my son's third-grade class?"

"Oh," I said disingenuously. "You mean gangs?"

I was becoming cruel. People now saw me as dangerous. I got quieter, meditating, reading. I distanced myself at the university, isolated myself within the town. I realized that, along with my own misanthropy, it was the ignorance and social homogeneity up here that was the cause of all this. I felt like I'd had a revelation. I told my acquaintances in Eugene that I could no longer tolerate being the only person of color they knew. We dropped each other and I started feeling better.

Now, I nod to folks, but barely anyone engages my conversation. People in the supermarkets assume I'm a foreign student on academic sojourn. I'm not supposed to be here—I'm not part of their community, but just passing through, using the post office or dry cleaner. I have become a stranger in their village. An exile.

My conversations come largely on the telephone now, with other writers, jazz and literary critics, and documentary filmmakers.

Many of them are white, some black or Jewish, and a few Asian Americans. Another few come from abroad. They are of wider acquaintanceship. The phone chatter lasts me for a while—I laugh and get good stories, find out about new things to read and listen to, hear the latest in their lives, and gossip about publishing—but it isn't enough. I still get restless.

These days, to supplement this tricky, exilic kind of life,

I've started making regular trips to Los Angeles. Sometimes I go on invitations to speak to students at UCLA or out in Claremont, to address a museum club and bookstore audiences in Pasadena and North Hollywood. Just as often, though, I make my own arrangements so I can stroll along the Third Street Promenade, cruise the 405 freeway and Santa Monica Boulevard, eat barbecue ("You don't need no teef to eat my beef!") and Chinese takeout, trying to reenter, as an adult, the world I grew up in.

This past winter I was on my way to Riverside, riding a shuttle from the Ontario airport. I was alone in the van with the driver, a young, streetwise guy who needed a haircut. He kept tucking and retucking his brown hair behind his ears, while the wind whipping in from the open driver's-side window repeatedly undid his work. He said that he was going to community college at night, taking courses in criminology. He was trying to prepare himself for work in law enforcement or as a prison guard. His name, he told me, was Presco Montoya.

"Presco?" I said.

"Pretty interesting name, huh?" he answered.

"Yeah," I said. "But I've heard it before. I used to know a Filipino cabdriver named Presco."

"You got it," he said. "Presco's short for Precioso—you know, Precious One. My mother's Filipina from Manila—she's romantic to the bone. My father's Chicano and tough, *pero*. They met overseas when he was in the military. They come home then, had me, and I grew up in El Monte."

I was liking anything he said by then because of the music in his voice, the way he formed his sentences, the torque and torsion of his speech. It had the city in it and a touch of some kind of twang I guessed might be from relatives who came from "the Valley"—which meant the San Joaquin Valley in my old circles. I told him I knew El Monte, that I used to go to dances there at the Legion Stadium when I was a teenager.

"Oh, yeah," he said, glancing up to the rearview mirror. He wanted a better look at my face, I guess. "You know, my uncle used to hang out there back in the sixties a lot, *vato*."

He was letting his voice catch even more of a lilt.

"You know Rosie, of Rosie and the Originals?" he asked, looking in the rearview again, searching my eyes for a reaction. "Sure, I know them," I said, laughing softly. "Ahh, let me see . . ."

"Well," he said, "she used to come over to our house a lot when I was a kid."

I was impressed. I thought back to some oldies I'd slow-danced to in the sixties.

" 'Angel Baby,' " I said, selecting the right tune from my memory.

"She used to go out with my uncle, you know?" Presco said. "I remember they would *lean* against the door of the pickup."

And the way he said that—slowing his speech way down, *decelerando,* shifting his hands on the wheel, scrunching up his face and his shoulders—made me laugh. I saw his uncle leaning a foxy lip-glossed Rosie up against the Turtle Waxed cherry red door of a citified pickup chopped low for cruising. She wore a sparkling sequined dress, and he was planting some deep, love-searching kiss down her throat, his rough hands riding up on her nyloned, barrio-soul-singer's leg. It was the L.A. version of a Cinzano poster, a kind of family photograph from the old days, and I got it simply by passing the time with the limo driver.

In L.A., whether I'm walking up the ramps and through the turnstiles in Dodger Stadium or ordering chow fun at the Far East Café in Little Tokyo, I feel a little grateful, even excited, to be reinhabiting uncelebrated zones of the familiar.

A Japanese American friend might pick me up at my hotel, pulling up to the curb by the lobby in a Lexus the color of silver fox. We'll drive over to the West Side, stroll through the downscale streets where the community nurseries and Nisei import shops used to be in the fifties, and then find a place where we can order a nouvelle-sushi lunch. We'll talk about my trying a screenplay, doing some work that will be seen by millions. Distracted, I'll notice that the waitress looks like the sitcom Morticia Addams, except that what I thought were the cutout black sleeves of her dress are really dark, spidery tattoos covering her arms. Jiving with her, I find out her name is Sachiko, that she's the daughter of a community activist I used to know. It's a frail, almost absurd connection, but a connection nonetheless.

And inevitably, there will be someone—maybe a guy named Sol, short for Soldofsky, who went to Uni High—who tells me some intricate, speech-syncopated story about his ex-girlfriend Vivian-from-the-Valley, who, once a publicist for Tom Snyder, is now housewifed to Sol's schlemiel cousin Stephen-from-Scarsdale, big deal, and they're rich as thieves, don't work for it, have a house in Topanga, buy their groceries at Bristol Farms Nieman-Marcus-for-tomatoes markup crazy.

It's not solely the style of the telling that does it for me, but Sol will wave a hand in a concomitant gesture I'll recognize as the Jewish sign of a sentimental love of place from the Lower East Side, itself evocative of my own infinite memories, then lean, some lazy, old-fashioned way, up against the outer brick wall of what used to be the Lighthouse jazz club out near the Hermosa Beach pier, and I'll be home suddenly, feeling the fog funky-chicken in from slow offshore breakers I can't see but hear, like a good pulse running in my blood. I'll turn and smile to my companion then, take a drag from the cigar I got at the beachside stand, invoke the night in 1968 when I was busted at the Old Burbage Theater for watching a performance of Michael McClure's play *The Beard*, and walk up the strand with him, feeling puffs of wind fill up my sports-coat pockets like handfuls of spiritual change.

In L.A., moments like these occur for me all the time now. I seem to need their humble affirmations in order to survive. My sons, sweet innocents in their unpitiable cloisters of sameness and comfort, need to know these things, too. They need to know that diversity is not danger. I need to bring them into this brave new world.

THE MULATTO MILLENNIUM

Danzy Senna

Strange to wake up and realize you're in style. That's what happened to me just the other morning. It was the first day of the new millennium and I woke to find that mulattos had taken over. They were everywhere. Playing golf, running the airwaves, opening their own restaurants, modeling clothes, starring in musicals with names like *Show Me the Miscegenation!* The radio played a steady stream of Lenny Kravitz, Sade, and Mariah Carey. I thought I'd died and gone to Berkeley. But then I realized. According to the racial zodiac, 2000 is the official Year of the Mulatto. Pure breeds (at least the black ones) are out and hybridity is in. America loves us in all of our half-caste glory. The president announced on Friday that beige is to be the official color of the millennium. Major news magazines announce our arrival as if we were proof of extraterrestrial life. They claim we're going to bring about the end of race as we know it.

It has been building for a while, this mulatto fever. But it was this morning that it really reached its peak. I awoke early to a loud ruckus outside—horns and drums and flutes playing "Kum ba Yah" outside my window. I went to the porch to witness a mass of bedraggled activists making their way down Main Street. They were chanting, not quite in unison, "Mulattos Unite, Take Back the White!" I had a hard time making out the placards through the tangle of dreadlocks and loose Afros. At the front of the crowd, two brown-skinned women in Birkenstocks carried a banner that read FOR COLORED GIRLS WHO HAVE CONSIDERED JEW BOYS WHEN THE NEGROES AIN'T ENOUGH. A lean yellow girl with her hair in messy Afro-puffs wore a T-shirt with the words JUST HUMAN across the front. What appeared to be a Hasidic Jew walked hand in hand with his girlfriend, a Japanese woman in traditional attire, the two of them wearing huge yellow buttons on their lapels that read MAKE MULATTOS, NOT WAR. I trailed behind the parade for some miles, not quite sure I wanted to join or stay at the heels of this group.

I guess I should have seen it coming. Way back in the fall of 1993, *Time* magazine put on its cover "The New Face of America," a computer-morphed face of fourteen models of different racial backgrounds, creating a woman they named Eve. The managing editor wrote:

The woman on the cover of this special issue of *Time* does not exist except metaphysically. . . . The highlight of this exercise in cybergenesis was the creation of the woman on our cover, selected as a symbol of the future, multiethnic face of America. . . . As onlookers watched the image of our new Eve begin to appear on the computer screen, several staff members promptly fell in love. Said one: "It really breaks my heart that she doesn't exist." We sympathize with our lovelorn colleagues, but even technology has its limits. This is a love that must forever remain unrequited.

Of course, anyone could see that women just like the computer face they had created did exist in Puerto Rico, Latin America, and Spanish Harlem. But the editors at *Time* remained unaware of this, seeming to prefer their colored folk imaginary, not real. As I read the article, it reminded me of an old saying they used to have down South during Jim Crow: "If a black man wants to sit at the front of the bus, he just puts on a turban." Maybe the same rule applied here: call yourself mixed and you just might find the world smiles a little brighter on you.

Mulattos may not be new. But the mulatto-pride folks are a new generation. They want their own special category or no categories at all. They're a full-fledged movement, complete with their own share of extremists. As I wandered at the edges of the march this morning, one woman gave me a flyer. It was a treatise on biracial superiority, which began, "Ever wonder why mutts are always smarter than full-breed dogs?" The rest of her treatise was dense and incomprehensible: something about the sun people and the ice people coming together to create the perfectly temperate being. Another man, a militant dressed like Huey P. Newton, came toward me waving a rifle in his hand. He told me that those who refuse to miscegenate should be shot. I steered clear of him, instead burying my head in a newspaper. I opened to the book review section, and at the top of the best-seller list were three memoirs: *Kimchee and Grits,* by Kyong Washington, *Gefilte Fish and Ham Hocks,* by Schlomo Jackson, and at the top of the list, and for the third week in a row, *Burritos and Borsht,* by a cat named Julio Werner. That was it. In a fit of nausea, I took off running for home.

Before all of this radical ambiguity, I was a black girl. I fear even saying this. The political strong arm of the multiracial movement, affectionately known as the Mulatto Nation (just "the M.N." for those in the know), decreed just yesterday that those who refuse to comply with orders to embrace their many heritages will be sent on the first plane to Rio de Janeiro, Brazil, where, the M.N.'s minister of defense said, "they might learn the true meaning of mestizo power."

But, with all due respect to the multiracial movement, I cannot tell a lie. I was a black girl. Not your ordinary black girl, if such a thing exists. But rather, a black girl with a Wasp mother and a black-Mexican father, and a face that harkens to Andalusia, not Africa. I was born in 1970, when "black" described a people bonded not by shared complexion or hair texture but by shared history.

Not only was I black (and here I go out on a limb), but I was an enemy of the people. The mulatto people, that is. I sneered at those byproducts of miscegenation who chose to identify as mixed, not black. I thought it wishy-washy, an act of flagrant assimilation, treason, passing even.

It was my parents who made me this way. In Boston circa 1975, mixed wasn't really an option. The words "A fight, a fight, a nigga and a white!" could be heard echoing from schoolyards during recess. You were either white or black. No checking "Other." No halvsies. No in-between. Black people, being the bottom of the social totem pole in Boston, were inevitably the most accepting of difference; they were the only race to come in all colors, and so there I found myself. Sure, I received some strange reactions from all quarters when I called myself black. But black people usually got over their initial surprise and welcomed me into the ranks. It was white folks who grew the most uncomfortable with the dissonance between the face they saw and the race they didn't. Upon learning who I was, they grew paralyzed with fear that they might have "slipped up" in my presence, that is, said something racist, not knowing there was a Negro in their midst. Often, they had.

Let it be clear—my parents' decision to raise us as black wasn't based on any one-drop rule from the days of slavery, and it certainly wasn't based on our appearance, that crude reasoning many black-identified mixed people use: if the world sees me as black, I must be black. If it had been based on appearance, my sister would have been black, my brother Mexican, and me Jewish. Instead, my parents' decision arose out of the rising black power movement, which made identifying as black not a pseudoscientific rule but a conscious choice. *You told us all along that we had to call ourselves black because of this so-called one drop. Now that we don't have to anymore, we choose to. Because black is beautiful. Because black is not a burden, but a privilege.*

Some might say my parents went too far in their struggle to instill a black identity in us. I remember my father schooling me and my siblings on our racial identity. He would hold his own version of the Inquisition, grilling us over a greasy linoleum kitchen table while a single, bright lightbulb swung overhead. He would ask: "Do you have any black friends?" "How many?" "Who?" "What are their names?" And we, his obedient children, his soldiers in the battle for negritude, would rattle off the names of the black kids we called friends. (When we, trying to turn the tables, asked my father why all his girlfriends were white, he would launch into one of his famously circular diatribes, which left us spinning with confusion. I only remember that his reasoning involved demographics and the slim chances of him meeting a black woman in the Brookline Public Library on a Monday afternoon.)

But something must have sunk in, because my sister and I grew up with a disdain for those who identified as mulatto rather than black. Not all mulattos bothered me back then. It was a very particular breed that got under my skin: the kind who answered, meekly, "Everything," to that incessant question "What are you?" Populist author Jim Hightower wrote a book called *There's Nothing in the Middle of the Road but Yellow Stripes and Dead Armadillos.* That's what mulattos represented to me back then: yellow stripes and dead armadillos. Something to be avoided. I veered away from groups of them—children, like myself, who had been born of interracial minglings after dark. Instead, I surrounded myself with bodies darker than myself, hoping the color might rub off on me.

I used to spy on white people, blend into their crowd, let them think I was one of them, and then listen as they talked in smug disdain about black folks. It wasn't something I had to search out. And most white people, I found, no matter how much they preach MLK's dream, are just as obsessed with color and difference as the rest of us. They just talk about it in more coded terms. Around white folks, I never had to bring up race. They brought it up for me, and I listened, my skin tingling slightly, my stomach twisting in anger, as they revealed their true feelings about colored folks. Then I would spring it on them, tell them who I really was, and watch, in a kind of pained glee, as their faces went from eggshell white, to rose pink, to hot mama crimson, to The Color Purple. Afterward, I would report back to headquarters, where my friends would laugh and holler about how I was an undercover Negro.

There had been moments in my life when I had not asserted my black identity. I hadn't "passed" in the traditional sense of the word, but in a more subtle way, by simply mumbling that I was mixed. Then the white people in my midst seemed to forget whom they were talking to, and countless times I was a silent witness to their candid racism. When I would remind them that my father was black, they would laugh and say, "But you're different." That was somewhere I never wanted to return. There was danger in this muddy middle stance. A danger of disappearing. Of being swallowed whole by the great white whale. I had seen the arctic belly of the beast and didn't plan on returning.

One year, while working as an investigative journalist in Hollywood, I even made up a list, evidence I've long since burned. These days such a thing would mean sure career death—luckily, it was never published. It was an exposé of who is passing in Hollywood. I called it "And You Thought It Was Just a Tan?" There were three categories:

Black Folks You May Not Have Known Are Black

Mariah Carey
Jennifer Beales
Tom Hanks
Carly Simon
Slash
Arnold Schwarzenegger

Johnny Depp
Michael Jackson
Kevin Bacon
Robin Quivers
Elizabeth Berkeley
Paula Abdul

Black Folks Who May Not Know They Are Black

Mariah Carey
Jennifer Beales
Tom Hanks
Carly Simon
Slash
Arnold Schwarzenegger

Johnny Depp
Michael Jackson
Kevin Bacon
Robin Quivers
Elizabeth Berkeley
Paula Abdul

Black Folks You Kinda Wish Weren't Black

O. J. Simpson
Michael Jackson

Gary Coleman
Robin Quivers

Needless to say, my list wouldn't have gone over too well with the M.N. posse. But I put decent research into the article and was proud of my results. It was nearly published in a local news weekly, but the editors balked at the last minute, for fear of lawsuits. I bet they're thanking their lucky stars now that they didn't print it. Essentialism is out. In this age of fluidity, it doesn't pay to be blacker than thou.

Just the other night, I was taken in for questioning by some M.N. officials. They wanted to question me about my "dark past." I tried to explain to them in as clear terms as possible why I had done it: denied my multiculti heritage for this negritudinal madness. I tried to explain to them that in Boston in the 1970s, racism was pervasive, blatant, dangerous, palpable. The choice of multiracial was simply not an adequate response to racism. In my mind, there were only two choices—black or white. Those choices were not simply abstractions. They had real consequences and meaning in my everyday world.

But the M.N. officials didn't buy it. They kept me at the station all night, in a small white room with a bright light. In the corner, there was a video monitor showing Grover and a gang of toddlers singing that old *Sesame Street* song over and over again: "One of these things is not like the other / one of these things isn't the same . . ." One of the agents, a big guy with a blond Afro and orange-tinted glasses, kept shouting at me, his spittle spraying across my face, "But why black? I mean, why didn't you identify as white if you were gonna identify as only one thing? Isn't that reverse racism?" I told him that multiculturalism should be about confronting racism and power, not about plates of ethnic food.

The Grover gang was beginning to have its desired effect. I was beginning to sing along, despite myself. " 'One of these things is not like the other . . .' " But I clenched my eyes shut and tried my best to explain to the man. I told him that all this celebration of mixture felt to me like a smoke screen, really, obscuring the fundamental issue of racism, and for that matter, class divisions. It seemed to me we spent so much time talking about kimchee and grits, we forgot to talk about power.

But the agent only whispered to me (his breath smelled of falafel), "Class analysis isn't quite as sexy as a grinning mulatto on a golf course." He even admitted to me that multiracialism was a terrific marketing tool, the best way to sell to as many types of people as possible. "It's ingenious!" he shouted, grinning, carried away by his own ideas. "This will change the face of marketing forever!"

But my experience, I told him, feeling broken now with exhaustion, could never be reduced to cute food analogies (Wasp cooking, I've come to realize over the years, can go well with almost anything because it has no flavor). My mulatto experience, I argued, was difficult not because things were confusing, but rather because things were so painfully clear. Racism, as well as the absurdity of race, were obvious to me in ways that they perhaps weren't to those whose racial classification was a given. Racism, I told him, is a slippery devil. Like Madonna, it changes its image every couple of years. Today, sans burning crosses and blatant epithets, racism is harder to put one's finger on. But I know it when I feel it. In all this mulatto fever, people seem to have forgotten that racism exists with or without miscegenation. Instead of celebrating a "new race," I told the agent, can't we take a look at the "new racism"?

When I was finished with my monologue, he just laughed. He told me I was imagining things. He told me there was no such thing as "new racism." He told me that if I couldn't show him a burning cross, he didn't want to hear about it. Then he was gone, locking the door behind him. The room was completely empty except for a video display monitor in one corner and a camera pointed at me in the other. At some point during that long, agonizing night, the video monitor switched from Grover and the gang to something far more sinister. It was a montage of Gary Coleman, Michael Jackson, Julie Andrews, and Sinbad, their faces flashing across the screen quicker and quicker until they seemed to blur into the smiling face of Juan Epstein. Eventually I fell into a fitful sleep and had a nightmare that I was buried under forty feet of snow.

But their tactics must have worked. I'm no longer a black girl. At least according to my new driver's license and birth certificate. The "black" has been smudged out and the word "quadroon" scribbled in. I told the woman at the DMV—auburn cornrows, vaguely Asiatic features—that I wasn't comfortable with that term "quadroon." I told her, as politely as I could, that it reminded me of slave days, when they used to separate the slaves by caste. She just laughed and told me to be happy I got "quadroon." "You don't know how lucky you are, babe," she said, puffing on a Marlboro and flipping through her latest issue of *Vibe* magazine. "They're being picky who they let use that term. Everybody's trying to claim something special in their background—a Scottish grandfather, a Native American grandmother. But the M.N. is trying to keep it to first-generation mixtures, you know. Otherwise things would get far too confusing." Then she had me sign some form, which I barely read, still reeling from my night before the video monitor. It said something about allowing my image to be used to promote racial harmony. I left the DMV in a daze.

These days, there are M.N. folks in Congress and the White House. They've got their own category on the census. It says "Multiracial." But even that is inadequate for the more extremist wing of the Mulatto Nation. They want to take it a step further. I guess they have a point. I mean, why lump us all together as multiracial? Eskimos, they say, have forty different words for snow. In South Africa, during apartheid, they had fourteen different types of coloreds. But we've decided on this one word, "multiracial," to describe, in effect, a whole nation of diverse people who have absolutely no relation, cultural or otherwise, to one another. In light of this deficiency, I would like to propose the following coinages. Perhaps the Census Bureau should give them a try.

Variations on a Theme of a Mulatto

Standard Mulatto: white mother, black father. Half-nappy hair, skin that is described as "pasty yellow" in the winter, but turns a caramel tan in the summer. Germanic-Afro features. Often raised in isolation from others of its kind. Does not discover his or her "black identity" till college. At this point, there is usually some physical change in hair or clothing, and often speech, so much so that the parents don't recognize their child when he or she arrives home for Christmas vacation. (E.g., "Honey, there's some black kid at the door.")

African American: The most common form of mulatto in North America, this breed is not often described as mixed, but is nevertheless a combination of African, European, and Native American. May come in any skin tone, and of any cultural background. Often believe themselves to be "pure" due to historical distance from the original mixture, which was most often achieved through rape.

Jewlatto: The second most prevalent form of mulatto in the North American continent, this breed is made in the commingling of Jews and blacks who met while registering voters down South during Freedom Summer or at a CORE meeting.

Jewlattos will often, though not necessarily, have a white father and a black mother (as opposed to the more common case, a black father and a white mother). Will also be more likely to be raised in a diverse setting, around others of his or her kind, such as New York City (Greenwich Village) or Northern California (Berkeley). Have strong pride in their mixed background. Will often feel that their dual cultures are not so dual at all, considering the shared history of oppression. Jewlattos are most easily spotted amid the flora and fauna of Brown University. Famous Jewlattos: Lenny Kravitz and Lisa Bonet (and we can't forget Zoe, their love child).

Mestizo: A more complicated mixture, where either the black or white parent claims a third race in their background (e.g., Native American or Latino) and therefore confuses the child more. The mestizo is likely to be mistaken for some other, totally distinct ethnicity (Italian, Arab, Mexican, Jewish, East Indian, Native American, Puerto Rican) and in fact will be touted by strangers as a perfect representative of that totally new race. (E.g., "Your face brings me right back to Calcutta.") The mestizo mulatto is more prevalent than commonly believed, since they often "disappear" into the fabric of American society, wittingly or unwittingly passing as that third, "pure," totally distinct race. It takes an expert to spot one in a crowd.

Gelatto: A mixture of Italian American and African American, this breed often lives in either a strictly Italian neighborhood if the father is white (e.g., Bensonhurst) or in a black neighborhood if the father is black (e.g., Flatbush). Usually identifies strongly with one side of the family over the other, but sometimes with marked discomfort becomes aware of the similarities between the two sides of his cultures, and at this point, often "flies the coop" and begins to practice Asian religions.

Cultural Mulatto: Any American born post-1967. See *Wiggers.*

Blulatto: A highly rare breed of "blue-blood" mulatto who can trace their lineage back to the *Mayflower.* If female, is legally entitled to membership in the Daughters of the American Revolution. Blulattos have been spotted in Cambridge, Massachusetts, and Berkeley, California, but should not be confused with the Jewlatto. The Blulatto's mother is almost always the white one and is either a poet or a painter who disdains her Wasp heritage. The father of the Blulatto is almost always the black one, is highly educated, and disdains his black heritage. Unlike the Jewlatto, the parents of the Blulatto are most likely divorced or separated, although the black father almost always remarries another blue-blood woman much like the first. Beware: The Blulatto may seem calm and even civilized, but can be dangerous when angry. Show caution when approaching.

Negratto: May be any of the above mixtures, but is raised to identify as black. Negrattos often have a white mother who assimilated into black culture before they were born, and raised them to understand "the trouble with whitey." They will tend to be removed from the white side of their family and to suppress the cultural aspects of themselves that are considered white. Will tend to be more militant than their darker brothers and sisters and to talk in a slang most resembling ebonics circa 1974. Has great disgust for the "so-called mulatto movement" and grows acutely uncomfortable in the presence of other mulattos. Despite all of this posturing, there is a good chance that they have a white lover hidden somewhere in their past, present, or future.

Cablinasian: A rare exotic breed found mostly in California. This is the mother of all mixtures, and when caught may be displayed for large sums of money. The Cablinasian is a mixture of Asian, American Indian, Black, and Caucasian (thus the strange name). A show mulatto, with great performance skills, the Cablinasian will be whoever the crowd wants him to be, and can switch at the drop of a dime. Does not, however, answer to the name Black. A cousin to other rare exotic mixes found only in California (Filipino and Black; Samoan and Irish; Mexican and Korean). Note: If you spot a Cablinasian, please contact the Benetton Promotions Bureau.

Tomatto: A mixed or black person who behaves in an "Uncle Tom-ish" fashion. The Tomatto may be found in positions of power, being touted as a symbol of diversity in otherwise all-white settings. Even if the Tomatto has two black parents, his skin is light and his features are mixed. If we are ever to see a first black president, he will most likely be a Tomatto.

Fauxlatto: A person impersonating a mulatto. Can be of white, black, or other heritage, but for inexplicable reasons claims to be of mixed heritage. See *Jamiroqui.*

Ho-latto: A female of mixed racial heritage who exploits and is exploited sexually. See any of Prince's Girlfriends.

The categories could go on and on, and perhaps, indeed, they will. And where do I fit into them? That's the strange thing. I fit into none and all of the above. I have been each of the above, or at least mistaken for each of them, at different moments in my life. But somehow, none of them feel right. Maybe that makes me a Postlatto.

There are plans next week to paint the White House rainbow colored. And just last month, two established magazines, both bastions of liberal thought, had cover stories predicting "the end of blackness." Not too long ago, *Newsweek* officially declared it "hip" to be multiracial. Race relations have been boiled down to a game of semantics—as if all that matters is which box one checks on the census.

And me? I've learned to flaunt my mixedness at dinner parties, where the guests (most of them white) ooh and aaah about my flavorful background. I've found it's not so bad being a fetishized object, an exotic bird soaring above the racial landscape. And when they start talking about black people, pure breeds, in that way that used to make me squirm before the millennium, I let them know that I'm neutral, nothing to be afraid of. Sometimes I feel it, that remnant of my old self (the angry black girl with the big mouth) creeping out, but most of the time I don't feel anything at all. Most of the time, I just serve up the asparagus, chimichangas, and fried chicken with a bright, white smile.

THE DOUBLE HELIX

Roxane Farmanfarmaian

Call me the foreigner. Though I was born a child of deep, strong roots, I have no sense of cultural belonging. I grew up in Europe, in a country that was not my own. In my parents' homelands, on the other hand, I felt no sense of self-recognition. Their worlds were thousands of miles apart, and both extreme. "What home is this?" I would wonder, seeing nothing of myself in them. And yet, like haunting background music that I could barely hear, the symmetries between my parents' worlds, repeated with uncanny consistency, implied a unity I could not grasp. Was there a purpose to their patterns, I wondered, seeing nothing beyond the haphazard coincidence of nature. Or was it simply that one always searches for parallels, trying to find the familiar in the unknown?

As a child, I was oblivious to the contradictions between my ancestral worlds. But as I grew older, I felt increasingly lost among the people who were supposed to be my countrymen, and at sea in the cities that held my heritage.

My mother was born a Mormon, my father a Muslim. This almost always is cause for amazement in those just brought into the know. I respond like a spitting snake, pointing out that the religions share not only their initial *M*s, but that their women wear special garments, that they both eschew certain foods, and, of course, that they both believe in the practice of polygamy.

Polygamy was, in fact, one of the elements that brought my parents together when they met in New York back in the fifties. My father, an outspoken critic of Iran's regime at the time, was cooling his heels as an exile, living in a small apartment on the Upper East Side of Manhattan. My mother, fresh from Salt Lake City, was attending Columbia University's Teachers College while making ends meet as a governess. They met at a production of T. S. Eliot's *Murder in the Cathedral* being staged in the university's chapel. A few weeks later, he invited her to his apartment for tea. There, in the powder room, she saw a watercolor of Brigham Young sitting in the middle of a wide bed, a line of wives stretching out on either side of him. Stunned to see the father of the Latter-day Saints so prominently displayed in the home of a Muslim, she let out a cry.

"It reminds me of my father," he explained. "He had a harem—with nine wives."

The parallels between the worlds of my parents did not end with Brigham Young. Once, while I was still in college, I flew from Tehran directly to Salt Lake City. It was not something I'd really planned to do. I'd spent the summer in Iran, and flew into New York intending to go straight on to university. But somehow I'd miscalculated my dates and, upon arrival, realized that classes did not start for another week. I called my mother from Kennedy Airport. As mothers will, she told me to come right out. Sixteen hours after stepping onto an Iran Air flight out of Tehran—and because of the time change, only a few hours later in the afternoon—I stepped off an America West flight in Salt Lake City.

I could have been disembarking at the same place I had boarded from. The mountains, rising into the twilight, were twins of the ones I'd just left. The ranges were both snow-capped, with the cities' lights running down their slopes like molten lava into the dusty plain. The air was the same dry air, tinged with the taste of salt from the wind off the saline lakes that lay embedded in their deserts. Iran's brackish lake lay farther off than Salt Lake City's, and dried up and cracked in the summer. But still, it gave off the same acrid smell.

It always struck me as one of those ironies that I, so tenuously American, should be from Utah, such a totally American place and yet, in all the United States, there is no more foreign a place, either. My mother's family are apiarists, and it is the honeycomb that is the emblem of Utah. It is also home to the Rainbow Arch, which graces so many of the posters hanging in travel agencies around the world. Yet it is the Mormon religion that is the true hallmark of Utah. And Mormons make other Americans feel slightly uncomfortable. Maybe it's the fact that the Book of Mormon is drawn from golden tablets which were miraculously unearthed by the teenaged Joseph Smith in the forests of New York, and which then as miraculously disappeared again before anyone else could see them. Or perhaps it is because Mormons don't drink coffee because they're not supposed to consume caffeine, but have been allowed to drink Coca-Cola ever since the church bought a goodly number of the company's shares. Or, most onerous of all, is it because, in the midst of a perfectly normal conversation, the Mormon missionary zeal will suddenly spring out like an attacking pit bull, forcing the victim to wriggle away as best he or she can?

To be fair, both faiths are deceptive in order to get around their rigid doctrines. Is it any more self-serving on the part of the Mormon religion to ban the consumption of alcohol and yet allow private clubs to serve liquor to anyone who joins for a day, a week, or a month, than for the Muslim religion to ban prostitution but allow the purchase of a wife for a day, a week, or a month?

Not surprisingly, for a person born into two of the most fanatic religions in the world, I turned out rather religiously bland. To be honest, neither of my parents is particularly devout. I am glad of it. But it did weaken my footing in trying to find my place in their cultures. In Utah, strong religious conviction is imperative: you are either of the faith or not, and if not, and you've chosen to leave the faith behind, you even have a name—you are a "Jack Mormon." Feeling freed from the manacles of religion—especially such a controlling one—I considered myself above my Salt Lake relatives. Without realizing it, I replaced my need to belong with preemptive disdain—an attitude that ensured that I could not be rejected because I'd already done the rejecting. This was dangerously self-serving, but since I lived abroad, I did not need to reckon with this false sense of superiority for many years. Instead, as an expat based in Holland, I hopped blithely from one nation to another, simultaneously from nowhere and everywhere like so many others of my ilk: the army brats, the Eurotrash, the diplomatic crowd, and all the rest who were the human equivalents of the Eurodollar. In The Hague, midway between my parents' homelands, I attended an American school and thought of myself as American. Yet, when my friends said they were from Ohio or Texas, I did not say I was from Utah. No, I was just generally American.

Culture shock, with a capital *C,* came when I moved to the States for college. The realization that I was not American, no matter how general, was blistering. I didn't understand the Whopper jokes; I didn't know who Topper was; I'd never seen a Corvair. When Easter came around, and everyone gathered to watch *The Wizard of Oz* on TV, I retired alone to my room, unable to relate to a movie whose characters bore no resemblance to the way I'd imagined them since childhood, and alienated by a culture that had fostered a tradition around a film I'd never seen.

That first year of college was one of the loneliest of my life. After living through it, however, I was more American than I'd ever been. At the same time, I made an important discovery: that I was rather happy I wasn't as American as I'd previously thought I wanted to be. The America that had held such an aura for me was the one defined by Tootsie Rolls, and Ked sneakers, and even *Bonanza*—none of which could easily be obtained, or viewed, abroad. Once I was in America, however, these became commonplace, along with the avalanche of other products that filled the supermarkets and the time on TV. I soon felt saturated with the consumerism and the waste, and tired of the constant advertisements, and the claims to be the biggest and the best in the world. Perhaps one has to be a foreigner to clearly see a culture. For me, the emphasis on "things" ran through American life like too much fat in an overrich meal. It was a constant irritant, and I recoiled, hankering for the more family-oriented, simpler life I'd grown up with. I was different from most other Americans, I realized, in some ways I did not want to change.

When it came to feeling Persian, on the other hand, I thought I had no illusions. I was, to my own mind, clearly an outsider. I did not speak the language; I had no Iranian friends; I did not pretend to know the culture. This was before the revolution and the hostage crisis. It was not politically incorrect yet to be from Iran. Still, there were pitfalls. Deep inside, unnamed, unrecognized, I had a sense of entitlement. Because my father's family was large and powerful, because it had been instrumental in Persia's modern history, and could track its ancestors back as far as the 800s, I felt the country was stamped upon my bones. Like brown hair or a flair for languages, I believed I had somehow genetically inherited an innate Persian sensibility. Though outwardly I was a foreigner, I subconsciously presumed that once I returned to my fatherland, I would quickly feel I belonged.

I was mistaken. This was made crystal clear the summer I spent in Tehran before I flew on to Salt Lake City. It was the first time I'd gone alone, the first time I'd gone without my father there. And I was lost. My savvy as a world traveler forsook me. I was more estranged in Iran than anywhere I'd ever been.

My roommate from college came through to visit for a couple weeks. It was an opportunity to explore Iran, and, acting the knowledgeable host, I suggested we travel to Yazd, the capital of the Zoroastrians, a midsize town located somewhere in the middle of the central plain. Upon our arrival, we drove to the one hotel I'd been told existed there, only to find it shut. Thank God I'd thought to get the name of a friend of a friend before leaving Tehran, and he kindly put us up for the night in his office. To this day, I don't know where regular tourists stay when visiting Yazd's Zoroastrian fire monuments and its houses with their unusual wind towers.

Our first night, we went to the local bazaar, a dark cavernous place, and bought dried figs for dinner. We slept on cots set up in the office hallway. The next night, we did the same. Two nights were enough. The following morning, we decided to decamp to Isfahan, where I knew there were sumptuous mosques, a glittering bazaar, and a four-star hotel called the Shah Abbas in an old, stately caravansary.

The friend of a friend said he'd drive us. In fact, it was his chauffeur at the wheel, while he sat in the front seat and talked at us for six hours as we drove across the bleached stones of the desert.

"I went to the University of Nebraska," he said. "I lived for four years at the Holiday Inn. I never had to make my bed. And I ate french fries and ice cream every night for dinner."

I looked out the window, mortified, as though he epitomized all Persians and his words reflected directly on me. My roommate, on the other hand, thought him a fool—if a kindly one—and simply ignored him.

Going to Isfahan was a good choice. Though neither of us could understand the words, we listened to a storyteller in the hotel courtyard that evening, his singsong voice punctuated by the hubbly-bubbly pipes being smoked by many of the other listeners. The air was languid, the stars close, and we could always tell when we'd reached a good part in the story because the smokers would suddenly start inhaling quickly and the pipes would gurgle loudly in unison.

The next day, however, my sense of equilibrium vanished at the airport. Expecting to get a routine confirmation of our ticket change through Isfahan, I was met with a typical Middle Eastern scene: a mobbed departure desk, no one in line, everyone shouting at the harried clerk, who paid no mind to who was first or second but only to whoever shoved their tickets most insistently into his face. Instantly, I knew I'd gone about the tickets all wrong. I should have had them confirmed earlier by someone in the hotel, paid a little bakshish, and avoided this scene altogether. Instead, I now had to claw my way through this melee. I felt I had let my roommate down—acting as though I knew my way around when in fact I was just an impostor, as ill at ease as she—if not more so—among my countrymen.

It was not until three years later, caught amid revolution and religious revival, my Persian family fleeing and my American countrymen taken hostage, that I came to understand my roots as an Iranian. I'd moved there just in time to catch the turmoil. Thank God I did, for it was the last chance I had to get to know the country. I stayed for two years. As Iran lurched toward political Islam, I developed a circle of friends, published a liberal English-language magazine, and traveled to hot spots around the country. Despite the guns in the streets, I grew used to driving around in the back alleyways, and came to understand the women in their tentlike chadors. Once, on a visit to the holy city of Qom, I even wore one myself, which caught the wind in its folds and elicited catcalls from some youths lurking nearby.

The revolution caught me once again in a personal conflict of national identity: Iran rejecting America—or was it the other way around? I was as much at risk of being arrested in the streets of Tehran for being an American as for being a member of the Persian elite. I felt shame for both my countries. But at last, I felt love for one.

That stay in Iran was a watershed for me. Although the country was lurching in a direction I could not condone, I felt a common identity with the passions and sentiments of the people. I loved the Persian wit, the street jokes about Ayatollah Khomeini and his wife and all the other mullahs who were so seriously taking over the country. I loved the ancient architecture, the food, and the strange third-world contrasts that would serve up a camel train caught in a traffic jam on the Tehran beltway. As more and more of my family fled the revolution, while I stayed, I felt less and less the impostor. In the past, everyone had seemed so much more "Persian" than I was. Now, I felt I knew something about Iran that only an Iranian could know—which gave me a sense of credibility. I no longer felt embarrassed that others spoke the language better than I did, or had memories of childhood summers on the Caspian, or had gone on camel trips across the desert. They had left, while I stayed on to experience the turmoil—and the baring of the country's soul. I knew what the villagers were saying about the demonstrations, how people reacted to the postrevolution drivel on TV, and where the last place was in town to get a glass of wine with dinner. I no longer needed to pretend that I belonged.

And yet, in my heart of hearts, I knew that it was more than that. Such intimate details I knew about Utah, too, and still I did not feel the same sense of belonging there. One summer in particular I had tapped its inner sanctum, selling encyclopedias door to door in hundred-degree heat. I saw inside the houses of hundreds of people, spoke to them about their families and their hopes, and asked them for money. They were good people, generous people, who gave me water and cake, and lived with too many children and too little time. But I did not feel they were my people.

Was it the sense of history that permeated all aspects of Iran that I related to so well? Was it the excitement of revolution that gave me a sense of real involvement? Or was it the fact that I had to lose Iran, and that I would have felt the same about Utah if it instead had been the one I had had to leave? I do not know. But when the Iranian revolution ejected me, and most of my Persian family, I left with a heavy heart, knowing that I was at last leaving a homeland behind me.

Today, I still cannot go back to Iran. The political situation makes me at once an outcast and a wanted woman. Finally, however, I understand the symmetry that, like a double helix, seems to turn my mother's country into my father's, and back again. I have come to grips with my need for reflected identity. Though Utah never has drawn me the way Iran did, it now offers me the legacy of both. Now every time I fly into Salt Lake City and disembark from the plane, I look up at the mountains, and at the city cascading down their slopes, and for one fleeting moment I taste the salt air and feel I'm stepping onto the dusty plain of Tehran.

CALIFORNIA PALMS

lê thi diem thúy

Before my mother arrived in the United States from Vietnam, I perceived myself to be an American. Whatever that is. I'd acquired a taste for dill pickles, macaroni and cheese, was an expert at the Hula-Hoop and roller skating backwards. I thought this entitled me to glide along like I imagined everyone else gliding along—merrily—and with no past to speak of. Not only did my mother prompt me to question my taste in American food by reacquainting me with condensed milk, ginger fried fish, lichee nuts, and noodle soup for breakfast, her presence also pointed to an entire history I thought I'd thrown overboard and left for sunken treasure or so much useless luggage adrift in the watery vaults of the Pacific. I thought

I had succeeded in making myself light, releasing my longing for Vietnam in order to secure a place in America. Now here was my mother, newly arrived and already dragging memories right out of the sea, shaking them loose on the shore before holding them up to the light and handing them back to me. While my father had instilled in me the belief that we might never go back to Vietnam, my mother came and insisted that we could never leave it.

When my mother arrived in the States in 1980, she had lost three children, survived two wars, was separated from her mother and father, brothers and sisters, and the land of her birth by an entire ocean. My father and I had escaped Vietnam in 1978. During the two years between our departure from Vietnam and my mother's arrival in the United States with my younger sister in 1980, my father and I had sent my mother portraits of ourselves decked out in our best clothes, standing in front of big cars and fancy houses in the wealthy neighborhood of La Jolla, a virtual independent republic of San Diego, California. Through so many smiling images, we led her to believe that the hacienda-style house stretching out behind the two giant California palms was indeed our home in America.

She arrived to find we had no house. What's more, I claimed she wasn't my real mother. I held on to this belief for months. Even coupling it with the suspicion that this man and woman who assumed the roles of my father and mother were in reality Communist spies, and that the young girl of two or three who was supposedly my sister wasn't really my sister but some child who was cast to be the younger sister just as I had been cast to be the older sister in what appeared to be the portrait of a struggling Vietnamese family newly arrived in America.

Where this elaborate drama came from, I do not know except to say that in my worldly travels as an eight-year-old in what were still the Cold War years, I had picked up the common wisdom that the opposite of an American was a Communist. Also, I had a vivid imagination. I was convinced that entire rooms changed once I'd stepped out of them, like a turning stage that twirled one living room away and brought another living room forward, with the same actors in place but in changed costumes and changed characters, which meant that an entirely different drama was about to unfold.

My mother was not overly concerned with having been cast as an impostor mother. After all, she knew she was my mother. She set about correcting my odd Vietnamese—I'd taken to saying things like, "Can I help you shampoo the dishes?"— and acquainting herself with English via songs from television commercials. Her two favorite songs were: "This Bud's for you" and "G.E. We bring good things to life!" Which she pronounced "lie." She often sang these songs—in lieu of the traditional lilting Vietnamese lullaby—to the little girl who, oddly, seemed to like them, especially when my mother thrust a cupped hand in the air, as though toasting the little girl with an invisible twelve-ounce can of Budweiser.

On weekends, she had my father drive us to Thrift Village, a warehouse of secondhand clothes and shoes, fat couches and coffee tables, flower-patterned vinyl kitchen chairs, velvet paintings, and tall lamps sporting crushed or otherwise crooked lampshades. It was here that she found a portrait of Jesus with his eyes painted to follow me around the room, so that no matter where I was in our small apartment, whenever I turned to look at him, he, like a demented guard dog my mother had ingeniously convinced to assume the likeness of

Jesus, was staring right back at me. It was also here that my father picked out two framed prints, one of the New England countryside alive in the glory of fall foliage, the other of a mother leopard staring into the camera while her baby, protectively curled beside her, yawned. What, I wondered, did these prints have to do with being a Communist? Yet, it was also at Thrift Village that my mother showed signs of her criminality. She taught my sister and me how to steal.

At Thrift Village, there were no dressing rooms. If you wanted to see whether a shirt fit, you either slipped it on over your shirt or, through some acrobatic feat that consisted in twisting your arms so that the elbow of the right arm almost nestled inside the armpit of the left and vice versa, you were able to loosen your shirt enough so that it became a makeshift tent under which you could try on any number of other shirts. The best thing to do was to hang a long dress over your head and proceed from there, though this did have the effect of making Thrift Village look like a room full of the rear ends of donkeys groping for their more becoming front ends. My mother took advantage of this controlled chaos to pile one article of clothing after another over my sister and me. On top of our own shirts, she had us put on other shirts. Over our own pants, she slipped on more pants, and over those, skirts and dresses. Placing a hat on our heads and a stuffed teddy bear or a toy dinosaur in our arms, my mother pushed my sister and me out the opened doors of Thrift Village with instructions to run and shed the layers of clothes in the back seat of my dad's car. We shed all but our original clothes and ran back to be layered with more. In this way, my sister and I acquired outfits and wardrobes, costumes and new skins.

Though my father was not keen on the phenomenon of

my sister and me leaving the thrift store in the guise of two Michelin men and returning as our small-boned, skinny selves, I should have known from the moment my mother arrived in the States that she had the upper hand in determining the direction my family would take. As far as she was concerned, he had failed miserably at keeping things together. Not so much because the hacienda in La Jolla was a fiction but rather because he'd gotten two important details about my identity entirely mixed up.

Back in Vietnam, I'd had an older sister who was called Big Girl, whereas I was called Little Girl. Her given name was Thúy and mine was Trang. We weren't often called by our given names, which is why, supposedly, my father confused her given name with mine. In the States, I assumed the name thúy and celebrated my birthday on January 15. Neither my father nor I was troubled by this until my mother arrived to set us straight. For one thing, she let us know, my name was Trang and my birthday was January 12, not the fifteenth. For a fleeting moment, I entertained the possibility of celebrating my birthday twice in one week, but my mother laughed that one off. Then I thought she'd let me relinquish the name thúy which, pronounced "twee" in English, had caused people to laugh into their hands and make jokes about a certain small cartoon character named Tweety Bird. I didn't necessarily feel that Trang, pronounced like a combination of "train" crashing into "tang," was any better, but it was new and, more important, it was supposed to be my name. To this, my mother said no. My older sister, the original thúy, had escaped Vietnam with my mother and younger sister, but she had drowned at the refugee camp in Malaysia. My mother insisted that I keep the name because, due to my father's propitious mistake, it was a part of my older sister that had made it to America. Like a T-shirt stretched to make a tent, I felt my mother's deft logic expanding the familiar one-syllable note of thúy to make room for my dead sister.

The result was, sometimes I felt my name was like an already occupied bed, something I couldn't quite find my place in because someone else was sprawled out and deep in sleep across it. Other times, I felt I had no name or hadn't found my real name yet and was using thúy until then. For a while, I even went by the name of Tina because a friend of mine, an African American girl named Lakeisha, thought thúy was a weird and difficult name to remember. I came to think of names in general and of my name in particular as rough skin, loose approximations of the person underneath.

A name, like any word, can be misspelled, mispronounced, kicked around, and then caressed back to life. Sometimes my mother would say my name in such a way that it didn't seem to be spoken so much as sung and, in its singing, made to linger in the air like a musical note. Through such moments, I came to understand that language is alive as sound, as utterance and invocation. I knew that in one breath she was calling to me and to my older sister, to the past in the present, reaching across the ocean's vastness to touch a particular stretch of beach in front of my grandfather's house.

I remembered the house. The neighbor with the pigeon nest on her roof. A particular rainy Tet evening when I wondered if the firecrackers would light. I remembered a younger brother whom my mother had described as no bigger than a marble when he was first born and an older brother who drowned when I was still in Vietnam but whose death I refused to believe in because my mother had told me, "He fell into a hole in the sea," and I thought that just meant he was hiding under water. I remembered the night my father sat me down in my great-uncle's fishing boat and told me to wait there until he returned. It was the night my mother got into a fight with her father and missed the boat that was taking my father and me away from Vietnam.

My childhood belief that entire rooms disappeared behind me hadn't come out of thin air but out of my own experience of leaving Vietnam. After the days and nights at sea, the months at the refugee camp in Singapore, the year and then two with no signs of my mother or other members of my family showing up, as I had imagined they would, my life in Vietnam took on the aura of something remote, like a house I had walked so far away from that when I turned back to look at it, I could barely make out the house, let alone the toys I'd left in the courtyard or the people sleeping inside. Vietnam became a kind of darkness, a deep silence that would occasionally be interrupted by sudden memories of a rooster crowing or a pigeon cooing. I would see flashes of someone's face, sometimes my older brother's as he turned to see how close I had come to catching him during a game of chase on the beach. Such memories of Vietnam appeared like intense points of light occasionally capable of piercing through the dark canopy that had come to define my relationship to the past. By the time my mother and sister arrived, I had buried so much of my longing for Vietnam that I could almost believe I had entered the world as a fully formed eight-year-old, emerging from an untraceable black hole.

My mother was the one who alerted me to the simultaneity of worlds. She spoke about Vietnam as if it were right around the corner, as alive as where we were, if not more so. While school and mainstream American movies defined Vietnam as a war, from my mother I might have thought there had never been a war, that history hadn't twisted itself around us like a tornado, lifting us up into the heart of it, stomping out our past with a flick of its tail and then depositing us as far from home as possible. She treated the United States like some place we were passing through, made bearable by the belief that no matter how long or how difficult this journey would be, in the end we were still Vietnamese and we would eventually make it back to Vietnam. According to my mother, every ordeal was a test of our strength, meant to build character. Strange, inexplicable things happened. One night, we had boarded a boat in southern Vietnam. One day, we had landed by plane in Southern California. That was fate.

It was fate that had changed my position in the family from the fourth child to the eldest, and it was fate which demanded that—even though I was a child—I become the representative head of my family. My mother's conversational English at the time consisted of Yes, No, Maybe, Okay, and Why not?—terms that she used interchangeably to create a cloud of confusion between herself and the listener. My father, who was less verbose, favored nodding solemnly or beginning every explanation with, My name is . . . , I entered with, Excuse me, Pardon me, What time is it?, Where is, We're just looking for, and Thank you. Through the clarity of my pronunciation and the agility of my translation, I was navigating my family through the perils of daily life, from finding milk at the liquor store to locating the correct room to enter at the social services building or the hospital. My mother was impressed with my English. Whenever I spoke, she would gaze into the face of the listening American and observe how my words were smoothing the furrowed brow, unlocking the tight lips, sometimes even eliciting a warm smile. While it might have seemed to my mother that my polite yet directed banter could protect my family from dumbfounded stares and prompt dismissal, I felt that I couldn't truly protect us but was merely delaying our inevitable eviction.

At home, my parents applauded my ability to speak English as well as any American and yet not be an American. In public, I carried myself as the representative of a family most of whose members didn't speak English well but harbored no greater dream than to be Americans. I both hoped and feared that sooner or later I would be found out. The public would discover that my parents had no desire to become Americans, while my parents would realize that I didn't know how or what it meant to be Vietnamese in America. I could translate sentences from one language to another and back again: tell my mother what my teacher said, ask the sales clerk for what my father wanted. Within our family, I could live life in our small apartment as though it were a distant outpost of Vietnam. Yet every time I turned the television on or stepped out of the house, my parents and Vietnam seemed far away, otherworldly. I had been rowing back and forth, in a relentless manner, between two banks of a wide river. Increasingly, what I wanted was to be a burning boat in the middle of the water, visible to both shores yet indecipherable in my fury.

As early as the age of eight, I had begun to run away. It wasn't long before hunger and darkness brought me back home, but then I would go again, escaping the claustrophobia of my house to run barefoot through the streets. I'd wander new neighborhoods, look in on other lives, imagine my family stepping out of a station wagon, strolling across the green lawn to unlock the promise of our very own big house. Or, I imagined bringing strangers home to live with us so that they could share the burden of being a witness to my world. I wanted someone to tell me what they saw in my father's stoic silence, my mother's talk about fate, my sister's wide-eyed curiosity, and my own uneasy donning of a dead sister's name. Add to this my father's drinking, my mother's gambling, and their spectacular fights, which left my sister and me hiding in the bathroom until our fear died down. On the flip side of all the tumult was the obvious affection, how with my mother's urging my father could be convinced to sing. He would begin slowly, softly, a hint of a song approaching from far away, and then his voice would rise and he'd clap his hands together. We'd join my father, keeping time, following his voice as it searched all the tones, high and low and back again, moving like a solitary figure leading us through areas of darkness and of light.

I think I became a writer in part because I wanted to convey in English the quality of my father's voice as he sang a song in Vietnamese or the peculiar truth of my mother's accented English speaking for General Electric when she declared, "G.E. We bring good things to lie!" Similar to the way my mother has secured my sister's passage to this country by having me bear my sister's name, I have arrived at English through Vietnamese and can't hear one language without feeling the presence of the other. When I sit down to write, there is a part of me that isn't laying words down so much as dragging my grandfather's fishing boats, sand-and-salt-speckled, clear across the Pacific and right onto the page, and then there is the part of me that continues to stare out from those portraits my father and I used to send to my mother, of our fabled hacienda in La Jolla. I see myself, one of two bodies framed within the space between two enormous California palms, smiling a winning smile. The girl I was then asks the woman I am today, What do you see? Daring me to speak.

MORO LIKE ME

Francisco Goldman

What was it about just the sight of me that could have so provoked the Spanish police that they drove right up onto the sidewalk to stop me, intercepting my dreamy progress toward the newspaper kiosk on the corner? The mystery plunged me into a state of baffled and paranoid self-scrutiny. I played the sequence over and over in my mind, me on the sidewalk that very first morning in Madrid, trying to see myself as the police must have, trying to pick myself out from the other pedestrians loosely arrayed along that stretch of sidewalk as the police must have, trying to recognize myself with a silent shout of *That guy! There he is!* Or, *There's one! Don't let him get away!*

Which is, of course, why I remember so vividly what I looked like that morning, what I was wearing, my way of walking and demeanor, exactly twelve years ago this month (November), while so much else about that time has faded. (I forget, for example, the name of the woman whose apartment I was staying in, though I do remember that she was a friend of a Spanish friend in New York.) I'd come to Madrid at the height of the period known as La Movida, the explosion of trendy urban youth culture following the decades-long sleep of the Franco dictatorship. La Movida Madrid had seemed a hopeful place to come to in the aftermath of a failed marriage. One reason my marriage had failed was that I'd spent at least half its short duration in Central America, war years there, instead of in New York with my wife. In certain ways, Central America had taken over my life, and not just because I wanted to write about it, though I *had* been writing short stories using that setting for years, and also the occasional magazine nonfiction piece.

So another thing I don't remember about Madrid is how long I'd stayed in New York that time, where my wife and I had agreed to separate once and for all, after returning from Central America. But I'd been there recently enough, that first morning in Madrid, that my skin—I remember naming precisely its shade—was still "cashew brown." Browned by however long under the tropical sun, not yet completely yellowed and paled by however long of apartment living in New York. I was wearing a denim shirt, untucked, and jeans and boots. I was sleepy-looking with jet lag, unshaven, unshowered, my coarsely curly hair messy and wild looking. Hands in pockets and kind of dragging my feet along, as I tend to. And probably feeling the unanticipated chill in the air—I'd thought Madrid was going to be on the mild side even in November. And of course, I was full of the excitement and impatience that accompanies being just-arrived in a new place where you plan to make a fresh start: look for a room to rent, establish a daily routine, find new friends. In Madrid, I was finally going to begin a novel, and actually had a small publisher's advance, enough to live on for, I hoped, six months. Impatient to feel immersed, in a novel, a new city, a new life, the future, in the Madrid of La Movida! A lonely and productive half-year ahead, but not, I hoped, *too* lonely. I was off on the right foot, making my way down the sidewalk past the elegant stone buildings and skinny trees with their pale leaves and a newspaper kiosk up ahead on the corner and the anticipation of, in just a few moments, plunging into Madrid, into Europe: espresso, strong cigarettes, newspapers (*Herald Tribune* and *El País*) in some crowded café where I was going to fit in . . . well enough.

A police car drove right up onto the sidewalk to stop me. A gleamingly sleek and white European-looking police car. Maybe it just came to a screeching stop at the curb, doors flung open and bearded police bursting out of it to surround me—that sounds more believable. Except I feel pretty certain it *did* drive up onto the sidewalk, both or at least one of the front tires ridden up over the curb. Three or four police, all with beards. The significance of their beards was explained to me later on—it had something to do with General Franco, with some security branch still associated with loyalty to Franco-Fascist ideals. The one with the Irish-setter-red beard was shouting at me to produce some identification.

I'd left my passport in my host's apartment. But I had a press card in my wallet, issued by the Sandinista government press center in Nicaragua, a laminated rectangle of thin green cardboard, tiny snapshot pasted to it, name, passport, and accreditation—the *New York Times Magazine*—typed in (a story on "writers and power" in revolutionary Nicaragua, completed months before). Now these gray shirts were going to part around me, respectfully murmured apologies sprinkling down their beards like graham cracker crumbs.

Officer Redbeard dismissively handed the card back, saying, "Anyone can get one of these." Castilian accents being what they are, this came out as a petulant growl (five hundred years of Spanish history distilled in that growl, the fearsome haughtiness of bearded conquerers sounding a last faint echo in a bearded policeman's bullying pettiness).

Whenever in tense situations in Central America, I'd learned long ago to pretend to speak no Spanish, to jabber away in strenuously gringo-accented English. In the end, they drove off the sidewalk and away with just an admonishment to always carry my passport. My prebreakfast fantasy of life in a renascent corner of modern Europe had been replaced by something like a sense of perplexingly familiar though not-yet-identifiable unease, like something I'd had no right to forget chillingly remembered in the blood.

But what was it about just the sight of me that had so provoked them?

"*¿Eres moro?*"

"*Tienes cara de moro.*" (You have the face of a Moor.)

Or, "*¿Eres sudaco? ¿Peruano? ¿Mexicano?*"

This line of questioning was a constant refrain during the six months I spent in Madrid. But they'd almost always ask if I was *moro* first. By which they meant North African, mainly

Moroccan, though also Algerian, Somalian, Sudanese, Tunisian, Libyan, Egyptian . . .

"*No tengo nada de moro.*" That, along with "What's it to you," became my refrains, snapped back in their faces with as much provocation as I could put into a stare, ready for a fight and, eventually, nearly always trying to start one. *I have nothing of Moor.*

Which, strictly speaking, probably isn't even true. Less true of me, though, than of most of my Spanish interrogators, their genetic trees likely to be much more solidly planted in a Spain that, after all, until a mere five hundred years ago, was Moorish and Jewish, too—the axes of conquest, expulsion, and Inquisition did not tear that tree out by the roots. My Guatemalan mestiza mother and I get our *pelo malo* ("bad hair") from somewhere. Spanish Catholic and Maya on my mother's side. Jewish on my father's. To the Spaniards, I looked *moro*.

The taxi driver eyeing me in the mirror, or the clerk in the shirt shop, "*¿Eres moro? . . .*" The stranger seated next to me at the bar punctuating his interrogation, But you have the face of a Moor! "*No tengo nada de moro. Y ¿porqué te importa?*" These were just the minor, mundane, nearly daily incidents. It took me awhile, weeks maybe, to absorb the full absurdity of this situation. To first relinquish my disbelief, and then some of my outrage—to realize finally that the *fact* of my not actually being Moroccan was probably the least instructive, or offensive, aspect of this experience.

Of course, for nearly as long as I can remember, I've been sensitive enough to bigotry, from both my Jewish and Latin American sides, although growing up in the United States, I very rarely experienced the overt racial discrimination and even hatred that I felt everywhere during my time in Madrid. As if before, my own ethnically ambiguous situation had afforded a kind of protection, in the way a shifting target makes it easier to evade direct hits. In Spain, *moros* were the despised ethnic minority, treated in a manner that I, of course, had been taught to associate—all this to varying degrees, of course—with blacks in the United States, Jews in Nazi Germany, or even Mexicans and Central Americans in Governor Wilson's California. In the eyes of many Spaniards, I was a *moro.* That's why the police had stopped me—in the mood that day, perhaps, to collar a *moro* with less than orderly immigration papers. That was why, on a long weekend bus ride to Granada to see the Alhambra, the policeman who boarded the bus while I dozed kicked me awake, in the shin, and demanded to see my passport. Kicked me in the shin while I slept! I was so infuriated, I pulled my U.S. passport from my pocket and shot it toward his face with a fast backhanded swipe, stopping, I swear, just an inch short of his astonished gape. Just last year, when I found myself in Spain again, with V., fair-haired and Mexican—the cargo freighter we'd taken from Mexico had let us off in Valencia—a policeman stopped V. on the dark street we were walking down to warn her that she was being trailed by a *moro* . . . meaning me, of course, lagging a short distance behind with our luggage. Hah-hah, that was pretty funny. That's not a *moro,* that's my boyfriend! Hah-hah! We had some good giggles over that, and a round of loud laughter with horrified but amused friends in Barcelona later. By the way, this *moro* business doesn't happen to me in Barcelona; as Catalans, they have their own charged relationship with Castile; and perhaps because the city is a great port, accustomed to the intermingling of many peoples, they are more worldly, and easily able to distinguish a Hebrew mestizo from a *moro*.

One of the first things I eventually figured out was this: it doesn't matter what my features actually are, the bigot looks only for certain recognizable markers—in this case curly dark hair, brown eyes, perhaps a certain roundness to the face—and does you the favor of filling in the rest, like a cook spooning *moro*-filling into a prepared flat round crêpe. In that way, every bigot is faithful only to what he knows, and makes you want to weep for human ignorance. It's the way of the bigot—that crêpe-filling way—from the most vulgar to the most seemingly literary and subtle, filling you in with his reeking spoonfuls, plopping them down with smug authority. (And never noticing the relationship between my Mayan nose and way with money, my big Jewish ears and love of big game hunting, my Andalusian feet and tranquil limpidity of spirit.)

But during those first bewildering days and weeks in Madrid, it really was as if a grotesquely absurd fiction had replaced my ordinary reality: In a strange and unexpectedly cold and hostile city, I was experiencing overtly and manifoldly expressed racism against an ethnicity and culture not my own. And experiencing it in a way much dimmer, much less complex in its tensions and hurts, than a true *moro* must experience it. For starters, to a real Moroccan, this treatment probably wouldn't come as much of a surprise.

Yes, taxis were hard to get, especially at night. Maybe after the fifth or eighth time I'd buzzed to be let into a little shop or boutique and been denied entrance by the clerks inside, I began to realize how avoidance of such stress and embarrassment could become second nature. Do you buzz again? There's a cool leather jacket in the window, but the clerks inside look rigidly posed around that table at the back, deep in grim, tense discussion of the Soho Missile Crisis. Maybe I should have kicked in the door. But why draw more attention to myself? You just stop going to places with buzzers and look elsewhere for a leather jacket. I ended up buying mine at El Corte Inglés, Madrid's largest department store.

I read about it in the newspapers: a certain hostility to North Africans, Gypsies, and even South Americans *(sudacos)*. Reports of skinhead attacks. And sensational "undercover" accounts of young Moroccan males and their hashish-junk-sex-dealing lives, their squalid squatters' dens. A brief run of stories about Peruvian pickpockets and petty thieves allegedly preying on train passengers. Unemployment was high in Spain, especially among Spanish youth. Madrid youth at the time seemed most interested in bad Spanish rock and roll, heroin, transvestite chic, the rockabilly look, and basketball. (The Boston Celtics came to play an exhibition and Larry Bird said his favorite thing about Madrid was that the McDonald's served beer.) I remember, later on during my stay, standing out in front of that very McDonald's, on the Gran Vía, one of Madrid's busiest corners, and counting the number of dark-skinned faces that walked past, just to prove to myself how exaggerated Madrid's anti-immigrant hysteria actually was. You could stand there all day and by the end you might have counted as many "brown" faces as you would in a matter of minutes in almost any major American city's downtown.

I began to feel lonely. But this wasn't the romantic, productive loneliness I'd wanted. This was, for me, a new kind of loneliness, though one often referred to, in the melodramatic cliché, as "crushing." Certainly a bit of a letdown, considering the high hopes I'd brought with me. Within a week of my arrival, I'd moved into a rented room of my own, in a tiny apartment on Calle Noviciado that belonged to a young acting student who was spending most of his time at his girlfriend's; she was an elegant beauty with lushly cascading hair who had recently won the "Miss Jean" role in a Spanish equivalent of *Romper Room*. Gabriel, a Basque, was a good fellow, and a very serious student of acting, and I'd almost weep with gratitude whenever—maybe twice a month—he found time to go out to dinner. These were like movie meals, the new American roommate watching and listening with astounded admiration over the profoundly "European" way his friend had of enjoying his food: conversation would cease while Gabriel intensely and rapturously muttered and whimpered to himself in his unselfconscious pleasure over the wine, over whatever inexpensive tapas or meal we were gorging on, on our modest budgets. I let myself adopt that habit, and it certainly made for a noisier and heartier ambience during the meal after meal after meal I had alone. I realize I'm digressing (digressions being life's sun, as Sterne somewhere says; as in, the sun finally breaks through the overcast, leaden sky . . .), because bigotry is a depressing subject. Even by writing about it, you feel you are allowing it a little victory over you. While bigotry is certainly a part of too many people's lives, it feels like the opposite of life, and is so essentially idiotic that it doesn't seem worth even eloquently or passionately denouncing. I remember *feeling*—by which I mean taking it personally—in Madrid how much this was all about denying a person's humanity, his very existence, of humiliating and even castrating him every day: pretending that that's not a man out there, buzzing to be let into your little boutique, raising his hand for a cab, knocking at the hidden-away trendy rock club door, where of course, you idiot, they don't let *moros* in. And I remember thinking that if this really were a central, heavy, defining fact of my life, then I probably wouldn't want to be a writer at all; I wouldn't want to write about it and I wouldn't know how to ignore it. I'd be too sick of the daily weight of anger and absurdity to want to re-create it in words, and if I had to, then I'd find some other art, nonverbal, to pour myself into. I'd want to soar, unleashing celebration and fury and love and pain in some way that it would seem trivial to want to justify or explain.

At an outdoor Christmas bazaar in the Plaza Santa Ana, I bought handcrafted puppets for the children of some friends in New York. And I stood on a corner of the plaza while it prettily snowed and pulled the puppets from their paper wrapper to admire them, beautiful puppets—and a fat-faced Spanish burgher came up and literally snatched them out of my hands and asked me how much I wanted for them! He thought I was just some vagrant street vendor. Well, all right, an honest enough mistake. But it was the way he snatched them from my hands, as if he already owned them, and me.

I think it was a day later, at the tail end of the same snowstorm, that I spontaneously stopped to give a helpful shove to the rear fender of a stuck, wheel-spinning car, helping to free it. The driver paused and rolled down his window and, with a strikingly begrudging expression, gestured toward me, not to say thank you but to offer me a coin worth about fifteen cents.

Of course, not everyone in Madrid was an overt bigot. But I remember thinking that even if only one out of every hundred was, that was easily enough to wreck your day nearly every day.

I carried my notebook from one café to another, trying to start my novel. I carried that stuck wheel-spinning futility with me everywhere, wishing for someone to come and give me a helpful shove. . . . I liked the café, from whose second-floor window I could stare down the length of the Gran Vía—Chicote's, Hemingway's Spanish Civil War hangout, just a few blocks ahead, where they shot the hysterical flit who was spraying eau de cologne on people, a place where people indulged in apocalyptic binge drinking as the city and the Republic finally crumbled around them under Fascist bombs—I must have spent whole afternoons up there, just staring out the window. I liked another café in the Plaza Bilbao; I remember one transfixed ghostly moment when I looked around at the crowded tables through clouds of cigarette smoke marveling at how many Jewish faces I saw in that room. It might have been the Upper West Side in the 1950s, or Berlin or Vienna much earlier in this century; it was a genetic haunting, the Madrid of five hundred years ago peeking through its modern veneer. I went at least once a week to the Prado Museum, and scuffed for hours amid wind-blown leaves and those strange fantastical squirrels and the boat ponds of El Retiro, where real *moros* furtively circled through the shrubs and statuary, selling hashish; I was approached more than once myself by eager young Spaniards quietly wanting to know if I had any to sell. At night, nearly every night, I walked from one end of the city to the other, starting from my neighborhood and the Malasaña, sort of like Madrid's Lower East Side, its labyrinth of dark, wet, alleylike streets littered with junkies' discarded syringes. I'd cross the city's central artery, and the Plaza del Sol, and climb past the Plaza Mayor, or up the hill into the bar-packed neighborhood surrounding the Plaza Santa Ana. Doing *la marcha,* this was called, the night-to-dawn bar and disco crawl that seemed to be the defining experience of La Movida; like an entire society throwing an all-night house party while their parents are away. I went out alone, nearly every night, drifting in and out of crowded smoky bars and cafés like Poe's gas-lit man in the crowd, stunned, almost marveling at the previously unexplored depths of loneliness and alienation I was getting to know, amid all the raucous friendliness of the crowds, a friendliness that seemed (I know, *Stop your sobbing;* but I'm just telling a story, a *true* story) meant for nearly everyone but me. I admit I've never been much of a seducer or even a very successful flirt, but the way that Spanish woman, after I'd dared to strike up a conversation, grimaced and slid away with a palpable show of offended, shivering revulsion . . . that really freaked me out! (Conversely, I still vividly recall the delightful surprise of a single conversation in a corner of a nightspot with two charming, dark, curly-haired Portuguese girls, tourists; and a sweet yet intoxicatingly vampish Norwegian who, I found out later, after I already had a heart-pounding crush, was herself madly in love with an Argentine rock musician; and another tourist, German, who briefly—she was just passing through—became a friend after noticing me in a crowded bar where I sat alone reading Günter Grass's *Dog Years.*) Of course, I couldn't help but notice the friendly treatment other foreigners received, that young "white" Americans received. And I found myself experiencing a strange sensation of estrangement from them, my countrymen . . .

I am going to temporarily leave Madrid and my "happy ending"—in the final act, I make some surprising friends, and I finally get to punch somebody—and jump ahead to an incident that happened just a few months ago. I've had the experience, many times, of being mistaken for what I am not, though never as extremely as in Spain. And sometimes this has been kind of hilarious, and even poignant, in its glancing lesson about people's well-meaning and often completely patronizing willingness to be deceived: as when, while on a magazine assignment, I'd come in from the war zone in northern Nicaragua to the town of Jalapa. I was lounging on some steps and reading a Sandinista newspaper—I happened to be wearing a green T-shirt—when I looked up and saw a tour bus crammed with North American "Witness for Peace" activists stopped in front of me on the narrow mud street. Many passengers were leaning out the windows, snapping photographs of this visual proof of the success of the Revolution's literacy campaigns, while I gaped back at them over the propaganda sheet, confused at first by their grins and cameras and clenched fists and shouts of "*¡No pasarán!*" In Managua, sitting alone in the patio of my cheap hotel one night, reading an American novel, I was approached by a German, who exclaimed, "Ah! So the Revolution is teaching you to read English, too!"

But I've also had the even more disconcerting experience of being mistaken for what I am. It happened just a few months ago, when I was on a book tour following the publication of a new novel. I was being interviewed by a big-city newspaper, not far from the suburban town I'd spent most of my youth in; that newspaper had already run a friendly review of my book, with photo.

"Do you know a Teresa O'Donneloni?" asked my interviewer. My memory traveled back, back, back a quarter of a century, to the mainly Irish-Italian little town where I had the adolescence I think I won't be making a nostalgic movie about any time soon. Yes, of course, O'Donneloni! A cheerleader whom I'd wimpily befriended in tenth-grade English class, as if that way I might eventually trick her into going out with me. Her boyfriend, an Irish thug with a band of Irish and Italian thugs, once came to my yard deep in the night and, to get at *me,* stripped all the branches from the trunks of the young cherry trees my father had recently planted.

"Yes, I remember Teresa O'Donneloni," I said. "She went to high school with me."

"Well, we received a rather disturbing fax from her. She really seems to have taken offense." The reporters said that Teresa O'Donneloni had faxed the newspaper to say that she remembered me from high school as "a Jewish kid."

Uh-huh. Well, Goldman. Hello? My last name *is* Goldman.

I said, "I guess it doesn't surprise me that she would have thought that."

I began to understand where this was coming from. The newspaper had identified me as a Guatemalan American. You can't be Guatemalan and Jewish!—is that what she thought? Of course, the newspaper reporter had to check out this provocative lead; perhaps he would discover that I'd invented a whole nonexistent family past for myself? I suppose it was her own suspicion that this was so that had led her to fire off her outraged fax. Why should someone get a little bit of attention in the newspapers for being something I know they are not, she must have thought, with an almost admirably crusty Yankee cantankerousness and intolerance for faddish deceptions, getting out her big spoonfuls of "Goldman-filling"

I explained my family background to the reporter, reminding him that I was generally uncomfortable speaking about certain aspects of my family's past in interviews, but that I'd pretty accurately—as accurately as I ever will—portrayed it in the admittedly autobiographical depiction of Roger Graetz's early boyhood in *The Long Night of White Chickens,* my first novel. There the narrator recounts early childhood years in Guatemala, and how he was saved from growing up there when he contracted tuberculosis; his mother took him back to Boston for the better hospitals, where she also had a rapprochement with her overjoyed Jewish husband. (Soon pure fiction takes over, with the arrival of an eventually Wellesley-college-bound and finally murder-bound young Guatemalan orphan housekeeper.) But my just-published novel didn't have those autobiographical elements; it didn't even have Jews; it merely told a story involving a largely though not entirely Central American cast. Perhaps Teresa hadn't read that first book.

"In high school back then," I told the reporter, "in the seventies, there wasn't the ethnic consciousness there is now, and I can hardly imagine what, back then, would have motivated me to go marching through the halls of my high school asserting my 'Guatemalan roots.' That would have been a pretty good way to get beaten up." But yes, of course, I'd thought of myself as an American boy, which I was. And of course, I wanted to be called Frank, which is still the name I use with most friends and in most daily transactions that don't involve a formal, rolled-off-the-tongue unfurling of the necessary—necessary to *me*—whole shebang.

I didn't recall if Teresa O'Donneloni had spent much time in my house, though she may have; but that house certainly told what it told about my family, which is why some of my friends liked to call it "The Copacabana."

"You mean you were just trying to fit in," said the reporter.

"I don't think I was *trying* to do anything." How could I explain it to him, the completely out-of-it fog of those years, when I carried a D-minus average through high school, and my friends liked to call me "Sleepy" and "Sleepless" because that's what I was like . . . Was that only because I wasn't expressing myself ethnically? I doubt it. My parents' renewed marital conflicts and looming separation; the bullying ignorance that characterized my school, that town; illegal substances and the allure of minor juvenile delinquency, the clever thieving schemes and skipping school—we did have some fun, after all.

Where had I been since then, and how had I, and my country (my *countries*) changed? Half of those twenty-five years had been spent in Central America and Mexico. When living in the United States, I live in a city, New York, whose population will soon be 30 percent Hispanic. I wouldn't be comfortable anymore, Teresa, in the town we grew up in. I never really was anyway. Needless to say, I am not going to spend my writing career justifying to Americans how you can be half Jewish and *latinoamericano,* too.

But why does it seem to matter so much? (O'Donneloni hasn't been the only one.) What about the countless other half-Jewish writers? Did Proust put up with this? What about Frida Kahlo? Kahlo is as Jewish a last name as Goldman, though apparently not as recognizably so to gringos who vacation in Kankún, Yukatán, drinking piña koladas from koko shells in the shade of their kabañas. Frida and I have the same ethnic mixture, and considering how many of the original conquistadors were conversos (on the run from the Inquisition), our particular *mestizaje* is a New World classic combo. My father is Jewish, my mother is Catholic, but as I am not trying to practice both religions at once, there is no actual conflict. Of course, there are aspects of my personality in which I recognize the influence of either my father or mother, and their respective families. But attributing personality traits simply to ethnicity really does strike me as a little far-fetched. National characteristics, cultural or even geographic ones—a sense of place—have more resonance. I'm a citizen and a partisan of America, in the national and hemispheric sense respectively. In Mexico City, where I've spent almost half of the last six years, I'm also, strictly speaking, one more mestizo in the largest and most mestizo city on earth, and am happy enough to leave it at that and fade into the crowd. In traditional Jewish law, you are what your mother is, while, conversely, in the United States, a Jewish last name seems to raise certain expectations that having a Jewish mother does not. The language of ethnic self-consciousness is one of such relentless banality, absurdity—of pigeonholed *restriction*—in our culture that I suppose I can't really blame anyone for taking the opportunity to wriggle completely free of it. We could use a more inclusive notion of ourselves as being a "mestizo" nation, too. Lately, it often seems as if soon we'll all be made to display our ethnic ingredients on our foreheads—and on our book jackets—like FDA Nutrition Facts labels, so that everyone can know just what they're getting. *Let's see what this new magical realist Karmen Kukaracha is really made of!* Well, at least then nobody will need to ask.

Frank Goldman is not just "a Jewish guy," and frankly, never was. Like a last name, your facial features, what you look like, precede you through the world in another way. In New York City, a Hispanic was usually an Afro-Caribbean person, Puerto Rican or Dominican. But for the last twenty years the city has filled with people from the land bridge running through Mexico to the lid of South America whom I recognize on sight, just as they sufficiently recognize something in me, stopping to address me in Spanish on the street, on a subway platform, in a restaurant or shop. I like speaking Spanish, being addressed in Spanish, on the street, in shops. Like just that glancing sense of belonging. More than Latino, in the U.S. identity-politics sense of that word, I feel that I'm *from* Latin America, that I'm as much from *there* as from *here*. Of course, in American letters it is something of an old truism that a writer needs his *place*—a postage stamp on earth—that he can call his own. And I used to joke that if that was so, the place most naturally my own was Miami International Airport: Jews flying down from the north, Latin Americans up from the south, and there intermingling. What I think I did end up doing in my first book was only to begin to express why and how Central America had become a part of me—that landscape, those people and their history—joining it to *my* history, as I'd lived it there and here in the United States, and in that hybrid of both places at once that can only exist in imagination but which is definitely *a place*. And maybe that purely literary "place" is my one true place; my imagination's permanent address, where my true progenitors would be novels from the two separate though not unrelated literary traditions that have most shaped my particular tastes and ambitions: the Latin American novel, and . . . "everything else."

But something else began in me during those months eleven years ago—an acceleration of a process already under way—when Madrid said I was a *moro,* and I began to see how ambiguous my place in the world could really be. In Madrid, I began to feel estranged from white Americans, because they were having so much fun and I wasn't; because when I told them about *moros* and Spaniards, they usually didn't believe me, because they thought the Spaniards of La Movida were so friendly and open-minded and cool and nice! They'd say, "I haven't seen anything like that! Gee, you don't look Moroccan to me. . . . Well, yeah, I guess I can see how maybe . . ." An estrangement from people who simply don't understand, or won't believe, who are completely oblivious of how their sense of comparative safety and entitlement looks to those outside of it. A sense of suddenly finding myself on the outside of a world I used to feel I belonged in—did I push myself out, or was I pushed out?

I had a few friends, finally, in Madrid. A Massachusetts guy who had a job teaching English and was dating one of his students, a Cuban cabaret dancer. Silvio, a Colombian. And Basilio, the bartender in a favorite bar, and also a rock drummer, whose brother was the DJ in one of those small hole-in-the-wall after-hours rock hangouts I was always being turned away from when I came alone. I was with the English teacher the night, in a nightclub, a Spanish girl just laughed and said she didn't believe I was American. I lamely pulled out my passport as proof. And then she said (providing me with a line I used later, in my novel), "Well, my grandfather is English. That makes me more American than you." She didn't believe I was a writer, either; she didn't even believe I was literate; she said so. And then the guy who I'd just realized was her boyfriend butted in to say, "If you're really American, then what are the words to this song that is playing?" At that moment, a song by the Pretenders was playing. I told him that I'd put up with this nonsense from her because she was a woman, but not from him. I told him that if he said one more word to me, I was going to hit him in the face. He said another word, and I did, and it landed hard enough to knock him down, and some people, presumably his girlfriend among them, began to shout, but I was already being rushed away; my American friend had seen and grabbed me and was already pulling me out the door.

Real *moros* hung out near the bars and taverns around the Plaza Santa Ana. They sold cigarettes from small tables and later they'd escape the cold and the tedium by crowding into one of the nearby bars. They'd stand in a crowd of men in the corner of one bar or the other, drinking, talking, and laughing among themselves, a gang of friends. As I was usually by myself in these bars, I thought I would try to talk to them. I wondered, Well, if everyone thinks I'm a *moro,* what will the *moros* think?

We became friends. Night after night, I'd end my trudge up the hill to the Plaza Santa Ana by sharing drinks with my new crowd of Muslim friends. Or I'd stand outside with them for a while, talking around their little cigarette tables. Most of them were named Mohammed. There was Mohammed Somali, Mohammed Sudani, Mohammed Egipto, and so on. Mohammed Somali became, by far, my closest friend, for a while my closest friend in Spain. Tall and lanky, always in a suitcoat, he had the look of a Giacometti sculpture. He was a political exile who'd been granted asylum from the Barre regime; and he studied computer engineering, as many of them did. Mohammed Somali explained to me one night how it was that he and his friends seemed regular booze hounds, when according to Islamic law alcohol is sinful. He said, "Ahh Frrrrank! My friend! Very good question! When in Islamic country, then we obey Islamic laws. But Spain is not Islamic country! Islamic law only in Islamic country!"

One night, soon after I'd begun searching them out, we were gathered—about eight of us—into one of our two regular bars, the one famous for its murals.

The bartender came over and said, in as genial a way as he could under the circumstances, "Too many *moros!* There are too many of you, some of you have to leave or you all have to leave."

I exploded, in Spanish and English, asking what law there was that decreed how many *moros* at a time were allowed into a Spanish bar, demanding that he explain what exactly he'd meant by "too many *moros*," and, of course, calling him names. I may even have pulled out my laminated press card, used the line about doing a travel story on Madrid-by-night. When the bartender heard that aggressive American English jumping at him from my lips, he gaped as if at a talking dog! And of course he backed down, went away red-faced and fuming.

I'd been astonished by the docility with which my new friends had seemed ready to back down in the face of this astoundingly racist harassment. Though of course they had to abide it, and understood it as a daily condition of their residence in Spain. Still, my self-righteous outburst had won us, and them, an entertaining victory.

Mohammed Somali began to say that as a Christmas present he was going to give me a copy of the best book he'd ever read. But it had started out feeling like the dreariest Christmas season I'd ever spent.

I waited Christmas morning in the one open, greasy-aired

café that I could find in my neighborhood. Since I knew Mohammed Somali was bringing me his present, I'd gone out and bought him one, too, a colorfully woven thick wool cap from the same Christmas bazaar where I'd bought the puppets. I sat there smoking, eating olives from the little dish on the counter, sipping at a glass of tinto, and wondered what book this could be, the best one Mohammed Somali had ever read.

When he came, he pulled his present from a white plastic bag. A big paperback of the Koran, in Spanish . . . (duh).

We walked to the Plaza de España. Mohammed had heard that an overseas pay phone was out of order; as it was Christmas, no repairmen would be coming to fix it. I had to phone home, too.

Every *moro* and *africano* and *sudaco* in Madrid was patiently waiting in the orderly line running all the way around the plaza, shuffling their feet in place, rocking clasped arms against the cold. Mohammed Somali and I took our place at the end of the long, scruffy, murmuring line. That's how I spent Christmas Day in Madrid that year, the last week of 1985, waiting in line for hours for my free overseas phone call, the line lengthening behind us, ever so gradually shortening towards the front, as one man—they were almost all men—after another sent his voice "home" to Casablanca, Bulawayo, Cuzco . . . I had nothing else to do that day, and did need to phone home. I felt a funny sense of belonging. I suppose I'd earned it. Though for me a sense of belonging can be elusive, and often arrives just like that, as at least partly the product of my own imagination—which does not diminish the good feeling, the simple, fleeting grace.

THE ROAD FROM BALLYGUNGE

Bharati Mukherjee

When my two sisters and I were little girls living in a Bengali-speaking neighborhood in Calcutta in the late forties, our favorite children's rhyme, in translation, went something like this: "Sisters three are we / Three pretty flowers on a tree." I believe the rhyme was intended to instill in little girls the desire to be as fragile and as decorative as flowers. We, however, because we were trapped in a forty-five-member Mukherjee family household in which our mother was daily upbraided for having borne no sons, turned the rhyme into our special song of solidarity and defiance.

Before the fifteenth of August, when India became a sovereign nation, our block of Rash Behari Avenue constituted our entire world. Rash Behari Avenue is a wide, boulevarded artery in the comfortably middle-class neighborhood of Ballygunge, which includes the Dhakuria Lakes for boating and grassy stretches for strolling. Our block of one-, two-, and three-story stucco houses, many with storefronts, was self-sufficient. In addition to "variety" shops where we could buy everything from candies to smelling salts, our block accommodated a homeopath's and a doctor's storefront clinics, a photographer's studio, and a tea shop. The freshwater fish we ate twice a day came from nearby Gariahat Market, famous in the city for selling the freshest fish and vegetables. Our male cousins played vigorous boys' games in the muddy furrows of wartime trenches in the small park three houses down, while our girl cousins took singing or sitar-playing lessons at home. As the sun went down every evening, my cymbals-clanking sisters and I followed our widowed paternal grandmother as she, a stern champion of Hindu tradition, lit the cotton wicks of a multiheaded, cobra-shaped brass oil lamp and with the holy glow of lamplight chased ghosts out of every room.

Our block of Ballygunge was so homogeneously Hindu and Bengali-speaking that as a very small child I never saw any foreigner other than an Afghan peddler who came by once a winter with baskets of dried fruits and nuts. All the same, the Raj assaulted the innocent self-centeredness of my parochial childhood with its sloganeering: "British is Best"; "Britannica Rules." In that colonial context, I intuited that biculturalism was a fixed contest between two cultures of opposing values: *ours* and *theirs*. Even in Ballygunge, the Raj cast a bullying shadow. *They* arrested our neighborhood boys for reciting banned nationalist poems; in the trench-scarred park where members of a youth club worked out, *they* raided the clubhouse for homemade bombs. *We* avenged ourselves through films and novels in which the villain was a ruddy-faced, pith-helmeted, women-molesting, sadistic English planter of indigo or jute. Sometimes the contest touched me directly. In the kindergarten school run by Bengali-speaking Protestant missionaries that I, the middle sister, briefly attended, I saw Jack and Jill tumbling down the hill in an illustrated book of British nursery rhymes, and though Mira, my older sister, and I were always dressed in pretty, just-sewn frocks my mother kept turning out on her brand-new Singer sewing machine, I couldn't help envying just a little bit Jill's perky pinafore outfit made of cloth not available in fabric stalls in Ballygunge.

That envy for Jill's pinafore, I now realize, was exactly the emotion that the colonizer aims for. Colonial insistence on race-based biculturalism reinforces ghetto identity and ghetto mentality. Any erasure of the ghetto's boundaries becomes an erasure of personal identity; any border-crossing amounts to betrayal.

Before Independence, like most children on our block, Mira and I had never ventured into the necklace of ghettos beyond. We knew, of course, that Bengalis with Westernized attitudes and close connections to the colonial government lived in neighborhoods with English names, such as Sunny Park, Rainy Park, and Mandeville Gardens; Europeans corralled themselves in Chowringhee, a "White Town" of garden-ringed bungalows, spacious apartment buildings, swept-clean roads, and colonial monuments; Muslims clustered in beef-eating neighborhoods of twisted alleys full of *burqua*-wearing women and henna-bearded men; and Anglo-Indians, a small Eurasian community of Empire loyalists who claimed Britain (which they were not ever likely to make their pilgrimage to) as their "homeland," hovered in the shabby peripheries of Chowringhee, self-segregating themselves from us Hindus and Muslims.

If Mira and I had not come of age in the post-Independence Calcutta of the fifties when the euphoria of nation building threw reactionary women like my paternal grandmother temporarily off balance, we would have been married off as teenagers, as had been our mother, to carefully selected Bengali Brahmin bridegrooms. Our maternal grandmother had been seven years old on her wedding day, and her younger sister only five on hers. At seven, Mother's mother had been scorned as an aged bride by the community, the victim of the progressive views of a father eccentric enough to encourage literacy for women.

We sisters were born at a lucky moment in the city's history. Independence opened up business opportunities for Indian men of energy and vision like our father, who in the fifties came to be known in the Calcutta Chamber of Commerce as the Bengal Tiger. The pharmaceutical company that Father, a biochemist by training, had founded in the midforties, prospered, requiring the relocation of the manufacturing plant to a large site outside the city limits. Workaholic Father's need to be on site at all hours eased our nuclear family's breakout from the crowded household in Ballygunge. For Mother, the move meant quarrel-free permission to enroll us in a girls-only school where the cultivation of intelligence would be as important a goal as the refinement of femininity and manners. The school she picked was Loreto House, an exclusive English-language establishment run by Irish nuns who promised Mother, the muzzled feminist, "Our girls can compete with the best anywhere in the world."

My years in Loreto House School and Loreto House College exposed me to a postcolonial variant of Raj-style biculturalism that required continual and complex readjustments to ensure survival with psychic integrity. During the schoolday, except during French class, we spoke only English; learned only European history because no India-friendly but not Britain-unfriendly textbook of Indian history satisfactory to the Loreto House nuns had yet been published; performed Gilbert and Sullivan in music class; acted in plays by Shakespeare, Oscar Wilde, J. M. Barrie in perfectly mimicked upper-class British accents; memorized Christian scriptures, including the Acts of the Apostles; played unfeminine sports like volleyball and basketball; and sang songs like "Home on the Range" at school socials. At home, we spoke a mixture of Bengali and English, and on weekend visits to Ballygunge relatives, a carefully enunciated, formally phrased Bengali; we tried to keep up with Bengali-language plays, songs, movies, and celebrity gossip; we scouted the city for stores selling the trendiest saris. Biculturalism ballooned into triculturalism every Thursday afternoon when we took in the matinee at the Metro Cinema in Chowringhee. The Metro Cinema showed only MGM musicals, costumed extravaganzas usually starring Doris Day, and made us daydream of a backlot-constructed "America" where the big-boned heroine with the frank face and toothy smile pursued love and happiness without having to step over homeless families and maimed beggar children sleeping on sidewalks. Loreto House was my accidental laboratory for experimenting with how and what new cultural elements to incorporate into my Ballygunge-self and how and what to reject so I could survive adolescence in transitional times.

Father, who liked to think of himself as a benevolently despotic head of the family, was touched by the promise and excitement of those improvisational times. He took what he later described as the biggest gamble of his life: he sent each of us three sisters to American campuses to study whatever subjects we wanted for two years while he searched for bridegrooms for us.

Mira and my younger sister, Ranu, arrived as "foreign students" at what was then known as Idlewild Airport in the fall of 1960. Ranu, who had just turned sixteen, was met by a friendly alumna of Vassar College and driven to Poughkeepsie to start her sophomore year. Vassar dorms were filled with what I imagine were American equivalents of Loreto House women and Ranu expected to fit in with them, but their cultural tolerances turned out to be totally alien. When Ranu learned that she had to fulfill the school requirement that entering students be photographed in the nude, she rushed back in tears to India.

Mira changed planes at Idlewild Airport for Detroit, gritted her teeth when she saw how different a neighborhood downtown Detroit was from Ballygunge, made friends with other international students, got her graduate degree in child psychology and preschool education, and just as Dad announced that he had found the perfect East Bengali groom for her, she surprised him by marrying a Bombay-born, Marathi-speaking Indian graduate student getting his business administration degree at Wayne State University.

I arrived in the United States exactly a year after Mira had.

On my way to the University of Iowa in Iowa City, where I was to study for a master of fine arts degree for two years, I stopped off in Detroit to visit with Mira. In that one year away from Mukherjee-style benevolent patriarchy, Mira had evolved into a confident, independent-thinking woman who had stepped out of the secured perimeters of our Calcutta compound into a bold, unchaperoned new world. The night I arrived in Detroit, she gathered her friends in her tiny apartment off Woodward Avenue for a "Welcome, Bharati!" potluck dinner. The kitchen alcove was crowded with Hong Kong Chinese, Algerians, Moroccans, Tunisians, Chaldean Christians, Indians from states in India that we Bengalis had traditionally patronized, two white American women, and one African American man. Except for the three native-born Americans, all the guests—like Mira, like me—were "foreign students" on student visas, though the few who were nearing the end of their medical school or engineering school degree programs were hoping to stay on as immigrants.

I stayed two weeks with Mira, then continued my journey to Iowa City. Before my two years of study at the Writers' Workshop were over, like Doris Day in my favorite MGM matinees, I found love and happiness with a fellow student, which led to a lunchtime marriage in a lawyer's office above a coffee shop. Because the man I so impulsively married happened to be an American citizen of Canadian parents, I was forced to choose between life with my husband on an alien continent and life back in India, my homeland. I chose husband over homeland. I don't think I had any idea when I first made that choice that I was acknowledging my willingness to transform myself from expatriate to immigrant, from aloof spectator to responsible participant, and in that process to transform the America I'd adopted into a homeland I would be proud to claim.

It is assumed in many parts of the world that to become an "American" demands jumping into the mythical melting pot—a kind of cultural electric chair—and committing psychocultural suicide. Resistance to change, to a McWorld of blue jeans and hamburgers, the deliberate barricading of oneself within one's original culture, is seen as heroic. In those circles, expatriation is a sign of integrity. Using the Old Culture as a shield against the New is a temptation I understand, but which I deplore.

Mira, who has lived in Detroit since 1960 and who now practices there as a child psychologist, and her Indian-born husband belong in the circle of expatriates. In the late nineties as the United States embroils itself in shrill debates over the rights of legal immigrants, Mira rages to me over the phone: "I feel used. I feel manipulated and discarded. This is such an unfair way to treat a person who was *invited* to stay and work here because of her talent . . . For over thirty years, I've invested my creativity and skills in the improvement of *America*'s preschool system. I've obeyed all the rules, I've paid my taxes, I love my work, I love my students, I love the friends I've made. But I want to go home to India when I'm ready to retire. I still I feel I have an Indian heritage. I feel some kind of an irrational attachment to India that I don't to America."

I wonder if Mira's "irrational attachment" comes from having lived the past thirty-seven years in a bicultural city like Detroit, where the only cultures that matter are African American and European American, and where to be an Indo-American is to feel irrelevant.

In bicultural, bilingual countries like Canada, Belgium, or

Sri Lanka, the debate about "nationhood" automatically generates bitterness, and sometimes blood. In theory, bilingualism should be an advantage, a gift; yet bilingual nations face the greatest challenge to stability. Slovakia has already made a "Slovak Only in Public Spaces" decision. In officially bilingual Canada, the war between the Anglophones and the Francophones continues to be fought in a climate of catastrophic national breakup.

I recognize Mira's pain as real. I understand her survivor's need of nostalgia for a homeland she doesn't have to live in and experience the gritty aggravations of every day. But in multicultural states like California, where I make my home, her expatriate stance of stubborn resistance to America seems a sad waste. A tragedy for all Americans, not just herself. In cities like San Francisco, where immigrants from Central America and South America jostle elbows with refugees from Cambodia and Vietnam, I've eavesdropped on thickly accented, enthusiastic conversation about "drive-through diagnostics" and "bun management" between people wearing fast-food-company logos on their shirt pockets. I want to think that in our multicultural United States, immigrants like them will play the stabilizing role that pride and history deny the major players.

The point is not to adopt the mainstream American's easy ironies nor the expatriate's self-protective contempt for the "vulgarity" of immigration. The point is to stay resilient and compassionate in the face of change.

REFLECTIONS ON
MY DAUGHTER

David Mura

I write about my daughter often in my poems, in part because she is our oldest. In one poem, "Listening," I describe the events around the town of a Japanese ancestor. The poem ends with the ancestor listening to his wife's pregnant belly and links that listening to what I myself was doing at the time I wrote the poem. The child inside my wife's belly was Samantha, and the poem is dedicated to her. I tell audiences that I was so obsessed with her coming presence that I made a tape of my voice. Then I had my wife place the headphones of the cassette player on her belly, so our daughter would be familiar with my voice as well as hers.

The same image—my listening to my wife's belly—also

ends my poem "The Colors of Desire," but instead of focusing on ancient Japan, this poem links the Japanese American internment camps in Arkansas with the racial politics in the American South. At the same time, it explores my own problematic sexual desires for white women and for pornography. At one point, the poem asks this question: "Father, mother, / I married a woman not of my color. / What is it I want to escape?" The poem's last lines contrast the legacies of racial history with the image of my wife's belly and ask the following question about our daughter's identity:

> And if what is granted erases nothing,
> if history remains, untouched, implacable,
> as darkness flows up our hemisphere,
> her hollow still moves moonward,
> small hill on the horizon, swelling,
> floating with child, white, yellow,
> who knows, who can tell her,
>
> oh why must it matter?

The past, the present, and the future. A world beyond race, a world within race. Where is it her life will go?

Recently, on a trip to a small midwestern city, I spoke to a Chinese-Hawaiian American who had moved into a white middle-class neighborhood with her daughter, who is half European American. The woman said that the first time her daughter went out to join the neighborhood children who were playing across the street, the children ran away from her. This happened a couple times, and each time, her daughter asked why this was happening. She told her daughter that the other children must have had to go in to supper or that their parents were calling them.

With a courage and patience I don't think I could muster, this woman then went across the street, knocked on doors, introduced herself, and told the parents what had happened, and asked if they knew why their children wouldn't play with her daughter. The parents seemed embarrassed and said they didn't know why their children acted that way. The next time the woman went with her daughter across the street, perhaps the children's parents had talked to them, because they didn't run away. Still, the children refused to engage her or let her use their toys. When they had candy, they did not offer any. The woman, though, kept coming back with her daughter and then invited the children to her house and gave them refreshments. Gradually, after a long, slow process of letting the children know neither she nor her daughter were something to be frightened of, her daughter was let into the neighborhood circle.

Of course, her daughter still has to deal with the same sorts of reactions outside her neighborhood, at school, at the county fair, where white parents have picked up their children if they are sitting next to her daughter before a ride begins. I asked the woman if she ever explained to her daughter why this was happening. No, she said, she always tried to create some other reason for their behavior, because it would be too painful to tell her the real reason.

It's clear it didn't matter to the neighborhood children that her daughter was of mixed race and part white. They saw her dark skin and they ran. This is one reason that there are many places in this country that neither I nor my wife would live in. It's not just that I don't want my children to go through such experiences; obviously, neither did this Chinese-Hawaiian American woman. It's also that I don't think I would have the patience or restraint to deal with such open racism.

At the same time, I do want my children to know that racism exists and to be prepared for it. I want them to know about the legacy of race in America. I want to train them for the world many white Americans don't think exists or want to see.

I think back to the time Samantha was four and I was reading her *Baseball Saved Us,* by Ken Mochizuki, a book that narrates the experience of a young Japanese American boy and his family coming to the internment camps in World War II. It explores the depression and social breakdowns that occurred after people were taken from their homes on the West Coast to barbed-wired enclosures in desolate and out-of-the way areas farther inland. At one point the boy's brother sasses back to his father, a major breach of Japanese familial rules, and the father decides that the young people need to have a baseball diamond, a place where they can reclaim some sense of normalcy. The boy of the story is neither very big for his age nor very skilled, but he manages to improve and hit a crucial home run in a camp game.

But after the family leaves the camps, the boy's difficulties continue. Now he is the only Japanese American on his school team, and when the team visits another town and he comes up to bat, he hears people yelling "Jap."

As a third-generation Japanese American, I found this book difficult to read. Partly, it brought up the whole experience of the camps and seemed to reawaken a deep emotional tie to that experience that I'm always surprised I feel. For instance, when I visited the internment camp exhibit at the Smithsonian a couple years ago with another sansei (third-generation Japanese American), we found we were both in tears by the end of the exhibit, a response neither of us had expected. After all, like much of their generation, neither of our parents had talked much about the camps. But perhaps that was one of the reasons why the exhibit so struck us: we were entering the forbidden, the silenced past; we were regaining a lost part of our heritage and ourselves.

Mochizuki's book on the camps also brought up my own memories of wanting to fit in as a youngster, of wanting to be accepted as normal, like the other boys in our white suburban neighborhood. It wasn't that I was ever the brunt of direct racial insults; it was more that I knew I was somehow different from most of the other kids at school or from the stars of the sitcoms or the westerns I worshiped as a child. It was a curious position: For instance, I identified as a matter of course with John Wayne fighting the Indians or even fighting the "Japs" in World War II movies. And yet I knew somehow that I didn't look like John Wayne and that I was never going to be John Wayne. The problem was I had no language to talk about how all this affected me or how I was being inculcated with a view of America that excluded people of color.

When I read the section in *Baseball Saved Us* about the racial insults, I told Samantha that "Jap" was like other racial insults to other people of color, and I also explained to her the terms "nigger" and "spic." I said that one reason Japanese Americans were put into the camps was because of the racism in the country, that there was a long history of hatred of Asians, particularly on the West Coast. I wanted to make Samantha aware that prejudice existed, and yet, at the same time, I didn't want to create in her a sense of fear or paranoia. I was trying to strike an uneasy balance.

Samantha then asked again about who in our family had been put in the camps. She was particularly impressed that her grandparents had been in the camps. I told her that my parents had not talked about the camps to me as a child but that I wanted her to know about them. It was important to remember what had happened in the past.

I don't know exactly how much of all this she understood. For a few weeks, the book was a favorite of hers, and we read it over several times. With each reading, my own sense of pain lessened. And I could feel the story sinking into Sam's consciousness, her sense of who she is.

As I read *Baseball Saved Us* to Samantha, I know she didn't feel a strong connection to the whites in the book—the guards who sit on the rifle tower and watch the camp games, the young boy's white teammates, or the opposing team and fans who hurl racial insults. I didn't talk to her much about how she is both Japanese American *and* European American. The lessons of the camps, their legacy of racism, seemed difficult enough to absorb.

As I look back, I see other reasons for my neglect of the "white" side of her identity. For one thing, I grew up wanting desperately to emulate the white mainstream. By high school, I reached the point where, if a friend said to me "I think of you, David, like a white person," I would consider it a compliment. I know how strong the pressures often are to assimilate, to erase your own sense of difference.

But what was the nature of my difference? I knew the way I looked made others associate me with others I did not want to belong to—Japanese Americans and people of color—and how it made me feel less attractive than the whites around me. But that difference also included anything that had to do with Japanese culture—the food, which I had encountered only occasionally on holidays and which I proclaimed to hate, and the language and culture, which were not part of my everyday life and which I saw no reason to look into. The difference between these two—the way I looked and my Japanese heritage—were difficult for me to sort out consciously. In my eyes they both stigmatized me. Only later did I see the difference between them. By assimilating, I could erase my cultural sense of difference (the value of such an erasure is another question). I could not, though, erase the way I looked. Or how others regarded me because of that.

On my travels throughout the country, I encounter or hear of young Asian Americans and hapa (the Hawaiian term for "mixed-race") who want to pretend they are exactly like the whites at their schools and do not understand why I talk so fervently about the need to formulate Asian American identities. The pressures to assimilate obviously have continued.

At the same time, I vaguely sense that the problems facing the young hapa are different from mine in ways I don't completely understand.

Part of me wishes for things to be simpler, to say that since Samantha looks mainly Asian, this is how society views her, this is how she will be treated, this is what I have to prepare her for. When I look at her, I want to see her as Asian American; that's an identity I've worked very hard to learn about and accept.

Of course, all this leaves out how she will want to view herself.

In thinking about the identity of someone like my daughter, most people, myself included, often become confused by the terms "bicultural" and "biracial." My daughter is both, but the way these two aspects of her identity play themselves out differs in scope.

I have a friend whose father is European American and whose mother is a Japanese national. She says when you grow up in two cultures, you aren't split in half. Instead, there are two distinct beings inside of you. If you're separated from one of the cultures, that being dies, at least for a time. It has no light to bathe in, no air, no soil. It can, like certain miraculous plants and seeds, come back to life, but the longer it dwells in that state of nonbeing, the harder it is to revive.

This isn't exactly my daughter's situation. True, I am Japanese American, and my wife is three-quarters Wasp, one-quarter Jew. But I didn't grow up with a sense of Japanese culture or speaking Japanese. We were raised Episcopalian (my father converted in college), and not Buddhist or Shinto. My parents never drummed into us any particular Japanese ethos, and if I was pressured to study hard and get good grades, this seemed less the handing down of an Asian educational philosophy than my father's embracing of the Horatio Alger myth: anyone can succeed in America if they work hard. Also, my high school was filled with academic-minded Jewish kids whom I had to compete against.

As for my wife and me, there isn't a great cultural or value gap between us; that's one of the reasons we've been together for so long, over twenty years. We're fervent liberals; we're secular-minded, children of the sixties; we both grew up in white middle-class suburbs; we share a taste for irony and are suspicious of the irrational or mystical. Susie's always felt her Wasp background was rather bland.

In terms of our children's background, she's generally just as assertive as I am about teaching our children about their Japanese American heritage. Part of the reason for this is that we can assume our children will learn about their Wasp background, since that background is deeply embedded in the school curriculum and the mainstream media.

"This culture is Wasp culture," Susie says. "We don't have to teach them about it."

There have been times, though, when we've wondered about this neglect. When Samantha turned three, it became apparent one day that she thought Susie was Asian. Susie asked if Samantha thought Susie's father and mother were Asian.

"Yes, they're Asian American, too."

Susie asked about her brother and sister, and Samantha said that she thought they were Asian too. Susie thought a moment, then asked, "Well, then, who are the whites?"

"The bad guys?" Samantha replied.

We both laughed when Susie told me about this. Still, it brought up certain questions: Did Samantha's answer reflect something of the ways we've taught her about her identity? Will she one day accuse us of teaching her to neglect her Wasp background? Will she find silences and gaps in my pictures of her family's past and who we are?

On some level, the silences are there. I don't know if I could talk to my daughter about her Wasp background without being quite negative. Perhaps that's another reason I avoid it.

My feelings, though, do come out in my writings, which

she'll someday read. There's a poem I've written about my
wife's grandfather, whom I have dubbed a redneck Yankee.
When my wife and I first visited her Wasp grandparents, this
grandfather crept into the room where she was sleeping—we
were unmarried at the time—and whispered, "Don't make
a mistake with your life, Susie." My poem deals with this
incident.

Not surprisingly, this same grandfather was also prejudiced
against Jews. As a result, he was never told that his daughter
had married someone who was part Jewish.

Recently, we've learned new facts about the Jewish side of
my wife's family. One is that distant relatives died in the Nazi
death camps. Samantha's immediate response was, "I had relatives who were in the concentration camps in Europe and in
the camps in America."

These past few months, she's been especially interested in
books about Judaism, and she asked that we celebrate Passover
this spring. She seizes on the fact of her Jewish background as
another mark of difference, as something special. She likes the
connection she now feels with a young Jewish friend of ours,
who came over to our house for Passover dinner. She asks if it
would be better if she were one-quarter Jewish instead of one-
eighth. She's obviously proud of the ways she can point to her
multiple heritages. At the same time, already a budding feminist, she wants to know why it is she can't wear a yarmulke and
her brothers can.

And yet, in the end, both the Japanese ethnic background
and a sense of Judaism as a practiced religion are for the most
part absent from her daily life. Despite our attempts to teach
her, she learns about these two aspects of her identity at a remove. A decade ago, my wife and I spent a year in Japan and

we've often talked of returning for a prolonged visit, but we never really do more than talk about it. Although we now participate in many Asian American events, there's not enough of a Japanese American community in Minneapolis for her to re-create a childhood anywhere near the one my parents went through. Oh, we read her Japanese fairy tales—about Momo-taro, the boy who sprang from a peach, and the Moon Princess who springs mysteriously from a tree in a forest—and we watch Japanese movies from time to time. Her favorite place to eat is a Japanese restaurant. There are Japanese prints and pottery decorating our home. But she's not growing up learning to speak Japanese, nor do we socialize with Japanese nationals. Overall, neither the cultural practices nor the values of our home are very close to those of my Japanese grandparents.

Similarly, my wife wasn't raised as a Jew; that part of her identity remained hidden for a long time. The Judaism Samantha learns, like her Japanese culture, comes mainly from a book.

In the end, it's probably not the bi- or multicultural side of Samantha's identity that will bring up so many questions. Instead, it's the way her parentage and her identity are tangled up with the issues of race. The conflicts in my identity as a Japanese American are derived not from any clash between Japanese and American values; instead, they reside in the way my parents were affected by the internment camps and in how I grew up in a culture which, as bell hooks has observed, is permeated with notions of "white supremacy." Similarly, my wife and I have often discussed the ways race—not cultural difference—factored in our mutual attraction. Having met her when I was still in denial about my identity, I dated only white women in a mistaken attempt to prove I was thoroughly assimilated. She, on the other hand, grew up with a father who traveled throughout the globe and with a family whose church in Atlanta was active in the civil rights movement. She has said that some part of her probably felt that to be with someone white would have been "too boring." To be with someone black, though, would have been "too taboo." I came with the right amount of "otherness." I looked different, but I didn't speak or act differently; we had both grown up with the values of white suburbia.

Who will Samantha find attractive? Who will she marry? How will that be affected by the ways she chooses to identify herself? Or will she simply want to declare herself free from the racial categories that affected her parents, the forces of desire that created her? And if she does want to declare herself free of these categories, will she be able to do so?

One Saturday last year, Samantha talked to us about how Hollywood was not making films with Asian or Asian American heroes. Therefore, she and her friend Diwa—who's Thai-Filipino American—were going to shoot a video about Asian Americans. They decided to film the story of Ruby Bridges, one of the young black girls who desegregated the schools in the South (Samantha has a book about Ruby's story). Sam and Diwa played the crowd, picketing with signs saying WHITES ONLY. Then they played Ruby and her teacher as Asian Americans desegregating a school. What is interesting here is that they identified with Ruby Bridges and saw her struggle as linked to their own identities as Asian Americans. This is something I would not have done as a child.

I said to Diwa's mother, a Filipino American film scholar, "Maybe we're doing something right."

Still, the battle is not an easy one. There are very few cultural icons who reflect Samantha's identity as a young Asian American girl, much less one who is of mixed race. And yet the need to find mirrors for herself still remains. Currently, the favorite movie among Samantha and her friends is *Now and Then.* It's set in suburban Indiana in the sixties; the four young white girls in the film are in junior high and just approaching the question of sexuality.

Sam and her friends have seen this movie dozens of times. Though they are four or five years younger than the group in the film, they discuss which of the girls they would play. Sam identifies most with the girl who becomes an author, who dresses in black as an adult. This character is the most cynical and the tomboy of the group. The parents of one of Sam's friends are going through a divorce, just like the fourth member of the girl quartet. This character becomes a way of talking briefly about this event.

When I think of Samantha watching the movie *Now and Then,* I know that much of the appeal of this movie obviously has to do with being a young girl identifying with other young girls who are slightly older. At the same time, I'm troubled by the whiteness of the movie; it's set in a place where there are no people of color, even on the peripheries, even as servants.

I've talked with her about the way the media work, about racial stereotypes, about taking pride in who she is, about the need for Asian American heroes and role models and television and movie stars, about the absence of faces like hers in the media. I don't think she's ever going to decide to "pass," despite the fact that, unlike me, she is part white. But no amount of talk will make the media any different. And films like *Now and Then* will continue to provide her with mirrors of who she is.

But what of her being of mixed race? There are even fewer role models for that. Recently, Tiger Woods has catapulted into the national consciousness, but it's clear that for much of the public he's still seen mainly as black. Actually, Tiger is one-quarter Thai, one-quarter Chinese, one-quarter white, an eighth Native American, and an eighth black. If you total this up, Tiger is more Asian American than anything else. Tiger identifies himself as "Cablinasian," a term he made up to combine Caucasian, black, Indian, and Asian. He's said that it's a mistake for people to simply look at him as African American. But it's a social reality in this country that when you are part black and look the way Tiger does, you're going to be considered black.

With mixtures of Asian and white, the way people perceive you often depends on the individual's looks. People for instance tend to see Russell Wong, the movie star, as full-blooded Chinese, when he is actually half Dutch. On the other hand, people are often surprised to find that Keanu Reeves is part Chinese Hawaiian. Dean Cain, who plays Superman, that traditional all-white all-American figure, is actually half Japanese American.

Samantha looks Asian. When she was younger and she and my wife Susan were in the grocery, people would come up and say, "Oh, she's such a beautiful little girl. Where did you get her?" These incidents stopped, though, when our second child, Nikko, came along, since he more clearly looked of mixed race. The same is even more true of our third, Tomo.

There was a time a few years back when we first visited

Hawaii that I thought of living there. In Hawaii, more than half the children are hapa. When we visit there, Samantha, Tomo, and Nikko all look like the norm, the majority.

It could well be that Samantha, as she grows older, will begin to look less Asian. This often happens with such children. Whatever happens, if she looks even part Asian, she will probably have to deal with men who are attracted to the stereotype of Asian women as exotic, submissive, sensual. Moreover, there are choices she will have to make about how she identifies herself to others, how she presents herself to the world. I have a friend who's half Chinese American and half European American who says that whether people think she's part Asian or not sometimes depends on how she dresses. The more businesslike and middle-class she dresses, the less people see the Asian in her. In a way, she's presented with an odd choice each morning: How am I going to identify myself? How am I going to reveal or conceal my identity?

My daughter wants to be an artist. She has known this since she was four (she's eight now), and she works at her art with a fierceness and a concentration that tells me she may very well pursue this craft the rest of her life. She has a book by her bedside of works by women artists, and she has crossed out in the book a disparaging remark about women artists by Hans Hofmann. Last year, she created an installation made up of pieces of cut wood and chopped-up parts of her Barbie dolls. The installation was a protest against the sexism and silliness of Barbie and the fact that she sees Barbie, despite some poor attempts to diversify, as a product which shuts out people of color. As for her cultural heritage, she knows a little about Japanese art, and in some of her earlier works she sometimes used kanji as part of her abstract paintings. She takes art classes from a Japanese American woman artist. She's read books about Jewish culture and history, but I don't think she sees that side of her as a source for her artistry. Perhaps later. Perhaps not.

She goes to a school that is racially mixed. We've deliberately chosen to stay in the city and send her to public schools because we believe such a mixture is important. In her class of twenty-two last year, there were three Asian Americans, five African Americans, two Native Americans, three Arab Americans, and the rest were European Americans. Her best friend at school, Breanna, is the daughter of an African American man and a European American woman. Her best friends in the neighborhood are the daughter of immigrants from England and the daughter of a Chicano woman and a Jewish American man. Her oldest friend is Diwa, whose father is a Thai national and whose mother is Filipino American (though not born here).

It's clear Sam is growing up within a diversity that isn't reflected in the television she watches, nor even in the many multicultural books she reads. While those books contain characters from many different races—she's currently reading one about two African American cousins—they rarely put biracial or bicultural issues at the forefront. The best attempts of well-meaning educators and authors have not yet caught up with the rapidly shifting demographics of our country.

Other than with Diwa, Sam and her friends don't talk much about issues of race. The main division in her classroom last year—second grade—was between boys and girls. I've been told by friends with children at her school that the racial divisions begin to appear around sixth grade and the first boy-girl parties. A Chinese American friend, whose children are all hapa, said that although her sixth-grader invited his black friends to his party, all the other parties her son went to were without any of the black students. Most likely, this will be Samantha's experience, too. She'll probably find herself caught in a racial divide that will not take into account her own biracial identity but will simply ask her, Which side will you hang with—black or white?

Sam's best friend in school, Breanna, goes with her to a class for gifted and talented students. It's probably more their smartness and quiet natures, their joy in schoolwork, that bring them together, rather than their being children of culture or biracial children. I'm sure Samantha identifies more with Breanna than with the other Asians in class. Two years ago, when there was a boy in her class who had recently come from China, Samantha felt she had less in common with him than with her other classmates. With the other Asian Americans at her school, she has the most in common with those who are more assimilated, and less with the children of recent immigrants.

There was one girl in her class a couple years ago who was half Chinese American and half European American, and Samantha at times resented the fact that people would automatically pair them together in their minds and sometimes confuse them. Samantha also felt competitive with this girl in a way that she didn't feel with other students (the girl was also very bright). In her reactions, Sam seemed to be resisting a categorization and grouping imposed on her from the outside. And yet, I also wondered if it could have been simply that their personalities clashed; Samantha said that her differences with this girl simply had to do with the fact that her bragging annoyed her. At any rate, it was clear my daughter didn't see this girl as a mirror for herself, as someone she might bond with because of that.

When I recently asked Samantha if race played any role in her friendships, her immediate reply was her usual "Dad, you're weird." She then said that she thought I was being racist, that to choose friends on the basis of color was wrong. I pointed out to her that while there are many reasons I have the Asian American friends I do, one thing I do share with them is certain experiences dealing with issues of race and culture. The same was more loosely true in relationship to my other friends of color. I also pointed out that she'd participated in various events sponsored by a local Asian American arts group I'm a part of; that was one of the things she and Diwa shared. By the end of our conversation, she said she understood what I meant, but that most of her friends don't even know what "Asian American" means. When I asked her how she thought of herself, she replied, "I'm half and half. I'm half cream, half milk." And then she laughed.

In general, even as I try to understand the ways race, culture, and identity might affect her life, I sense that these things don't matter very deeply now. And yet, directions are already being cast, the basis for certain later decisions are being set. Those decisions will probably become clearer in sixth grade. They will become clearer when she begins dating. They will become clearer as she begins to formulate her identity through her art, through the questions her artistry will force her to face. I have many questions. All I can do is wait and hope.

But what are my hopes for her? They are not that she decide on any particular identity I might formulate for her. No matter how much I delve into these questions, I know whatever conceptions I may conceive can't foresee her life. That is one of the limits of being a parent. Eventually, you have to let go.

At the same time, I do hope that in searching for her own way of looking at herself she does justice to her own complexity and the complexity of her parentage. I hope that she finds a way of dealing with the world that does not deny racism and yet realizes the absurdities and divisions created by racial categories. Most of all, I hope that she finds within herself the courage to ask her own questions, no matter how troubling or difficult or upsetting to others, including myself. As an artist, as a biracial-bicultural child, may she find and create the necessary tools, the ones neither I nor the culture have provided her, to find her own way in the world.

LIFE AS AN ALIEN

Meri Nana-Ama Danquah

> I only now understand why it is that people lie about their past, why they say they are one thing other than the thing they really are, why they invent a self that bears no resemblance to who they really are, why anyone would want to feel as if he or she belongs to nothing, comes from no one, just fell out of the sky, whole.
>
> —Jamaica Kincaid, *My Brother*

I don't know where I come from. When people ask me, I have to stop and wonder what it is they really want to know about me. Do they want to know where I was born, where I grew up, where I have lived as an adult, where I live now? It troubles me to be so scattered, so fragmented, so far removed from a center. I am all and I am nothing. At the same time. Once, a long time ago, when I believed that answers were as easy as smiles, someone told me that home is where the heart is. Perhaps this is true. Love has always been a magnet. It is half the sky, the raggedy part that needs to be held up and saved. It is a name as long as history with enough vowels for each of its children to claim. It is the memory of wearing open-toed shoes in December. Of mango juice running a straight river from your hand to your elbow.

Love is a plate of steamed white rice and pig's-feet stew. As a child, this was my favorite meal. I would sit at the dining table, my legs swinging back and forth, and hum as I scooped the food into my mouth with my hand. I always ate the rice first, saving the meat in a towering heap on the side for last. After I had finished the rice, I would wash it down with some water or Coco-Rico, this coconut-milk soda my mum used to buy. Then I would greedily dig into the pile of pork and choose the largest piece. When my teeth had grazed all the flesh clean off the bone, I would hold it to my lips and suck it dry of its juice. I would bite down hard until it broke in half and I could touch the marrow with the tip of my tongue. Right then, right there, I knew my world was complete.

Several years ago, in what I can only assume was a temporary loss of sanity, I decided to become a vegetarian. Swept into the New Age organic, fat-free health obsessions of Los Angeles, the city in which I live, I vowed to never again eat another piece of meat. Not fish, not chicken, and certainly never pork. In preparation for what I believed would be a permanent change of lifestyle, I spent the morning of my first meatless day in the produce section of the supermarket stocking up on lettuce and carrots, and at the bookstore buying books like *Diet for a New America.* Throughout the day, whenever I grew hungry, I would pull out a carrot stick or rice cake and nibble, often squeezing my lips into a tight purse of dissatisfaction after swallowing. What I really wanted to be eating was fried chicken. It felt strange to not eat meat anymore; nothing I took in seemed to fill me.

"You'll get used to the change," a friend promised. "Pretty soon, the idea of putting that stuff in your body'll turn your stomach." We were at an Indian restaurant celebrating my newfound diet. I pondered what she said, scanned the menu, reading only the selections listed under the heading "Vegetarian," and ordered the Saag Paneer with Basmati Rice. When my dinner arrived, a gentle nostalgia descended upon me. The food—a creamy stew of chopped spinach—resembled kontumare, a Ghanaian dish I very much enjoy. I was, all at once, swept up by the force of habit—the habit, that is, of moving my head, torso, and legs in rhythm to a series of closed-mouth "Yums." Except the pot of gold at the end of my culinary rainbow was missing. There was no meat. And that absence left me feeling so cheated out of an integral part of the experience I was having that before returning to my apartment I stopped by an uncle's house and begged the leftover remains of his curried goat dinner.

My attempt to be an herbivore was but one in a long list of numerous attempts I have made to create or "try out" a new identity. In my twenty-four years of living in America, I have adapted to all sorts of changes. I have housed many identities inside the one person I presently call myself, a person I know well enough to admit that I don't know at all. Like a chameleon, I am ever-changing, able to blend without detection into the colors and textures of my surroundings, a skill developed out of a need to belong, a longing to be claimed. Once, home was a place, perhaps the only place, where I imagined that I really did belong, where I thought myself whole. That is not so anymore, at least not in the home that I grew up believing was mine. That word, "home," and all it represents has shifted in meaning too many times.

From the age of six, when I left Ghana and arrived in Washington, D.C., to be with my mother, who had been in the States already for three years, it was quite clear that some-day we would return. There was always talk of going back. There were always plans being made, sentences being spoken that began with words like "When I go home . . ." Even after my father joined us, America was still just a place of temporary existence, not home. And in consideration of our imminent departure, assimilation was frowned upon. My parents tried to fan the flames of our culture within me, in hopes that it would grow into a raging fire and burn fully any desire I had to be-come an American.

English was spoken only in the presence of people who could not communicate in any of our languages (Ga or Twi). It wasn't as if my parents forbade me to speak English, but if I addressed either of them in English, the response I got was al-ways in Ga. These days my father, now remarried to an Amer-ican, speaks to me primarily in English, unless I speak to him first in Ga, and even then chances are he will respond in En-glish. My mother still insists upon conversing with me in Ga. When it appeared as though I was losing fluency, she became adamant and uncompromising about this; in her mind, to for-get one's mother tongue was to place the final sever in the um-bilical cord. I do believe that she was right, but over the years I have praised and cursed her for this.

Although we didn't speak English in my house, we surely did sing in it. Music was a constant. We listened to reggae, calypso, high life, jazz, and sometimes R & B, especially Motown songs by Smokey Robinson, Marvin Gaye, or the Supremes. We also listened to country music—Kenny Rogers and Willie Nelson (which might explain my Jimmie Dale Gilmore and Lyle Lovett collections)—and disco. On weekends, my mother—wrapped like a burrito in a single piece of cloth and wearing traditional thong sandals—would listen to Manu Dibango while she was frying fresh fish or dipping a whole chicken she had just killed in our tiny kitchen into a pot of boiling water so its feathers would come off easily; or my father would sit—without shoes, socks, or shirt—in the living room playing Jimmy Cliff and Bob Marley records, his head swaying from side to side, his knees bouncing. Like my mother he, too, was in the company of animals.

On one wall of the living room where he sat and sang was the long, scaly skin of a baby python. On the other was the skinned coat of a wildcat, its head plastered in profile against the white wall, with an oval hole where the eye would have been. Not far from the wildcat were two bows; hanging inside the open arc of each one was a tall, slender pouch containing ten poison-tipped arrows. They were his pride and joy. Sometimes I would beg my father to pull down the arrows and let me touch one. When he did, I would hold it carefully, my small hand trembling as it wrapped itself around the thin stick. After a few minutes, he would take it from me and place it back in its pouch with the other arrows.

I remember asking my father once if he had actually used those very weapons to kill the snake and wildcat. I imagined that only someone with tremendous strength could do something like that—a warrior. I don't recall whether he said yes or no, but the image of my father holding his big, muscular arm high above his head and darting an arrow straight into the body of an animal became my pride and joy. But, like the pig's-feet stew, it was a pride that I was able to acknowledge and partake in only within the confines of our apartment. Most of the exposure I had to homes outside my own was through my friends who invited me over to play or eat dinner. Yet that was all it took for me to see how vastly different the life I led was from their lives. None of the Americans I knew in the suburbs of Washington, D.C. had dead animals and deadly "primitive" weapons tacked up on their walls. They had plaques, awards, framed photos of their smiling families. They had pets, animals that were very much alive and very much loved. They bought their food prepackaged in boxes or in cardboard trays. And there were no bare-chested warriors singing of the Zion train, no mothers peeling, slicing, chopping, killing. Taken out of the context of my home, my life—live chickens, reptile and wild-cat skins, bows and arrows—became a source of shame and embarrassment for me.

In this way, the split between the me who lived in that apartment and the me who had to learn how to survive outside it was immediate. It had to be. Initially, I suppose that I viewed that split simply as an external divide, straight and pronounced, like the threshold of our front door, marking the point of separation between two distinct realities. On one side was America, on the other was Ghana. And I didn't know how to bring them together, how to make one make sense *to,* let alone *in,* the other.

Why do you talk like that? Where are you from? Is that string in your hair? Newness is easy to detect, especially with immigrants. Everything about you is a dead giveaway. And people

constantly watch and stare through the scrutinizing lens of curiosity. That was a foreign thing for me, being questioned,
being eyed. From top to bottom, the eyes would travel. From
top to bottom, taking a silent inventory of the perceived differences: the way I wore my hair wrapped with thread as thick
as an undiluted accent, or in small braids intricately woven
like a basket atop my head; my clothing, a swirl of bright, fes-
tive colors dyed on fabric much too thin for the shivery East
Coast climate.

Being black made the transition from Africa to America
extremely difficult because it introduced another complex
series of boundaries. In a racially divided country, it isn't
enough for an immigrant to know how to float in the mainstream. You have to know how to retreat to your margin,
where to place your hyphen. You have to know that you are no
longer just yourself, you are now an Asian American, a Latin
American, an Irish American, or, in my case, a black American. (Only recently has the label become "African American.")
At the time of my emigration, the early 1970s, Washington,
D.C., a predominantly black city, was awash in a wave of Afro-
centricity. Dashikis draped brown shoulders and the black-
fisted handle of an Afro pick proudly stuck out in many a back
pants pocket. However, despite all the romanticizing and
rhetoric about unity and brotherhood, there was a curtain of
sheer hostility hanging between black Americans and black
Africans.

The black kids I encountered, in and out of school, were
the cruelest to me. While other children who were being
picked on for whatever trivial or arbitrary reason were called
a host of names tailored to their individual inadequacies
—Frog Lips, Peanut Head, Four-Eyes, Brace-Face—there was

no need to create a name for me. *You—you—you African! Go back to Africa!* Who I was seemed to be insult enough; where I was from, a horrific place to which one could be banished as a form of punishment.

The white Americans—children and adults—I met attacked me with verbal "kindness," not verbal cruelty. But it was no less hurtful or damaging. Their branding came in the form of adjectives, not nouns—special, exceptional, different, exotic. These words, which flowed so freely from the lips of teachers, parents, and fellow students, were intended to excuse me from my race, to cage me like some zoo animal being domesticated; these words, I realized years later, were intended to absolve those white people from their own racism. I was among the black people to whom many white people were referring when they said, "Some of my best friends . . ." I was complimented for not talking like "them," not acting like "them," not looking like "them"—"them" being black Americans, the only other physical reflections I had of myself besides my family. But, of course, that wasn't acceptance; it was tolerance.

The one place where I found acceptance was in the company of other immigrants. Together, we concentrated on our similarities, not our differences, because our differences were our similarities. Still, I secretly envied the other foreign kids because I believed that their immigrant experience was somehow more authentic than mine. Unlike me, they were not caught in the racial battlefield of black and white, their *ethnicity* was visible. Mine invariably faded to black. They spoke languages that were identifiable. Everybody's heard of Spanish, Korean, Chinese, even Arabic. The few people who had heard of Ga and Twi colonially labeled them dialects, not languages.

Of all the other immigrants, I got along best with my Spanish-speaking friends. For me, they were the middle ground between America and Africa. So when I grew tired of being pendulous, of going to and fro, I entered their culture and it became my home away from home.

In the second grade, I started taking Spanish lessons at my school, and the connection I already felt to that culture was quickly validated. One morning we were learning the Spanish words for breakfast, lunch, dinner, and all the foods usually served during those meals. The teacher, a heavy-hipped Nicaraguan woman with arms that looked like rolling pins, held up a card with a picture of a hazel-colored loaf of bread on it. When she flipped the card over to show us its name in Spanish, the word *pan* was written there in big, bold letters. My jaw dropped in amazement. *Pan* also meant bread in Twi.

One by one, I discovered other words, found other sources of affirmation, the biggest being the fact that I had the best of approvals, parental permission, to assimilate into that world. My mum was no stranger to it herself. She did the bulk of her shopping at bodegas, rummaging the shelves for suitable replacements for ingredients needed to prepare customary Ghanaian dishes. Often enough, she would take me along when she went to these stores, where stodgy men in blood-smeared aprons would greet us from behind their butcher blocks with smiles and deep-diaphragmed laughter. I felt a sense of freedom in the narrow aisles of those stores, with the tickling smells of hot peppers and the loud chorus of tongues that were kin to my own. I was both outside and inside the split, within the distance between home and here.

But it was not a steady resting place. The Latino kids were

also in motion, also trying to reach beyond themselves, searching for their own middle ground. And when I traced the pattern of their movements, it led me right back into my skin. Their middle ground, en route to whiteness—the ultimate immigrant assimilation goal—was black America. So I followed them there. By then, I had befriended two black American siblings, Karen and Allen, who lived with their mother in an apartment upstairs from mine. Allen (who is now married to a Ghanaian woman) and I were the same age, but I was closer to Karen, who was a year older. She taught me how to jump double-dutch and "snap" back when kids teased me.

"Tell 'em, 'Yo' momma,' " she'd advise.

"Your mama," I'd repeat, rolling my eyes and sucking my teeth the same as she had done.

Allen would always barge into Karen's room when she was in the midst of schooling me and poke fun. "You sound like a ole white girl," he'd say. And, at that time, that's the last thing I wanted, to "sound" white. I wanted to sound like Karen and Allen and all the other black kids at school. Every day when I left their place and went back to my apartment, I would stand in front of the bathroom mirror and practice speaking like them. I practiced and practiced until, finally, when I listened to the sound of my voice, I could no longer hear an accent. By then, I was in fourth grade.

When I rid myself of my accent, I suddenly internalized the divide, blurred the lines between continents and allegiances. There was no middle ground anymore, no threshold, no point of distinction between one reality and another. I had strayed so far away from the place I called my home that I could not find my way back. From that point on, every culture I made contact with seeped in to create one fluid geography within me. Yet as much as I imagined that I could claim them all, I still belonged to none of them. I didn't even belong to the one in which my family resided, the one that had once provided me the safety of a home base. Like everywhere else, I became the "other" there, unable to fully expand and unfold the many selves I now had, unable to ever again feel completely whole.

It seems fitting that, of all the cities I could have chosen to live in when I moved from the city where I grew up, I found myself in Los Angeles. This place is the most accurate external portrait of my internal existence. It is a place where everything is subject to change, where even the land is not stable. It is a city of illusions; what you see is not necessarily what is. People come to Los Angeles in search of their future, in spite of their past. Identities and images are created, killed, or altered here on a daily basis. Over a hundred languages are spoken; cultures overlap, blend, and produce hybrids. There are African American street vendors selling teriyaki burritos, and Mexican cooks in the kitchens of Jamaican restaurants. Far from being idyllic, it is a city at war with itself, a place where xenophobia and self-hatred run rampant. And I have never felt more at peace anywhere else. As the result of a recent incident with my six-year-old daughter, Korama, I began, for the first time, to accept myself, my history of traversal. I began to create a context for the cross-cultural life that I have led.

For whatever reason, in the course of one of Korama's kindergarten conversations, she let it be known that my favorite television program is *The X-Files*. That afternoon when I picked her up from school, she told me about the disclosure. "Oh. Okay, Korama," I said, releasing a slight breath of relief.

I was happy to know that she and her friends were now exchanging what I believed was less personal information about their parents. Just a few days before, she had spurted out, in a fountain of giggles, that her classmate's mother wore G-strings; and the day before that I learned of another mother's recent miscarriage.

"Mo-o-m," she whined, "it's not okay. They said you like that show because you're an alien. I tried to tell them that you weren't, but Hugo said I was wrong. He said that you're not from America, and that everyone who's not from here is an alien. Is that true? Are you an alien?" She stared at my head as if antennae would pop out at any time. I wasn't sure how to reply, but with the shrewdness that parenthood teaches you, I tried to figure out a way to answer her question without volunteering too much information that might, ultimately, confuse her. While I was mulling it over, she and I walked side by side in silence. With each step, I felt a distance growing between us. It was a distance much wider than the gap of generations that eventually settles between parents and children. And it was haunting.

For a moment, her stare was as disempowering as those of the American children whom I had encountered as a child, her questions as offensive. I wanted to arm myself against the pain of being reminded that I was "other." I wanted to beg that little girl before me to try, to just try to accept—if not love—me for who I was, the way I was, no matter how different that seemed from the way she was. But I knew I didn't have to, because she already did. "Yes," I finally said to Korama, "I am." I explained to her that in addition to creatures from outer space, the word "alien" was used to refer to human beings from other countries. I expected her to be a bit confused, but she didn't appear to be. She nodded, reached out for my hand as we approached the street we had to cross to get to our apartment, and the distance disappeared.

When I tucked her into bed that evening, she raised the subject again. "Mom, will you always be an alien?" she asked. And, again, I tried to find a straightforward, uncomplicated response, this time to a question I had been trying unsuccessfully to answer for over twenty years. "No," I told her. "Not if I become an American." Up until the second I said that, I had never so much as considered becoming a United States citizen. In the belief that I would one day return to the country of my birth, I had never made a commitment to being in the country where I have spent the better part of my life. I had always thought of naturalization as nothing more than a piece of paper one received after passing a test, a series of questions designed to assess one's technical knowledge of the country and the laws by which it is governed. If that's the case, I could live or die without that slip of paper, that change of nationality. It wouldn't make a difference one way or the other. I have lived my life as an alien, an outsider trying to find a way and a place to fit in. And it is only through that experience that I have come to think of myself not as a citizen of one country or another but, rather, of an entire world.

LOST IN THE MIDDLE

Malcolm Gladwell

I. Father

One summer Saturday, when I was growing up, my father piled my brothers and me into the family station wagon and took us to a barn raising. This was in rural southern Ontario, in the heart of Canada's old-order Mennonite country, where it was the custom when someone's barn burned down for friends and neighbors to put it back up. There were probably two hundred people there that day. They came from the surrounding farms in black horse-drawn buggies, the women in cheesecloth bonnets and gingham dresses, the men in white shirts and black pants. The women set up long picnic tables outside, and piled them high with bread and luncheon meat and pickles, and pies for dessert. The men swarmed over the skeleton of the barn, those on the roof and on ladders against the walls hammering away in unison, everyone else forming a long human chain, passing plywood and roofing metal and nails hand to hand to hand from the bottom to the top. It was a marvel of improvisational coordination, a communitarian ballet of burly clean-shaven Mennonite farmers in straw hats and loose cotton shirts, and in the midst of it all, in happy and oblivious contrast to everything around him, was my father—slender, bearded, and professorial, in the tie he never left the house without.

My father liked Mennonites. He would chat with the farmers who were our neighbors all the time, talking of crops or the weather or cows or pigs or any of the topics that have always, weirdly, held his interest. The old-order Mennonites of my hometown are rather like the Amish of Lancaster County in Pennsylvania. They live in the nineteenth century and keep to themselves. But they seemed to make an exception in his case. He would come home from the nearby college where he taught, or get up from working on some mathematical equation, and go outside and strike up a conversation with one of our black-suited neighbors—my father with his clipped English accent, the Mennonite in his guttural German dialect. I imagine that's how my father found out about the barn raising, since that's not something that a non-Mennonite would ever be invited to. My father probably asked, in his matter-of-fact way, and our neighbor probably felt compelled to respond. There is something in my father that does not recognize social barriers, and whatever that is makes him difficult to resist. I remember once when we were in Jamaica and my father took us for a long drive far into the mountains, where we all got out and had a picnic by a mountain stream. As we ate, children from a nearby village began to gather around, fascinated by the sight of what was probably the first pale, bearded Englishman they had ever seen. Before long, my father had organized all of them, and us, into a game, striding about explaining all the rules, energetically supervising a few dozen squealing, laughing nine- and ten- and eleven-year-olds, fitting in as happily and easily as if he had been back home in the hills of England, or, for that matter, chatting to a Mennonite and hammering nails in a barn raising. When we left that day, piling exhaustedly into our rented Volkswagen, I remember that the children ran after us down the road, as if my father were the Pied Piper.

My father's name is Graham Gladwell—Graham Maurice Leslie Gladwell. He is a mathematician and a gardener and an art lover and an adventurer and, in the end, a little bit of a mystery. I often wonder about what it is about him that permits him to cross so many barriers, because it's not immediately obvious. He is not charismatic or charming, in the traditional sense of those words. He is friendly, but he's also an egghead, a little bit awkward sometimes, a little bit of a dreamer, a little more comfortable inside than outside his thoughts. Some people, I suppose, might try and break down barriers out of a kind of earnestness, a missionary zeal, but that doesn't quite describe him either. There is something very self-conscious about the work of a missionary, and there is nothing self-conscious about my father. He does not bridge differences because he wants to bridge differences. He bridges them because he doesn't see differences at all: when he put on his tie and went to the barn raising, or played Pied Piper to the children on that Jamaican hilltop, he didn't feel out of place because I don't think it ever occurred to him that he should feel out of place. In the most rare and wonderful way, my father is blind, and when I finally understood this about him long after I had grown up, I think I finally understood how it was that my father came to marry my mother.

My father met my mother in England in 1958. They were both students at University College in London. My father was very young. He had started college at the age of sixteen. My mother was three years older. She had taught for several years in her native Jamaica before traveling to Britain to begin university. They met in the university's Christian Union, and she was attracted to him because, despite his youth, she felt there was something serious about him, something profound. They did not date in college. They met each other in groups. Once my father invited my mother to coffee, mistaking her for her twin sister, who was also at University College. Another time, he took her back to his parents' house, where she was greeted warmly as an "overseas student." Many of my father's friends in those years were overseas students. In the language of those days (which seems impossibly quaint now), he was an "internationalist." Once my mother graduated, they began a period of frantic courtship. Two weeks later, my mother returned to Jamaica to teach again, and my father informed his parents that they intended to marry. It was a difficult moment. My grandparents had grave objections to mixed marriages. They objected, citing New Testament verses to the effect that God had set boundaries for the habitation of nations. "It's wrong for Graham to have a black child," my grandmother told my mother. "It is wrong for you to have a white child." It is easy, I think, with the benefit of hindsight, to think of my grandparents as bigoted or small-minded. But that was not it at all.

They were simply expressing what my father, apparently, could not see, that his decision to marry my mother was a revolutionary act. When my father made it clear that he would not be moved, they acquiesced. His three sisters were my mother's bridesmaids. Her wedding veil was my grandmother's wedding veil. Today, like many happily married couples, my parents have grown alike—not just in affect and expression but also in color. My mother's native brown seems to have faded a little, and my father's whiteness has grown darker. But their wedding pictures from long ago are photo negatives. My father's color leaps out from the page—a startling, starched white. My mother's features seem fuller, her skin richer and darker. They are not two shades of brown. They are black and white. My parents' wedding pictures are radical in a way that their marriage today is not. I remember once reading an article about a famous case in Virginia in which a white man married a black woman and was prosecuted under state antimiscegenation statutes. I was just skimming it idly, thinking of it as just another artifact of Southern racism, until I realized that the date the couple was prosecuted was the same year my parents were married. It was hard for white to marry black in the 1950s because mixed marriages were so unmistakably political. For my father, though, I think it was easy. The surest way to commit a revolutionary act, after all, is not to perceive what you are doing as revolutionary.

II. Mother

My mother is not black, but brown. Her father's mother was part Jewish, in addition to black, and her mother's mother had enough Scottish in her that my grandmother was born with straight hair to go with her classically African features. The proper term for my mother is actually "middle-class brown," which is a category of special meaning in the Caribbean. From the earliest days of colonial rule, coloreds occupied a special place in Jamaica. They formed a kind of proto–middle class, performing various skilled and sophisticated tasks for which there were not enough whites. This was my mother's class— carpenters, masons, plumbers, small businessmen, and civil servants. She and her twin sister and brother grew up in the tiny village of Harewood in central Jamaica. My grandparents were teachers, and while they were by no means well off, they had the expectations of those who were. In my grandfather's library were Dickens and Maupassant. My mother and her sister were pushed to win scholarships to a proper English-style boarding school at the other end of the island; and later, when my mother graduated, it was taken for granted that she would attend university in England, even though the cost of tuition and passage meant that my grandmother had to borrow a small fortune from the Chinese grocer down the road. In my mother's first year at boarding school, she looked up "Negro" in the eleventh edition of the *Encyclopaedia Britannica.* "In . . . certain . . . characteristics . . . the Negro would appear to stand on a lower evolutionary plane than the white man," she read. And the entry continued:

> The mental constitution of the Negro is very similar to that of a child, normally good-natured and cheerful, but subject to sudden fits of emotion and passion during which he is capable of performing acts of singular atrocity, impressionable, vain, but often exhibiting in the

capacity of servant a dog-like fidelity which has stood the supreme test.

All black people of my mother's generation—and of generations before and since—have necessarily faced a moment like this, when they are confronted for the first time with the allegation of their inferiority. But it is wrong to think that this meant the same thing to my mother as it might have to a young black child in, say, the American South around the same time. She was living in a country where blacks were the majority, where they held positions of power and authority. She was attending an integrated school, where many of the best students were dark-skinned. Most of all, she did not entirely associate the word Negro with herself. She was, after all, *brown,* not black. It is this, I think, that begins to explain what seems like the strange reaction my mother had when she first met my father's family—which was to realize how similar it was to her own.

You wouldn't say that, of course, looking in from the outside. My father's father was in insurance. He owned a house in Kent, in the suburbs of London. He took the train to work every day. He loved long walks and dogs and gardening and wore tweedy jackets and small, wire-rim spectacles above a long Roman nose. My mother's father, on the other hand, was a large man who lived in a bungalow high on a hill surrounded by acres of Jamaican rain forest, and if you stood on his verandah and looked in every direction, the only sign that another human being lived within a day's drive was the church spire off in the distance. He rolled his own cigars, walked out in the morning and picked grapefruit off the trees in his backyard, and in his dotage would sit in a chair on his front porch with a

cat on his lap and receive visitors from the surrounding vil-
lages. One of my grandfathers was the personification of the
English middle class. And one of my grandfathers was the personification of the brown-skinned colonial petite bourgeoisie.
But it was my mother's feeling that these two things were not
that far apart: that in their libraries they would read the same
books, in their churches they would sing the same hymns, and
in their hearts they had the same hopes for their children. My
mother found in my father a kindred spirit, which was why it
was so strange to her that their marriage set off so many alarm
bells. In my mother's eyes, middle-class brown and middle-
class white were really the same thing.

My grandmother, my mother's mother, was in favor of my
parents' marriage. She had married a man lighter-skinned than
herself, and was forever proud of that fact. In Jamaica, for a
brown woman to marry a white man was an example of social
mobility. But for a brown woman to marry a black man, well,
now, there was a radical act. In my grandparents' house in
Harewood, the family often passed around a penciled drawing
of two of my great-grandparents: she was part Jewish and he
was part Scottish. The other side—the African side—was
never mentioned. Brown trumped black. That fact meant that
my grandmother never quite matched up to her fairer-skinned
in-laws. "Daisy's nice, you know," my grandmother's mother
would say of her daughter-in-law, "but she's too dark." My
mother had a relative, Aunt Joan, who was as fair as my great-
grandmother was. Aunt Joan married what in Jamaica is called
an Injun—a man with a dark complexion that is redeemed
from pure Africanness by straight, fine black hair. She had two
daughters by him—handsome girls with dark complexions.

But he died young, and one day, while she was traveling on a train to visit her daughter, she met and took an interest in a light-skinned man in the same railway car. What happened next is something that Aunt Joan told only my mother, years later, with the greatest of shame. When she got off the train, she walked right by her daughter, disowning her own flesh and blood, because she did not want a man so light-skinned and desirable to know that she had borne a daughter so dark.

My mother, in the 1960s, wrote a book about her experience. It was entitled *Brown Face, Big Master,* the brown face referring to her and the big master, in the Jamaican dialect, referring to God. In one passage in the book she describes a time just after my mother and father were married, when they were living in London and my eldest brother was still a baby. They were looking for an apartment, and after a long search my father found one in a London suburb. On the day after they moved in, however, the landlady ordered them out. "You didn't tell me your wife was colored," she told my father in a rage.

In her book, my mother describes her long struggle to make sense of this humiliation, to reconcile her experience with her faith. In the end, she was forced to acknowledge that anger was not an option—that as a Jamaican "middle-class brown," and a descendant of Aunt Joan, she would hardly reproach another for the impulse to divide others along racial lines. My mother did not find her marriage to my father any more radical than he did—although for an entirely different reason: not because she was oblivious to the complications of color but because those complications were all too familiar to her.

I complained to God in so many words: "Here I was, the wounded representative of the Negro race in our struggle to be accounted free and equal with the dominating whites!" And God was not amused; my prayer did not ring true with him. I would try again. And then God said, "Have you not done the same thing? Remember this one and that one, people whom you have slighted or avoided or treated less considerately than others because they were different superficially, and you were ashamed to be identified with them. Have you not been glad that you are not more colored than you are? Grateful that you are not black?" My anger and hate against the landlady melted. I was not better than she was, nor worse for that matter. . . . We were both guilty of the sin of self-regard, the pride and the exclusiveness by which we cut some people off from ourselves.

III. Son

When my father took us all to the barn raising, I remember that I stood to the side, by the car. There were other children, Mennonite children, there as well, playing happily in the sun. But I didn't join them. I was not a joiner as a child. I quit the Boy Scouts after a week, refused my parents' invitation to go away to summer camp, and generally kept to myself and my toys. I didn't fit in. This was not, at least in the beginning, a re-action to the fact of my mixed racial background, because I never thought about my racial background when I was young. Back then, "race" and all that it connoted was something uniquely American. I would read the old *Life* magazine every week and see pictures of civil rights marches, or black protesters, or Angela Davis with her sky-high Afro, and my only thought was how foreign it all was: it was of a piece with the Vietnam War and Richard Nixon and baseball. One of my mother's friends—a Jamaican woman—spent some time in Atlanta and told my mother that the racism was so thick down there that you could "cut it with a knife." I was six or seven at the time, and I was only dimly beginning to understand what racism was, but I couldn't get that image out of my head. Atlanta, I knew, was steamy and humid and fetid, and all I could think about was that it was the racism that was making the air so thick down there. The air was not thick in Canada. It was dry and light, blown fresh across the Great Lakes.

When I thought about what made me different, I put it down to other things—to the fact that we had just come from England, and that I talked funny, or that I wasn't a farmer like almost everyone else in our little town, or that I didn't play hockey (which, in rural Canada, is rather like living in Munich and not drinking beer). Mostly, though, I didn't know, and it wasn't until I was well into my teens that I began to get an answer. I was a runner then, a miler, and I would travel around the province with my track club. These were the years of the first great wave of West Indian immigration to Ontario, which meant that whenever we went to track meets in Toronto—where most of the immigrants settled—there were suddenly all kinds of black faces that I hadn't seen before in Canada. I won't lie and say that I felt some great and immediate kinship with these West Indians. I am, after all, only partially West Indian. But they gave some definition to my alienation. There was a West Indian on my track team—a magnificent long jumper by the name of Chris Brandy—who came up to me one day, looking closely at my hair and features, and demanded: "What *are* you?" The question was entirely unexpected, and I remember blinking and stammering momentarily overwhelmed by that word *what*. I had always thought that my singular alienation was the result of *who* I was. But now it occurred to me that perhaps it was the result of something entirely external—the result of nuances of color and skin and lip and curl that put me just outside the world of people like Chris Brandy and just outside the world of the people I grew up with in rural Ontario.

I am not like my parents. I do not have my father's gift for overcoming social barriers, nor my mother's gift for appreciating when differences are not relevant. I go back and forth now between my two sides. I never feel my whiteness more than when I'm around West Indians, and never feel my West Indianness more than when I'm with whites. And when I'm by myself, I can't answer the question at all, so I just push it out of my mind. From time to time, I write about racial issues, and always stumble over personal pronouns. When do I use "we"? In a room full of people I do not know, I always search out the ones who fall into the middle, like me, out of some irrational idea that we belong together.

I worry sometimes that this is the wrong thing for the child of a mixed marriage to feel. My parents conquered difference, and we would all like to think that sort of accomplishment is something that could be passed down from generation to generation. That's why we're all, in theory, so excited by the idea of miscegenation—because if we mix the races, presumably, we create a new generation of people for whom existing racial categories do not exist. I don't think it's that easy, though. If you mix black and white, you don't obliterate those categories; you merely create a third category, a category that demands, for its very existence, an even greater commitment to nuances of racial taxonomy. My mother never had to think about whether she was black. She was. I have to think about it, and turn the issue over in my mind, and gaze in the mirror and wonder, as I was so memorably asked, *what* I am.

By virtue of my upbringing, I can safely say I am free of racial discrimination. I cannot—without commiting an act of extraordinary self-hatred—ever believe that blacks are in any way inferior. But I am also, perhaps permanently, hostage to the questions of racial difference. Racial intermarriage solves one problem in the first generation, only to create another in the next—a generation that cannot ignore difference the way their parents did. I put myself, sometimes, in my father's shoes, back in the mid-fifties, and wonder whether I could have done what he did—marry someone, bridge a gulf of human difference, with my eyes entirely closed.

THE FUNERAL BANQUET

Lisa See

As a child, I spent a lot of time with my father's parents in Los Angeles's Chinatown. My grandparents—my grandmother especially—made sure that I learned Chinese traditions: how to eat duck feet, how to steam rice perfectly, how to respect and honor my elders, and, most important, how to identify everyone I was related to. When we went to wedding banquets, first-month baby parties, or funerals, my grandmother would take me around and introduce me. "This is your third cousin twice removed." I think—I know—my grandmother believed in this order of the world, for she lived as a Chinese wife, Chinese daughter-in-law, Chinese mother, Chinese grandmother, and Chinese great-grandmother.

But Stella Copeland See was Caucasian. Both sets of her grandparents had come out West and settled in Waterville, Washington, at the end of the last century. Her parents, itinerant workers, didn't achieve much in the way of the American Dream. Her father labored in the fields by day and earned extra money moonlighting as a barber. Her mother worked in a cook shed. Since they traveled from farm to farm, they left my grandmother hither and thither with different relatives. In 1920, they sent her down to Los Angeles at the age of fifteen to look after an aunt who was dying of tuberculosis.

Stella met my future grandfather, Eddy See, in high school. His family had already been in Los Angeles for decades. Eddy's grandfather had come to America to work on the transcontinental railroad. *His* son, Fong See, had come a few years later, opened a shop in Sacramento, then, in 1897, married my great-grandmother—a white woman who had run away from home. I use the word "married" loosely since it was against the law for Chinese and Caucasians to marry in California. This marriage was merely a contract drawn up by a lawyer. Many years later, in 1928, the miscegenation laws were still in place, so my grandparents drove down to Mexico to get married.

Over the years, my grandmother, whose early life had been so precarious and rootless, attached herself to the Chinese side of the family with a fierce tenacity. She shopped in Chinatown. She worked in Chinatown. For many years, she lived in Chinatown. Unlike her in-laws, neighbors, and friends, who were often striving to become more American, she made a deliberate choice to become more Chinese. Her modes of dress, speech, cooking, housekeeping, and child rearing were consciously modeled on what she saw around her. By the 1950s when I was born, she was more "Chinese" than most Chinese.

In her striving to re-create herself, she reached—at least to my eyes—a kind of Chinese perfection that went far beyond surface accoutrements and decoration. She had become Chinese not through her heritage or her blood but through her being.

When my grandmother died earlier this year, my father and I weren't quite sure what do, because she had always been adamant that she didn't want a funeral. "I just want to be cremated. I don't want anyone crying over me. I don't want anything!" But we had to do something, so my father and I began constructing a memorial that would be true to her wishes and still fulfill our desire for a celebration of her life.

Of course, it would have to be as "Chinese" as possible. My grandmother had taught me everything I knew about my Chineseness, about identity, about race. This meant that we would hand out candy at the end of whatever it was we did to wash away the bad taste of death and *lisee*—a red paper envelope with a coin inside—to bring good luck. Right away, there was a little flurry about the *lisee*. At my great-uncle Gilbert's funeral a few months earlier, my cousin had given out red *and* white money-filled envelopes. But Gilbert was one of the first Chinese American architects in this country, his father was one of the founders of the Kong Chow Association in Los Angeles, and his mother was the city's premier Chinese-language teacher. Gilbert's funeral had to be Chinese-custom perfect. But my grandmother's? I put in a quick call to a friend at the Chinese Historical Society, who said that "considering the circumstances"—meaning that my grandmother was a *lofan*—the red envelope would be enough.

But our biggest concerns were not over the *lisee* or what photos to put in the memorial photo album or whether or not we would put big bottles of Coke and 7-Up on each table or what difficulties might arise from having my father's two ex-wives and his current wife in the same emotionally charged room, but whether to serve roast duck or white chicken. My father and I wanted to observe Chinese traditions and have a traditional banquet (dropping the regular funeral service entirely), but both of us (and my grandmother, too, for that matter) had always hated traditional funeral dishes, which are relatively fat-free and bland in the extreme. Nothing could be more boring than the steamed white meat of a chicken. The same could be said for vegetables and noodles with little seasoning. In fact, this is perhaps the *only* Chinese meal where the guests don't pack up the leftovers to take home.

What my father wanted—and I agreed—was a dim sum lunch. Immediately, my father put his foot down when it came to two of my grandmother's favorite dim sum dishes. There would be no fried dumplings made of mashed taro root or triangles of sweet fermented white rice cake. "Nobody likes that stuff," he argued. "Grandma did, and I do, too," I retorted, but on this he would not be swayed. Again and again, we came back to whether or not to have a conciliatory dish of white chicken or go for the serious grease with a plate of roast duck.

"I love roast duck!" my father said. "I love that gooey fat!"

"But at Uncle Gilbert's funeral, the old people were very picky about what they would and would not eat. They don't want anything too rich."

"They don't have to eat it. They can have dumplings."

"Those are rich, too."

I have to stop here for a moment and say that my father and I tread very carefully around each other. We both loved my grandmother, but other than that, we've certainly "had our differences." So I can also say with complete honesty that on that day at the Empress Pavilion I knew I was getting on my father's nerves. "Fine," I said, "have the duck, but it isn't traditional." At which point he settled on the white chicken, ordering it in rusty Cantonese. (A couple of days later, my father called to say that he'd gone ahead and ordered the duck anyway.)

The day of the funeral finally arrived. The ex-wives strolled in and the other relatives flocked around to say hello. Ngon Fong—my great-grandfather's third wife and widow, my grandmother's stepmother-in-law and my own stepgreat-grandmother—hobbled in. Her eldest son, Chuen, came with his Japanese wife. Chuen's brother, Yun, looked frail from a recent round of chemotherapy. Uncle Tyrus, not a true uncle but an honorary one, put on a brave face. He was the last surviving member of an artistic and funny group that had included my grandparents and my favorite aunt and uncle. My cousin Leslee arrived with Joe, her sweet Caucasian fiancé, who had caused Uncle Gilbert to go nearly crazy because he was a *lofan*. (Not everyone in our family is open-minded about mixed marriages. Gilbert's own mother had fought his marriage to my half-and-half aunt for eight years. Despite his own experience, Gilbert wanted his daughter to marry someone 100 percent Chinese. After Gilbert's funeral, Leslee and Joe joked that Gilbert had chosen to die rather than have to go to their wedding.) At another table, my grandmother's sister-in-law, a Japanese American woman who'd been interned during the war and had flown in from Oregon for the funeral, tried to explain to her grown twin daughters who everyone was and how they were related.

Before the dishes were brought out, my father said a few

words about his mother, Stella See. He explained that we would not be having a traditional meal and that Stella didn't want a traditional funeral. "And certainly no Forest Lawn! Because if there's one thing I can say about my mother, it's that she knew how to hold a grudge." He went on to describe that grudge, although everyone there knew it.

When my great-grandfather died in 1957, the family had wanted to have him buried next to his Caucasian wife in Forest Lawn, but the cemetery was segregated. The cemetery offered to dig up this wife and move her to the nonwhite section. They offered to sell the family a casket with a diamond embedded in the top if they'd allow Fong See to be buried "in that nice flat area down by the fence." After six weeks of negotiating, arguing, and pleading, the funeral was indeed held at Forest Lawn, then Fong See was transported to another, older cemetery where he was buried with the city's other pioneers. My grandmother had never gotten over the injustice of it and so here we all were for dumplings.

It is not a Chinese custom to stand up at a funeral banquet and give testimonials or tell stories, but several guests, including my father's wives, did. First my stepmother, an African American woman, made a few remarks. Anne had barely sat down when my mother stood and rattled off a few anecdotes. Then my former stepmother—not about to be outdone—jumped up and began wending her way to the podium. Some might say that this parade was in bad taste. And I'll admit it—there was a certain amount of good-natured teasing. *(Oh, that dad of yours! Ha ha!)* But what did this display really say about our family? You could argue that multiple wives are a part of Chinese tradition. Certainly, my Chinese relatives still treat my mother, who divorced my father almost forty years ago, as the "number-one wife." But it's deeper than that. We learned the hard way that to survive in this sometimes hostile country you needed to hold on to family in whatever form it took. Over the years, even my uncle Gilbert—truly as bigoted as they come—had embraced me with my measly one-eighth blood as though I were his full-blooded Chinese niece. He taught me a lot about being shortsighted and stingy, but he also taught me about Chinese American history, beauty, and persistence.

But back to the funeral. Others, who were too shy to get up in front of the entire group, told stories to their table companions. One of these was Herman Liu. Back in the thirties, his father, Loy, worked in my grandfather's Dragon's Den restaurant. Loy eventually saved enough money to bring his son over from China. When the fourteen-year-old arrived, my aunt Sissee gave him the American name of Herman and enrolled him in school. My grandfather gave him his first taste of ice cream. Many years later, after Herman married and his wife got pregnant, my grandmother lobbied Good Samaritan into accepting this Chinese woman as the hospital's first-ever Chinese patient. My grandmother even named Herman's two daughters: Elizabeth and Margaret, for the two English princesses. On the day that Elizabeth was born, Herman and my grandmother were standing at the nursery window when another group came by to look at the newborns. When they saw the Chinese baby, one of these people "said something." Was this euphemism used only in our family or in Los Angeles's Chinatown, or is it common to all ethnic and racial groups? I don't know the answer, but I can say that when my grandmother heard that something she "raised such Cain" that she had to be physically restrained and was ejected from the hospital by burly guards.

Finally, the guests began to leave. The hostess in me feels compelled to tell you that they packed up every single leftover dumpling and every last piece of white chicken and duck and took them home. As they left, they thanked us for having dim sum. "It's not traditional," more than one person said. "But it sure was good for a change."

And my father responded, "It didn't have to be traditional. My mother was Caucasian after all."

I'm writing this piece at my grandmother's kitchen table. For the last few days, I've been coming over to her house in the morning, writing for a couple of hours, making a few business phone calls, then spending the afternoon dealing with my grandmother's stuff. This place was originally a shepherd's shack. In the early twenties, a bungalow was added to the property and my great-great-grandmother moved in. About ten years later, my great-grandmother Jessie, who was visiting, was sitting by a window, reached into the parrot's cage, grabbed that poor bird by the neck, and strangled it. There are two stories of what happened to her that day. One was that she had a complete mental breakdown; the other was that she had a stroke. Either way, she spent the rest of her life in an institution.

When my great-great-grandmother died in the early fifties, my grandparents and father moved in and began to change the nature of the house and the property from charming California bungalow with a neat lawn to Chinese peasant house with a Chinese peasant garden. Over the last forty or so years, the bamboo, palms, ferns, and exotic trees have completely obscured the house from the street. Another shed was built and storage areas were added in the house. One room was completely given over to boxes. Until my grandmother died and I started going through her things, I hadn't realized that that room had *any* windows, let alone three. Meanwhile, the two sheds were both filled to the ceiling and right up to their doors with . . . stuff.

It's been a true archeological dig. The first layer is simple day-to-day goods—pots and pans, books, toiletries. I was surprised when all of my grandmother's clothes fit into just one Hefty bag while her shoes and slippers filled another. The next layer or layers are all the other lives in that house. We found my great-grandmother's diary. Reading it, we determined that she must have slowly gone crazy over many years. We found the earthly belongings of the aunt who died of TB back in 1921: photos, taffeta gowns, hats with ostrich feathers, letters. We found the full estate of a friend of my grandparents, a man who was estranged from society not for his race but for his sexual preference. In the back room, I found boxes and boxes filled with his silver, china, buttons, oil-lamp collection, and personal papers. I also found a cache of pocket watches and other jewelry that belonged to Richard White, a soldier of fortune who talked my great-grandparents into selling Chinese antiques more than a hundred years ago. That suggestion became a family business which carries on to this day.

In and around these other lives are those of my grandparents. My grandfather was half Chinese and proud of it. You've heard the saying that the Chinese save everything? I think that phrase was invented to take into account my grandfather, because he stashed away yards of electrical conduit, barrels of old nails (some so old they're square), antiquated motors, pipes, wire, shipping crates, a case of cooking wine from Prohibition that must have been left over from the restaurant.

But it's my grandmother's things that captivate me. I'm not talking about the boxes of mason jars, luggage labels from every trip she ever took, postcards and stationery from around the world, or the drawers filled with used wrapping paper and ribbon from every present that had come into the house since the year one. (After the hardships of her own childhood and being married to a Chinese man all those years, you couldn't expect her to throw away anything, could you?) No, let us forget that tier and focus instead on the things that really mattered to Stella See.

My grandmother worked in our family's Chinese antiques store until she was eighty-five. All these years, she was never paid in money. (The Chinese can also be cheap, especially with their daughters-in-law.) But she was paid in things—what I and the rest of the family grew up calling "stuff" or "junk." As of this writing, here's what I've found: hundreds upon hundreds of Chinese porcelain and earthenware dishes in just about every known pattern, lacquerware, bamboo ware, Canton ware, five pigskin chests, Chinese baskets for keeping ducks, baskets for fish, large ladles for Chinese street vendors, ivory carvings, bolts of silk, trunks of embroideries and other textiles, vast quantities of antique American and Chinese clothes (collected by a woman whose own personal wardrobe fit into that one Hefty bag), about a hundred really fine Chinese teapots, crates of Chinese pewter. Every drawer, every envelope, every piece of clothing has to be opened, felt, searched. Inside some booties, I found carved pieces of jade. In a box in the small shed, I found all of my father's schoolwork from grade school. In an envelope tucked inside a cookbook, I found photos of this house as it used to be.

She left all of these things to me, I believe, because she knew they would remind me not only who I am but how I should live. She had first created her identity through material goods: her first Chinese necklace, her first pair of baggy black pants. The power of those objects sank into her, became a part of her until she became a part of them. I think that from the time when she took me around at those wedding banquets she understood that my identity, my sense of self, would have to be constructed from the outside in. By absorbing this "stuff"—the pewter, the silks, the porcelains—I, too, would be able to claim my true identity.

In the prologue for *On Gold Mountain,* I wrote that I didn't look Chinese but I was Chinese in my heart. When I wrote those words, I worried that I was being presumptuous and that the Chinese community would not take kindly to it. As in, "How dare you claim to be a Chinese when you don't look the part?" That didn't happen, because I didn't embarrass anyone. As one of my cousins once said, "If you do something or say something that is bad, it reflects on the entire family." That idea ripples out across all of Chinese culture. If you do something bad or embarrassing, it not only reflects on the family but on the entire race. (As an aside, think about the pressure that puts on Asian American writers as they sit down at their computers to write an article or book. Think about how that idea affects every career or life choice an Asian American makes.)

Still, I have had these bizarre moments when a couple of Chinese discuss my appearance in front of me as though I weren't there. "Her face is long. You know, some Cantonese look like that." Or, "She's slim, not fat like the usual American." "Look at her eyes. I had an uncle with eyes like that." "But her hair . . ." This last always brings the conversation to a disquieting close.

What I hadn't anticipated was that my statement about being Chinese in my heart would make Caucasians batty. "What do you mean you feel Chinese in your heart? You don't look Chinese!" Even more than their comments, I've been surprised and interested by the flashes of bewilderment—and sometimes disgust—on their faces. I think it comes down to this: Why would anyone *choose* to be other than white? Why would anyone forsake the inherent privilege that being white allows us in this country?

The other related question I've gotten these last couple of years is "Have you ever felt discriminated against?" Of course not. I have red hair, freckles. In this country, people look at a face and when they see white, they make a whole range of decisions based on the assumption that what they're seeing is true. I look white, therefore I am white. How easy it must be for me to say I'm Chinese in my heart when I haven't had to pay the price. No one's ever turned me down to rent an apartment based on the color of my skin. No one has ever called me a slant-eye, a gook, a Chinaman. No one has *ever* accused me of being good at math or computers or science because of my racial background.

Nevertheless, I have paid a price. If in the white world I'm white, in the Chinese world I'm white, too. I've had relatives—100 percent Chinese-blood relatives—say to me, "Oh, so-and-so is Caucasian just like you." I've had waiters in Chinese restaurants tell me I shouldn't order a particular dish because it's not for Caucasian tastes, or, even more insulting, put a fork by my plate. Those people look at me and, just like their Caucasian counterparts, see only my white face with these freckles. What I want to say to them is, "My great-grandfather worked on the railroad, goddamn it! I know how I'm related to every single one of my relatives. My family suffered from the old laws barring marriage between Chinese and Caucasians, barring the ownership of property (making us land poor but 'stuff' rich), barring the immigration of our other relatives long before you or your family ever thought about America." These are not charitable thoughts, but I have them just the same.

Things have changed since my great-grandparents, grandparents, and even my own parents got married. Mixed marriages and biracial children are now extremely common. I've seen it in the faces of people who come to hear me speak in bookstores in Minneapolis, Denver, Seattle. I've seen it in the world faces of the nurses at Good Samaritan Hospital. I've seen it in the faces of the kids my children play with. Those kids may look one way, but how can I or anyone else tell whose side of the family they'll take after when the mother might be from Baltimore, Bombay, or Beijing and the father from Bozcaada, Budapest, or Bogotá? In the 1990s, I'm still an aberration, but in another ten, twenty, thirty years, Americans will look at each other and—just like they do with me now—really not know who someone is by their face. When I say that in lectures, there's a moment when I see smiles on faces and people nodding agreeably. Very quickly, that turns to a collective look of confusion as people play this out in their minds. What would it be like to shake someone's hand and not know what they are?

You may have noticed that I have labeled everyone in this piece. My white grandmother. My Japanese aunt. My African American stepmother. Our family is strong because of its many races and cultures. It's strong because we have survived everything the larger culture has thrown at us. When the larger society is fighting your very existence, your strength can only come from friends and family, from mixing and accepting, from extending and including. Part of that requires knowing what people are whether they look the part or not. These are things my grandmother taught me.

I hope at the dim sum banquet for my funeral my sons will stand up and say, "We're here today instead of Forest Lawn because our mom—like our great-grandmother—sure knew how to hold a grudge." I hope there's a colleague or two who will talk about my writing and how my belief in Chinese traditions and culture grew out of my filial ties to my family. Finally, I hope someone will say, "She never forgot where and what she came from. At heart she was always a Chinese peasant." And then I hope my sons, grandchildren, and great-grandchildren will go to my home and begin their own excavation project into my life and those of our ancestors so that they, too, might discover—remember—who and what they are.

A WHITE WOMAN OF COLOR

Julia Álvarez

Growing up in the Dominican Republic, I experienced racism within my own family—though I didn't think of it as racism. But there was definitely a hierarchy of beauty, which was the main currency in our daughters-only family. It was not until years later, from the vantage point of this country and this education, that I realized that this hierarchy of beauty was dictated by our coloring. We were a progression of whitening, as if my mother were slowly bleaching the color out of her children.

The oldest sister had the darkest coloring, with very curly hair and "coarse" features. She looked the most like Papi's side of the family and was considered the least pretty. I came next, with "good hair," and skin that back then was a deep olive, for I was a tomboy—another dark mark against me—who would not stay out of the sun. The sister right after me had my skin color, but she was a good girl who stayed indoors, so she was much paler, her hair a golden brown. But the pride and joy of the family was the baby. She was the one who made heads turn and strangers approach asking to feel her silken hair. She was white white, an adjective that was repeated in describing her color as if to deepen the shade of white. Her eyes were brown, but her hair was an unaccountable towheaded blond. Because of her coloring, my father was teased that there must have been a German milkman in our neighborhood. How could *she* be *his* daughter? It was clear that this youngest child resembled Mami's side of the family.

It was Mami's family who were *really* white. They were white in terms of race, and white also in terms of class. From them came the fine features, the pale skin, the lank hair. Her brothers and uncles went to schools abroad and had important businesses in the country. They also emulated the manners and habits of North Americans. Growing up, I remember arguments at the supper table on whether or not it was proper to tie one's napkin around one's neck, on how much of one's arm one could properly lay on the table, on whether spaghetti could be eaten with the help of a spoon. My mother, of course, insisted on all the protocol of knives and forks and on eating a little portion of everything served; my father, on the other hand, defended our eating whatever we wanted, with our hands if need be, so we could "have fun" with our food. My mother would snap back that we looked like *jibaritas* who should be living out in the country. Of course, that was precisely where my father's family came from.

Not that Papi's family weren't smart and enterprising, all twenty-five brothers and sisters. (The size of the family in and of itself was considered very country by some members of Mami's family.) Many of Papi's brothers had gone to the university and become professionals. But their education was totally island—no fancy degrees from Andover and Cornell and Yale, no summer camps or school songs in another language. Papi's family still lived in the interior versus the capital, in old-fashioned houses without air conditioning, decorated in ways my mother's family would have considered, well, tasteless. I remember antimacassars on the backs of rocking chairs (which were the living-room set), garish paintings of flamboyant trees, ceramic planters with plastic flowers in bloom. They were *criollos*—creoles—rather than cosmopolitans, expansive, proud, colorful. (Some members had a sixth finger on their right—or was it their left hand?) Their features were less aquiline than Mother's family's, the skin darker, the hair coarse and curly. Their money still had the smell of the earth on it and was kept in a wad in their back pockets, whereas my mother's family had money in the Chase Manhattan Bank, most of it with George Washington's picture on it, not Juan Pablo Duarte's.

It was clear to us growing up then that lighter was better, but there was no question of discriminating against someone because he or she was dark-skinned. Everyone's family, even an elite one like Mami's, had darker-skinned members. All Dominicans, as the saying goes, have a little black behind the ears. So, to separate oneself from those who were darker would have been to divide *una familia,* a sacrosanct entity in our culture. Neither was white blood necessarily a sign of moral or intellectual or political superiority. All one has to do is page through a Dominican history book and look at the number of dark-skinned presidents, dictators, generals, and entrepreneurs to see that power has not resided exclusively or even primarily among the whites on the island. The leadership of our country has been historically "colored."

But being black was something else. A black Dominican was referred to as a "dark Indian" (*indio oscuro*)—unless you wanted to come to blows with him, that is. The real blacks were the Haitians who lived next door and who occupied the Dominican Republic for twenty years, from 1822 to 1844, a fact that can still so inflame the Dominican populace you'd think it had happened last year. The denial of the Afro-Dominican part of our culture reached its climax during the dictatorship of Trujillo, whose own maternal grandmother was Haitian. In 1937, to protect Dominican race purity, Trujillo ordered the overnight genocide of thousands (figures range from 4,000 to 20,000) of Haitians by his military, who committed this atrocity using only machetes and knives in order to make this planned extermination look like a "spontaneous" border skirmish. He also had the Dominican Republic declared a white nation despite of the evidence of the mulatto senators who were forced to pass this ridiculous measure.

So, black was not so good, kinky hair was not so good, thick lips not so good. But even if you were *indio oscuro con pelo malo y una bemba de aquí a Baní,* you could still sit in the front of the bus and order at the lunch counter—or the equivalent thereof. There was no segregation of races in the halls of power. But in the aesthetic arena—the one to which we girls were relegated as females—lighter was better. Lank hair and pale skin and small, fine features were better. All I had to do was stay out of the sun and behave myself and I could pass as a pretty white girl.

Another aspect of my growing up also greatly influenced my thinking on race. Although I was raised in the heart of a large family, my day-to-day caretakers were the maids. Most of these women were dark-skinned, some of Haitian background. One of them, Misiá, had been spared the machetes of the 1937 massacre when she was taken in and hidden from the prowling *guardias* by the family. We children spent most of the day with these women. They tended to us, nursed us when we were sick, cradled us when we fell down and scraped an elbow or knee (as a tomboy, there was a lot of this scraping for me), and most important, they told us stories of *los santos* and *el barón del cementerio,* of *el cuco* and *las ciguapas,* beautiful dark-skinned creatures who escaped capture because their feet were turned backwards so they left behind a false set of foot-prints. These women spread the wings of our imaginations and connected us deeply to the land we came from. They were the ones with the stories that had power over us.

We arrived in Nueva York in 1960, before the large waves of Caribbean immigrants created little Habanas, little Santo Domingos, and little San Juans in the boroughs of the city. Here we encountered a whole new kettle of wax—as my mala-propping Mami might have said. People of color were treated as if they were inferior, prone to violence, uneducated, un-trustworthy, lazy—all the "bad" adjectives we were learning in our new language. Our dark-skinned aunt, Tía Ana, who had lived in New York for several decades and so was the authority in these matters, recounted stories of discrimination on buses and subways. These American were so blind! One drop of black and you were black. Everyone back home would have known that Tía Ana was not black: she had "good hair" and her skin color was a light *indio*. All week, she worked in a *factoría* in the Bronx, and when she came to visit us on Saturdays to sew our school clothes, she had to take three trains to our nice neighborhood where the darkest face on the street was usually her own.

We were lucky we were white Dominicans or we would have had a much harder time of it in this country. We would have encountered a lot more prejudice than we already did, for white as we were, we found that our Latino-ness, our accents, our habits and smells, added "color" to our complexion. Had we been darker, we certainly could not have bought our mock Tudor house in Jamaica Estates. In fact, the African American family who moved in across the street several years later needed police protection because of threats. Even so, at the local school, we endured the bullying of classmates. "Go back to where you came from!" they yelled at my sisters and me in the playground. When some of them started throwing stones, my mother made up her mind that we were not safe and began applying to boarding schools where privilege transformed prejudice into patronage.

"So where are you from?" my classmates would ask.

"Jamaica Estates," I'd say, an edge of belligerence to my voice. It was obvious from my accent, if not my looks, that I was not *from* there in the way they meant being from somewhere.

"I mean *originally.*"

And then it would come out, the color, the accent, the cousins with six fingers, the smell of garlic.

By the time I went off to college, a great explosion of

American culture was taking place on campuses across the country. The civil rights movement, the Vietnam War and subsequent peace movement, the women's movement, were transforming traditional definitions of American identity. Ethnicity was in: my classmates wore long braids like Native Americans and peasant blouses from Mexico and long, diaphanous skirts and dangly earrings from India. Suddenly, my foreignness was being celebrated. This reversal felt affirming but also disturbing. As huipils, serapes, and embroidered dresses proliferated about me, I had the feeling that my ethnicity had become a commodity. I resented it.

When I began looking for a job after college, I discovered that being a white Latina made me a nonthreatening minority in the eyes of these employers. My color was a question *only* of culture, and if I kept my cultural color to myself, I was "no problem." Each time I was hired for one of my countless "visiting appointments"—they were never permanent "invitations," mind you—the inevitable questionnaire would accompany my contract in which I was to check off my RACE: CAUCASIAN, BLACK, NATIVE AMERICAN, ASIAN, HISPANIC, OTHER. How could a Dominican divide herself in this way? Or was I really a Dominican anymore? And what was a Hispanic? A census creation—there is no such culture—how could it define who I was at all? Given this set of options, the truest answer might have been to check off OTHER.

For that was the way I had begun to think of myself. Adrift from any Latino community in this country, my culture had become an internal homeland, periodically replenished by trips "back home." But as a professional woman on my own, I felt less and less at home on the island. My values, the loss of my Catholic faith, my lifestyle, my wardrobe, my hippy ways, and my feminist ideas separated me from my native culture. I did not subscribe to many of the mores and constraints that seemed to be an intrinsic part of that culture. And since my culture had always been my "color," by rejecting these mores I had become not only Americanized but whiter.

If I could have been a part of a Latino community in the United States, the struggle might have been, if not easier, less private and therefore less isolating. These issues of acculturation and ethnicity would have been struggles to share with others like me. But all my North American life I had lived in shifting academic communities—going to boarding schools, then college, and later teaching wherever I could get those yearly appointments—and these communities reflected the dearth of Latinos in the profession. Except for friends in Spanish departments, who tended to have come from their countries of origin to teach rather than being raised in this country as I was, I had very little daily contact with Latinos.

Where I looked for company was where I had always looked for company since coming to this country: in books. At first the texts that I read and taught were the ones prescribed to me, the canonical works which formed the content of the bread-and-butter courses that as a "visiting instructor" I was hired to teach. These texts were mostly written by white male writers from Britain and the United States, with a few women thrown in and no Latinos. Thank goodness for the occasional creative writing workshop where I could bring in the multicultural authors I wanted. But since I had been formed in this very academy, I was clueless where to start. I began to educate myself by reading, and that is when I discovered that there were others out there like me, hybrids who came in a variety of colors and whose ethnicity and race were an evolving process, not a rigid paradigm or a list of boxes, one of which you checked off.

This discovery of my ethnicity on paper was like a rebirth. I had been going through a pretty bad writer's block: the white page seemed impossible to fill with whatever it was I had in me to say. But listening to authors like Maxine Hong Kingston, Toni Morrison, Gwendolyn Brooks, Langston Hughes, Maya Angelou, June Jordan, and to Lorna Dee Cervantes, Piri Thomas, Rudolfo Anaya, Edward Rivera, Ernesto Galarza (that first wave of Latino writers), I began to hear the language "in color." I began to see that literature could reflect the otherness I was feeling, that the choices in fiction and poetry did not have to be bleached out of their color or simplified into either/or. A story could allow for the competing claims of different parts of ourselves and where we came from.

Ironically, it was through my own stories and poems that I finally made contact with Latino communities in this country. As I published more, I was invited to read at community centers and bilingual programs. Latino students, who began attending colleges in larger numbers in the late seventies and eighties, sought me out as a writer and teacher "of color." After the publication of *How the García Girls Lost Their Accents,* I found that I had become a sort of spokesperson for Dominicans in this country, a role I had neither sought nor accepted. Of course, some Dominicans refused to grant me any status as a "real" Dominican because I was "white." With the color word there was also a suggestion of class. My family had not been among the waves of economic immigrants that left the island in the seventies, a generally darker-skinned, working-class group, who might have been the maids and workers in my mother's family house. We had come in 1960, political refugees, with no money but with "prospects": Papi had a friend who was the doctor at the Waldorf Astoria and who helped him get a job; Mami's family had money in the Chase Manhattan Bank they could lend us. We had changed class in America—from Mami's elite family to middle-class spics—but our background and education and most especially our pale skin had made mobility easier for us here. We had not undergone the same kind of race struggles as other Dominicans; therefore, we could not be "real" Dominicans.

What I came to understand and accept and ultimately fight for with my writing is the reality that ethnicity and race are not fixed constructs or measurable quantities. What constitutes our ethnicity and our race—once there is literally no common ground beneath us to define it—evolves as we seek to define and redefine ourselves in new contexts. My Latino-ness is not something someone can take away from me or leave me out of with a definition. It is in my blood: it comes from that mixture of biology, culture, native language, and experience that makes me a different American from one whose family comes from Ireland or Poland or Italy. My Latino-ness is also a political choice. I am choosing to hold on to my ethnicity and native language even if I can "pass." I am choosing to color my Americanness with my Dominicanness even if it came in a light shade of skin color.

I hope that as Latinos, coming from so many different countries and continents, we can achieve solidarity in this country as the mix that we are. I hope we won't shoot ourselves in the foot in order to maintain some sort of false "purity" as the glue that holds us together. Such an enterprise is bound to fail. We need each other. We can't afford to reject the darker or lighter varieties, and to do so is to have absorbed a definition of ourselves as exclusively one thing or the other. And haven't we learned to fear that word "exclusive"? This reductiveness is absurd when we are talking about a group whose very definition is that of a mestizo race, a mixture of European, indigenous, African, and much more. Within this vast circle, shades will lighten and darken into overlapping categories. If we cut them off, we diminish our richness and we plant a seed of ethnic cleansing that is the root of the bloodshed we have seen in Bosnia and the West Bank and Rwanda and even our own Los Angeles and Dominican Republic.

As we Latinos redefine ourselves in America, making ourselves up and making ourselves over, we have to be careful, in taking up the promises of America, not to adopt its limiting racial paradigms. Many of us have shed customs and prejudices that oppressed our gender, race, or class on our native islands and in our native countries. We should not replace these with modes of thinking that are divisive and oppressive of our rich diversity. Maybe as a group that embraces many races and differences, we Latinos can provide a positive multicultural, multiracial model to a divided America.

A MIDDLE PASSAGE

Philippe Wamba

The tree cannot stand up without its roots.
— Congolese proverb

It ain't where ya from, it's where ya at.
— Rakim

In my early teenage years, when my family would travel to Los Angeles from our home in Dar es Salaam, Tanzania, to spend part of the summer with relatives on my mother's side of the family, my cousin Chris and I would amuse ourselves by hanging out at the mall, going to the movies, or just cruising the streets of Westwood, Venice, or Inglewood in his father's Volkswagen hatchback. Sometimes we'd run into high school friends of his, and Chris always enjoyed introducing me with a mysterious flourish. "This is my cousin Phil," he'd say, and then pause for emphasis. "He's from Africa." We were always amused by the reactions; eyebrows would dart upward in surprise ("Word? For real?") and people would peer closely at me for a better look. When they addressed me, they'd tend to speak in an exaggeratedly loud, slow, and deliberate voice, "Ple-eased to me-eet you," contorting their mouths with each word as though they hoped I could read lips. Chris and I still laugh at how one friend of his who gave us a ride somewhere mimed for me to put on my seat belt, gesturing with her hands and widening her eyes, pronouncing the word carefully, as though addressing an infant: "Se-eat be-elt." Chris and I would usually play along for a while, he pretending to speak to me in Swahili and calling me "N'jawa" (an "African" name of his own invention), and I acting like I had trouble understanding English and speaking with a thickly stereotypical accent ("I yam veri hepi to be in Amerika"), but eventually we'd tire of the game or I'd slip inadvertently, lapsing into American as a song I liked came on the radio: "Yo, turn that up, man, that's my jam." Eyes would narrow with suspicion and fists would perch angrily on hips. "I thought you was from Africa?" they'd accuse. And I'd be obliged to tell the whole story, that yes, I was from Africa, but that I had actually been born a mere few miles away.

Later in my life, when I visited cousins on the other side of my family in Brazzaville, Congo, I was welcomed as "*notre frère américain*," an American brother finally come to visit his African family. My cousin Richard, a couple of years younger than me and clearly excited to meet me, showed me around the city and forgave me my atrocious French, displaying a few words of his own halting English so I wouldn't feel so bad. I was proudly introduced to his friends as "*mon frère Philippe, l'Américain*" and spent much of my visit answering questions about life in the United States. It's expensive there, yes? How much does food cost? How much does an apartment cost? How much money do you make? The whites treat black people very badly there, yes? I fielded the inquiries as best I could over bottles of the local beer, a potent pilsner called N'gok. My fondness for the brew became a bit of a joke among my cousin and his friends because its manufacturers had once promoted it with an odd and strangely appropriate advertising slogan: "*N'gok: la bière qui séduit les Américains*" (N'gok: the beer that seduces Americans). I heard that joke a few times before I left Brazzaville, and my cousins even presented me with a N'gok-logo print shirt as a parting gift. Of course, my cousins knew that I wasn't entirely "American," that my father, their uncle, was born and raised in Zaire (now the Democratic Republic of the Congo), and that my brothers and I had partly grown up in Tanzania, where our parents worked as educators. As we toured Brazzaville, I often mentioned that parts of the city reminded me of Dar es Salaam, and we would often compare words in Kikongo and Swahili to check for similarities in meaning (though I could not understand the Kikongo conversations that often surrounded me, I could usually pick out the handful of words that the two Bantu languages share). But my cousins nonetheless chose to identify me primarily with America, the land of my birth and the homeland of my mother, to them a much more exotic and romantically unfamiliar place of origin than Tanzania, a poor African country like Congo.

It can be difficult to define yourself when those around you are so eager to do it for you. Throughout my life, African Americans have usually chosen to regard me as an African, while Africans have tended to see me as an African American. In establishing my own sense of self, I have had to plot a middle course.

My father came to the States from Congo on an international student scholarship, and first saw my mother, a French major, at a French Club meeting at the western Michigan state college they both attended. She was impressed with his seriousness and extensive book knowledge; he appreciated her curiosity about Africa and her intelligence and ambition. Although an aunt had warned her that African men beat their wives and practiced polygamy, my mother disregarded her; like many of her peers, she had overcome the fear and disdain with which many older black Americans regarded Africa. She saw the continent as a motherland she had never known, and eagerly educated herself about my father's country and culture. Though my father was often at a loss for what to make of the African Americans he met at college, whom he often considered frivolous and unfocused, he felt that he had enough in common with my mother to build a sound foundation for the future. My parents were married in 1966, in an inelaborate Western ceremony attended by my mother's family and assorted friends. They stayed on in Michigan, where my older brother, Rémy, was born later that year. Even though my mother's family had accepted my father, one of her aunts still called up anxiously after the baby's birth. "Is he too dark?" they wanted to know.

I was born in 1971 in Pomona, California, where my parents lived briefly while my father finished his master's degree. When my father completed his studies in California, he got a job at Brandeis University, and we moved to the Boston area, establishing ourselves in the predominantly white, middle-class communities of Waltham and West Newton, where my younger brothers, Kolo and James, were born. My early childhood was a fairly typical American suburban existence in an environment of shady, tree-lined streets, clean, well-tended public parks, and attractive aluminum-sided family homes with driveways. My brothers and I attended the local public schools (where we were usually some of the only black kids in the hallways), we played soccer, baseball, and basketball and rode bikes after school, and wasted countless hours watching *The Brady Bunch* and *Gilligan's Island*. We hung out with the white kids in our neighborhood, picked up Boston accents ("Come ovah heah, youse guys"), shoplifted candy at the local Cumberland Farms, played hooky and smoked cigarettes in a nearby cemetery, and learned to appreciate white-boy rock groups like Kiss and Aerosmith. But at the same time, we were initiated into African American culture of the 1970s by our mother and friends who lived in Boston's predominantly black communities of Roxbury and Dorchester, while our father and his nearby relatives provided us with an education on Africa.

As a kid, I had no reason to feel that the various cultural strands that colored my life were exceptional. But I did have to find a way to live with all of them in a way that made sense to me. My brothers and I absorbed an interest in issues of ethnicity and culture from our parents and the world around us, and we referred to diverse cultural cues to construct an identity for ourselves. Culture was a highly embattled space in our childhood environment, but as kids we took it all in stride, barely realizing the breadth and variety of the sources that informed our outlook.

The differences between our American and African heritages were codified in specific ways, and we learned to understand and appreciate them early on. Since before I can remember, my parents usually spoke French to each other and English to my brothers and me, and while we picked up a few French words here and there, during my early childhood there was always a sense of linguistic division in the household. My father spoke English, his fourth language after Kikongo, French, and Lingala, with a Zairean accent, and when my brothers and I wanted to sound stern, we would chastise one another in what we thought was a pretty good approximation of my father's deep-voiced, accented English. We would also try to repeat French phrases we heard around the house, but to us the language was gibberish, even though Rémy had allegedly spoken fluent French as a youngster in Zaire, where my parents lived briefly before I was born. To complicate matters, my father spoke Kikongo with visiting Zairean friends and relatives, a language that was unknown to my brothers and me and barely comprehensible to my mother.

To my parents and Zairean relatives, I was always "Philippe," a foreign-sounding French mouthful that didn't make me feel very American. Rémy took to calling me "Phil," and it caught on among my mother's side of the family and my American playmates, a name I preferred at school and in public because it made me feel I was no different from the Johns, Roberts, Kevins, and Joeys in my class. I also knew that I had an African name as well, but I didn't know what it meant, and I only heard it when my father read to me from letters he received from Zaire that included warm greetings for "Philippe Kiatuntu." I would probably have been mortified if any of my friends had stumbled onto my alter ego.

I took an interest in the cultural backgrounds of my friends, learning to identify the Irish Americans, Italian Americans, and Jews among my playmates, and became almost obsessed with the process of cultural labeling itself. Like my mother, my black friends referred to themselves as "Afro-Americans" or just "black." My brothers and I were outspokenly proud to be black, an outlook we inherited from our parents, who fed us black consciousness with our baby food. Our childhood heroes included Malcolm X and Muhammad Ali, and in the often intolerant world of Waltham, Massachusetts, Rémy and I had to fight to defend the honor of our race on more than one occasion; we had a number of memorable scuffles with neighborhood kids who called us "niggers." But as black kids with a bicultural heritage, we also realized that there were all types of black people, so while we accepted the label "Afro-American," we decided that for us "Zairo-American" was more accurate, although few seemed to know what we were talking about.

It was my mother who usually cooked the family meals, and though she sometimes dabbled in recipes she had learned when she lived in Zaire with my father and Rémy for three years in the late 1960s, the bulk of her culinary repertoire came out of her experience growing up black in Chicago and Detroit. Her specialties included macaroni and cheese, cole slaw, black-eyed peas, pepper steak, fried chicken, spaghetti, and meat loaf, with the occasional pot of "peanut butter greens," a delectable concoction my mother based on a popular Zairean dish, thrown in for good measure. Conversely, when my father cooked, Zairean food reigned; he specialized in huge pots of beans and salt fish, which we ate with mounds of sticky rice or foufou, a starchy, doughy Zairean staple my brothers and I learned to love. My father's meals always made liberal use of pilipili, finely ground hot peppers that adorn most African foods, and he would encourage us to try as much as we could stand, saying that in Zaire children who couldn't eat pilipili were the object of scorn. My brothers and I came to regard dinners as an either/or choice, Zairean or American, depending on who was cooking.

Both of my parents were enthusiastic fans of music, and when my brothers and I were kids, each played items from their respective collections constantly. If I was arriving home from school and heard the strains of some song wafting down the stairs, I could pretty much figure out who was playing the record before I entered the living room. My mother was into Motown and other black soul and also loved jazz; her favorites, the music I grew up on, included Stevie Wonder, the Jackson Five, Aretha Franklin, James Brown, War, Chaka Khan, Natalie Cole, Donna Summer, Ramsey Lewis, Cannonball Adderley, and Wes Montgomery. My mother played and danced to her music often, sometimes deejaying her own individual dance parties on weekend afternoons, when she would use me as a dance partner to attempt to re-create the steps of her youth, the mashed potato, the monkey, the jerk, and her favorite, the bop.

My father also loved to dance, but his tastes ran toward Zairean dance orchestras headed by legendary bandleaders like Tabu Ley, Franco ("le Grand Maître"), Joseph Kabasele, Grand Kallé, and Sam Mangwana. He also loved Cuban salsa by performers like Johnny Pacheco, funky African jazz by Manu Dibango and Fela Anikulapo Kuti, and the Caribbean folk songs of Harry Belafonte. The somewhat odd exceptions to my father's almost completely African Caribbean musical bias were the lounge-style croonings of Nat King Cole, a perennial favorite, and the lovelorn ballads of Roberta Flack. My brothers and I still know the words to almost every song by both of these artists, the result of years of involuntary exposure. It was only as an adult that I learned the names, and to appreciate the music, of the non-American performers of my father's listening repertoire. As a college student in New England, far from Tanzania and deeply homesick, I rediscovered African music as a comforting cultural link to my home and family, but to me as a child, my father's music seemed distinctively foreign: loud, upbeat soundscapes of horns and drums under melodies in strange languages that my brothers and I would jokingly imitate. And my father's dancing style was a far cry from my mother's bop: at home he would typically dance to his music while he rearranged his thousands of books in the living room, smoothly shuffling forward toward the bookcase, rotating his hips in time to the music, and spinning fluidly when the band launched into an insistent soukous guitar solo. My mother would dance to Zairean music with my father at African parties, but she seldom, if ever, played any Zairean records on her own.

My father's younger sister and her family moved from Zaire to nearby Lynn in the mid-seventies, and they joined a community of Zaireans in the Boston area, a diaspora attracted to America by education, jobs, and the lure of prosperity. My family quite often attended the Zairean gatherings that commemorated holidays and special events. These parties always featured Zairean friends and relations with names like Bawa, Sadi, Konzo, and Mafwa speaking loudly in Kikongo, Lingala, and French, blaring uptempo Zairean music, and lots of Zairean food, often cooked with ingredients that had been brought to the United States by recently arrived Africans. Foufou, salt fish, mbika (a dish made from pounded pumpkin seeds), mfumbua (a coarse spinachlike vegetable cooked with peanut butter), cassava, and boiled plantains were some of my favorites. My father still loves to tell the story of the time he and one of my uncles decided to slaughter a goat for one of these parties, and responded to an intriguing "Goat for Sale" ad in a local paper. When my father went to pick up the intended centerpiece of our prospective feast, its owners introduced the animal by name (Joe) and asked if they would be able to come and visit him in his new home. "What?" asked my father incredulously, thinking he must have misunderstood the question. "But we're going to eat him!" Needless to say, the deal fell through. My father and uncle left emptyhanded, laughing at the foolish Americans who kept food as a pet, while Joe's shocked family muttered disgustedly about the savage Africans.

Whether we could procure a goat or not, the parties were always enjoyable. The adults, the men dressed immaculately in pleated pants, pointy-toed shoes, and colorful dress shirts and the women in tight African-print dresses that hugged their substantial hips, would dance to Zairean music until daybreak, and we kids would eat and run around playing until we passed out on the couch or in the beds of our cousins. The events had a sense of nostalgia in that what linked the guests was a common and distant place of origin, a far-off, fondly remembered homeland they re-created in microcosm at parties like these. My father and his friends would trade reminiscences and speak animatedly about Zairean politics, enjoying the familiar food and music, and relishing the opportunity to speak the languages they grew up with. My brothers and I were always included as part of the family, as Zaireans who would one day return "home" along with everyone else. I was always self-conscious in my inability to speak French or Kikongo, and realized that I wasn't as Zairean as my Kinshasa-born cousin Dina, for example. But I embraced the sense of cultural identification and delighted in the idea of an estranged home in Africa that I would someday visit.

For some holidays, my family would drive to Cleveland to visit my mother's father and stepmother or to Detroit to visit her mother and sister. These reunions were similar in spirit to the Zairean parties, but quite different in substance. Legions of cousins with names like Skip, Beth, Butch, and Chris and older relatives like Uncle Clarence, Grandmother Martha, and Aunt Sweetie would fill my grandfather's large house for huge meals of fried chicken, collard greens, baked beans, potato salad, cornbread, and homemade preserves washed down with sweet iced tea. Rémy, my cousin Chris, and I would discuss the latest dances and popular music (Rick James, Parliament Funkadelic, Chic, and Kool and the Gang, among others) and play video games while the younger kids ran around playing noisily and the grown-ups shared loud jokes and card games. I remember that my mother would really unwind at these gatherings, spending laughing, affectionate time with her sisters and younger brother, using exclamations like "Ooh, chile" and terms of endearment like "fool" and slipping into ebonics-flavored discussions of old times.

To me, the gatherings on each side of my family felt the same; they had a warm sense of family and inclusion, though the sounds, smells, and sights of each environment were quite different. But I also knew that the two worlds were separate; when we immersed ourselves in one, it was as if the other did not exist. Relatives on my father's side were aware of their American in-laws, but they had virtually no contact with them. My nuclear family, a fusion of at least two cultures, bounced between them without really unifying them.

It was a devastating tragedy that brought the two sides of my family together for the first time in my memory. In 1979, my older brother Rémy, who was then thirteen, was diagnosed with leukemia. He spent the better part of a year in and out of area hospitals, where a constant stream of family members visited him, sitting with him, praying for him, and willing him to recover. My entire family suffered through Rémy's illness, and when he died in late 1979, countless relatives and friends pulled together in a unified expression of support and love. I was barely eight years old when Rémy died, but I remember his funeral vividly. And thinking about that day now, one thing stands out in my mind, more than picking the sad faces of Rémy's friends out of the crowd as I walked with my family down the aisle of the church in my too-big borrowed suit, more than the sour, salty taste of the tears on my cheeks as I listened to speaker after speaker bemoan the tragic loss of one so young, and more than the strange guilty thrill of riding in the dark, plush interior of the limousine to the cemetery. My brother's funeral is the only occasion on which I can remember seeing both sides of my extended family together, my father's Zairean friends and relatives alongside my African American mother's relatives in from Ohio and Michigan.

I remember that at the funeral my mother's sister Anne read a touching eulogy about how Rémy's spirit would live forever. And I remember that my dad's cousin, Uncle Fukiau, read a tribute to Rémy in French that was punctuated by African exclamations of agreement from the Zaireans in the audience and greeted with polite applause from those who couldn't understand the words. I remember being aware of the obvious differences between the two sides of my family, noting how easy it was to tell who was on what side from their physical features, how they dressed, the way they carried themselves. At first, it seemed strangely incongruous to see them all there, as though one group had come to the wrong funeral or something.

But I realized that it was a desire to mourn Rémy's death and to claim him as part of themselves that united them all. I think my brothers and I had always unconsciously dichotomized between the two sides of our identity, and we slipped from one to the other depending on the context, keeping our dual heritage neatly divided. But on the day we buried my brother, and in the midst of my sadness, I felt whole in a way I never had before.

If my brother's funeral provided me with a more unified sense of self, the next great change in my life complicated matters still further. In 1980, still reeling from the shock of my brother's death, my family moved to Dar es Salaam, Tanzania, where my father got a job teaching history at the national university.

Tanzania was a new playground. My brothers and I roamed the white sand beaches and swam in the Indian Ocean; we played tag in cashew nut trees and learned Swahili from our playmates. It was a glorious time of new discovery and exploration.

The new environment forced me to confront the question of my identity in unprecedented ways. When my new friends wanted to know where I was from and to what tribe I belonged, most were usually satisfied when I said that I had been born in America and that my father was a Mukongo from Zaire and my mother an American. But some insisted that a child inherits the nationality and culture of the father, while others said that since I was born in the United States, I was an American. These sorts of responses added to my confusion.

On one occasion soon after we had moved to Dar es Salaam, my mother, my brothers, and I took a shortcut to the store through a poor neighborhood just outside the university campus, where my family lived in faculty housing. As we walked through the complex of dingy, state-owned bungalows, barefoot children playing in the dust saw our American sneakers and jeans and the other subtle signifiers of our American-ness, and pursued us, playfully chanting "*Wazungu, wazungu!*" I spoke enough Swahili at that point to know that *wazungu* referred to non-Africans in general, and to white people in particular. The taunts wounded me. Why did they see us as outsiders when we were blacks returned from America to our rightful homeland? I wondered. After that experience, I took pains to blend in, wearing shorts, thong sandals, and T-shirts like most Tanzanian boys my age; after I adjusted my wardrobe, and after I learned enough Swahili to sound like a native, I was rarely ever "exposed" as a foreigner again.

But I was unable to fully transform myself into a complete Tanzanian. In my third-grade class, which was primarily conducted in Swahili, the teacher once used the black spiritual "Swing Low, Sweet Chariot" as part of an English lesson; when the class laughed at the unfamiliar sounds and joked around jovially, mangling the lyrics and deliberately distorting the melody, I was offended. Didn't they know that this was a song that had been sung by African American slaves and as such should be approached reverentially? I seethed with silent indignation.

A similar chord was struck by my first trip to Zanzibar, a

small and beautiful island off Tanzania's coast, where slaves from the mainland had been held in caves before being exported to Saudi Arabia and Europe during the East African slave trade. Because Zanzibar has a rich and ancient history, my brothers, my mother, and I made a weekend trip to tour the island. As we inspected the dank, dark slave caverns, one of many stops on our guided tour, I was almost moved to tears. Maybe my mother's ancestors had been held in this very cave before being taken to America, I remember thinking. And I wondered if the fact that my family had now returned to our estranged homeland mattered to anyone but us. Our guide seemed bored. I saw the site as a tragic torture chamber where my own relatives might have suffered hundreds of years ago; I wondered what our guide, or any other Tanzanian, saw when they looked at the caves. Did they see a blood-drenched pit where their abducted kin had been held against their will, or an ancient ruin where distant and vaguely recalled historical dramas had unfolded long ago? And did they see my family as the descendants of their enslaved ancestors or as just another group of tourists, exploitable sources of income for whom they felt nothing?

Despite such experiences, within two years of moving to Tanzania I felt at home, learning near flawless Swahili, playing barefoot soccer with my new friends, and becoming more distanced from my American identity, although I was rarely permitted to forget it (my peers were quick to refer to my brothers and me as "*wamarekani*"—Americans). Though still at least partial outsiders in our new environment, as my brothers and I assimilated the nuances of Tanzanian culture, we added a third heritage to our cultural background. As my then four-year-old brother James put it, we were now "half American, half Zairean, and half Tanzanian." We soon added another language, and another linguistic dividing line, to our household: my parents continued to speak to each other in French and English, while my brothers and I spoke English and the occasional French phrase to our parents, and English and Swahili to each other.

Such a cocktail as ours was not really unusual in a city that was home to a host of cultural mixtures. Swahili language and culture, in fact, draw from African, Arab, East Indian, and Portuguese sources, and Dar es Salaam, an ancient trade outpost for Africans from the interior, has for centuries been a crossroads for various peoples and cultures, colonized in turn by the sultans of Oman, the Germans, and the British. I soon began to feel right at home as just another mongrel in a city of mongrels. Shortly after we moved to Tanzania, my mother got a job teaching at the local international school, which catered to the children of diplomats, aid agency employees, and a general community of international transients; the International School of Tanganyika (named before the country's 1964 merger with the island of Zanzibar), which my brothers and I began attending in 1981, was the United Nations of Tanzanian schools, and many of my classmates and friends there seemed as mixed up as I was. My Tanzanian best friend in seventh grade counted Germans, Maasais, Yemenis, and Comoro Islanders among his ancestors, yet was ethnically unexceptional in a Dar es Salaam community in which bloodlines were often murky. Another close school friend was the son of a Trinidadian mother and a Tanzanian father, yet another was a Tanzanian–Sri Lankan mix, and down the street from my family's house near the university campus lived a German-Ghanaian family whose children wore the badge of their cultural confusion in their bright blond Afros. In such company, I gradually came to feel less conflicted about my own background; it was an environment in which it seemed okay to have diverse cultural roots and make no apology for them.

Kolo and James were five and three respectively when my family moved to Tanzania, and neither of them have much memory of my family's years in the Boston area—most of their earliest formative experiences were in Dar es Salaam. When we moved to Dar, Kolo began attending Tanzanian nursery school, where he began to learn Swahili and school songs and rhymes he still remembers. I didn't admit it for many years, but it is clear to me now that his grasp of the Swahili language and culture is more advanced than my own. Kolo says he now sees himself as an "African American," with a special emphasis on the "African," and he considers it a matter of course that when he completes his studies in the United States he will return to Dar es Salaam to work and live, and perhaps eventually settle in Zaire. In terms of "degrees of acculturation," my brother James, all but an infant when we moved to Dar es Salaam, is even more Tanzanian than Kolo. James has virtually no memories of life in Boston (and, sadly, few memories of Rémy), and has considered Dar es Salaam his home for as long as he can remember. His Swahili is completely fluent, and he also speaks some Arabic, which, after English, is Dar es Salaam's third most widely spoken language. He even converted to Islam recently, adopting the name Saleem and joining Dar es Salaam's religious majority. Although he identifies with African American and Zairean culture as well, for all intents and purposes James is a Tanzanian in language, culture, and spirit, and he, like Kolo, takes it for granted that he will return there to live when he finishes school in the United States.

I spent the first eight years of my life in the United States and the next eight in Tanzania, returning to America to attend school when I was sixteen. Dar is my family's current home, but to me it is only one of many possible homes. Growing up in Dar es Salaam as a bicultural expatriate who nonetheless came to identify with Tanzanian culture, I realized that identifying myself was a personal process I would have to go through alone, and that it had little to do with my siblings or even my parents. By the time I left Tanzania for the United States in 1987, I had begun to think of myself in terms that were somewhat independent of culture and country, although I was still confused and disoriented, caught between the communities of my ancestry and those of my experience.

Matters came to a head during my undergraduate career at Harvard University, where I struggled to find a community in which I felt comfortable. I felt alienated in Black Student Association meetings, where I self-consciously came to realize how little I shared with members of the various African American campus cliques, and though I fared better among Harvard's African students, I still didn't feel "African" enough to be accepted as a bona fide Tanzanian or Zairean. Even though I tended to identify more strongly with my African side, having lived in Tanzania for eight highly formative years, I often felt stuck in the middle, both African and American and unable to bridge the gap between the two. African Americans usually saw me as an African, and though I didn't often admit it, many Africans, at Harvard and at home in Tanzania, considered me an American, or at best an inauthentic black hybrid. I eventually got bored with trying to find a comfortable fit in either.

I used to try to find succinct ways of responding to the question "Where are you from?"—simple one-word answers that would satisfy the curious. I envied my friends their ability to state one place confidently and simply say "New York" or "Kenya." I felt that most people I'd meet, at college, at parties, through acquaintances, and at work, weren't really interested in where I came from and were just politely making conversation, so I'd want to oblige them with a nice, neat response that would keep the dialogue going without revealing too much. Sometimes I would think that it didn't matter what I said to a particular person because I'd never see them again, and I would just name one of my various sources, for example, "Los Angeles," the place of my birth, and be done with it. Sometimes this would backfire, and the person would say, "Really? What part?" For a period, I even referred to myself as "a citizen of the world," a high-minded moniker, bred of my own boredom and frustration, that used to annoy people. I don't think I was ever successful with my attempts at the short answer. Gradually, I came to employ a variety of longer answers that got at the truth of my background but didn't tell the whole story and seemed grossly oversimplified.

Now I have decided that the succinct answer is always inadequate, and that the story of origin is always a complex saga. I recently read an article on Alex Haley's *Roots* that pointed out that the structure of a human family is more like a big, tangled bush than a tall, branching tree, and that Haley's search for "roots" was really more of a quest for a "route" back to Africa through his family ancestry. I, too, have come to reject the idea of a simple, dualized family heritage and the simple bicultural understanding of self I internalized as a child. My cultural influences, in terms of my genetic heritage and my personal experience, look a lot more like a bush than a tree—maybe a tumbleweed is an even more fitting analogy, since it helps to capture the sense of movement, migration, and mixing that has characterized and shaped my life.

I was born both African and African American, but it took years for me to negotiate the precarious currents of the middle passage between my American mother and African father and to understand what that duality could mean, how it would make me struggle to span four hundred years of history, thousands of miles, and worlds of experience ever since. For a time, I lived as a sophisticated cultural chameleon, attempting to blend with my shifting surroundings by assuming the appearance and habits of those around me. But even though a real chameleon may look like the green foliage it imitates, it never really becomes a leaf, and I could never fully transform myself into what I imagined a "real" African American to be, or into the "authentic" African of my mind's eye. In the end, I am both African and African American—and therefore neither. I envy others their hometowns and unconflicted patriotism, but no longer would I exchange them for my freedom to seek multiple homes and nations and to forge my own.

FOOD AND THE IMMIGRANT

Indira Ganesan

In an Indian household, a baby enters the world with a taste of sweet on the tongue. A drop of honey is provided for a good life. A baby's drool, in fact, is considered nectar. My memories of India are touched by sepia and taste—photographs of unknown relatives and a strange recall of foreign fruit. India is mangoes, milky tea, coconut sweets. It is poori, puffy pillows billowing in oil, to be sopped in potato and peas; it is dosa, rice-flour crêpes two feet long; steaming idlis wrapped in banana leaves for transport. It is tiffin, that colonial answer to afternoon tea, an hour-long predinner snack session. It is spicy hot samosas dipped in tamarind and date sauce, chopped onions and chickpeas, followed by strong North Indian chai.

To dream of India is to salivate in flavor, smell, taste. Hot, sour, sweet, salty, bitter—all must be accommodated, say the ancients. Food is ritual. On harvest day, milk is boiled and words are spoken over the foam for a good year. Tiny spoonfuls of flavored rice are arranged in neat rows on a banana leaf to satiate the birds, to assure a brother's health. Sweet porridge is offered to the gods, along with raisins and nuts, rock candy crystals.

These gods are bathed in a sequence of milk, honey, banana, dates, and water in Hindu temples. To see the face of Venkateswara covered in milk is divine, a friend of my mother's once told me. Every visit to the darkened temple brought prasadam from the priests, food we placed in our mouths after touching its holy essence to our eyes. Blessed is he who can eat.

Then there is America. A puritan church that frowns on gum chewing, that looks with abhorrence at its wafer-swallowing cousins of Catholicism. The cathedral of the giant supermarket. Fifty kinds of wheat-based cereal, twenty kinds of chips. Still, the food stores *are* amazing. My favorite stocks rose petal jam, jalapeño pesto, coffee from Vietnam. The vegetables are huge, the ads promote tea as a macho drink ("This ain't no sippin' tea," meaning, I suppose, a kind of tea in a can that can be guzzled in a single shot. The consumer then presumably crushes the can, tosses it, and sets off for a wild night with the boys.) Aisles and aisles of choice, of freedom, of quantity. Four-dollar organic butter, pure vegetable-oil spread, cream cheese, full fat, low fat, some fat, no fat. Instant rice, instant pudding, instant bread, instant cappuccino. One has to move very fast to leave the store with only eight items. To linger is to lose. Hours will pass deciding between brands of falafel mix, tomato paste, chocolate.

When my father arrived in America with seventeen dollars in his pocket, a university scholarship, and a wife and two children to support back home, he bought a carton of ice cream. Every night, he'd eat a few teaspoonfuls, happy with his hoard. When my mother followed, and this was in the mid-sixties, she took to frozen foods, marveling at the convenience. From her hand came curried A & P peas and carrots, spiced A & P chopped spinach and potato, and the very horrid A & P "mixed vegetables." Once in a while, as a treat, we'd get a TV dinner—macaroni and cheese, peas and pearl onions, stewed apples in tinfoil. I'd watch *Lost in Space* after clearing my TV tray, a few years ahead of Neil Armstrong, Tang, and Space Sticks.

By high school, I knew how to make brownies from a mix, and slice-and-bake cookies. This while my mother turned out gorgeous milk halvahs and gulabjamuns, carefully cutting sweets into diamond shapes after placing thin silver sheets on top. I remained unimpressed by her culinary expertise. I liked grilled cheese, and for a snack I looked to, perhaps fittingly, an Oreo cookie. Like Maxine Hong Kingston's narrator in *The Woman Warrior,* I too resolved to eat plastic, avoid the eccentricities of ethnic cuisine.

Pollution rules were one eccentricity. Hindus were very strict about hygiene and food, I learned. A Brahmin might bless his food by circling it with drops of water. He ate fastidiously, using the tips of three fingers, on a banana leaf that needn't be washed, just thrown away; he never shared food from his plate. I grew up with the Tamil word *etchel,* which loosely translates as "polluted with saliva." My grandmother, to my wonderment, would drink water from her tumbler by tilting her head back and pouring the liquid into her open mouth, never allowing the metal to touch her lips. So dexterous was she, she could swallow while pouring, like a bird.

There are still some holdovers to these customs in America—certainly, anyone from my mother's generation, and sometimes younger. My cousins and I have no problem with going to an Ethiopian restaurant and eating from a common bowl, but then we are cousins. While my brother and I would do the same with friends and just-met strangers, others might not be so flexible. In all cultures, sharing food is a basic step toward friendship, yet diners do not offer their food randomly to just anyone. The pollution laws take this a step further, so that by eating from another's plate or spoon, one becomes tainted with *etchel,* and therefore unclean. Likewise, in some orthodox Hindu households, menstruating women are not only forbidden to enter the shrine room or temple but are expected to eat their meals apart. To touch a menstruating woman is considered unclean. And of course, she is not to step into the kitchen.

This has led me to develop two sets of behavior for two sets of people. With American friends, I share food and utensils freely; with conservative Indian friends, I am more reserved. It is easy to share; it's not knowing the rules that's hard. When I'm in the kitchen with a new South Asian acquaintance, what can I assume? Can I offer her a taste off my spoon? By playing it safe, do I fall into a stereotype and deny her intimacy?

In my own home, I disregard the menstruation taboos. In my world, God, being female, realizes there is nothing shameful in letting go of eggs. But at my parents', I honor them as far the shrine room goes. Never have they expected me to eat apart. In India, I have seen my aunt eating by herself in the vestibule, and wonder, if she could have her way and overrule my more modern uncle, whether I, too, would be barred from the table. Would her rules carry across the waters?

At home ("India"), it's shoes off, no sleeping at sunset, and eating as soon as the food is served, not waiting for everyone else to be seated. When we have company, my mother rarely sits before the first course is over, despite pleas and reassurances that there's enough salt, enough napkins. Outside ("America"), it's shoes in the kitchen, napping anytime, passing the potatoes around the table, and a lot of forks. This schizophrenic behavior is essential to biculturalism. It's like owning two sets of silverware, wearing two kinds of coats. What happens, though, when an American strides with her shoes into an Indian kitchen? When I unthinkingly taste from the pot in front of my mother's friends and put the spoon back in? At home, we all flinch when a repairman walks into the kitchen with his boots, but say nothing. We are, finally, guests after all, despite our right to vote, and we don't wish to offend.

We were vegetarian at a time when yogurt was a rarity in the supermarket. A midwestern doctor looked at my naturally small frame and my Indian name, and declared me to be malnourished. An egg a day, boiled, was the cure. So for one year, I dutifully ate an egg with ketchup while watching *Dennis the Menace* on TV. Other Americans asked me if by vegetarian did it mean I only ate vegetables, thinking, presumably, of cellophane-wrapped bags of carrots and pale celery. Where was

Alice Waters then? Obviously, not in my neighborhood. One well-meaning mother of a playmate asked me to dinner and served me plain boiled white rice. With a fork. What did she know of rasam and sambar, the delicious lentil broth and gravies to flavor rice, the accompanying curried vegetables, the rice and yogurt with spicy hot pickled mango bits, all to be scooped up with spoons?

My experiences with meat have been rare but memorable. When I was five, on the trip over from India, our flight attendants went on strike, so the plane disembarked us at various airports to eat. I stared disdainfully at the plate of pasta and marinara the Italians had graciously offered; it was to be distrusted, all that lumpy red. Later, in St. Louis, at a kindergarten trip to the "big school's" cafeteria, I was loath to try watermelon. "Try a little," urged my poor teacher, promising me it was safe. I looked at the fleshy chunks and shook my head. But when she wasn't looking, I ventured a taste: delicious! But true to saving face, I resolutely refused to eat more in front of the teacher. My brother solved his problem with vegetarian foods that looked nonveg. Faced with a slice of pizza, he flipped it over, hiding all the sauce, and munched away.

In sixth grade, I had a crush on a boy named Michael. He had pale skin, freckles, a shag haircut, and a very slight resemblance to Bobby Sherman. At our class "International Day" luncheon, where our mothers made ethnic meals and wrote up recipes to match, infatuation drove me to try a bite of his mother's Swedish meatballs. They were dry and bland and awful. My mother's efforts weren't any better. She had prepared an Indian sweet covered in sugar syrup that had hardened considerably. My classmates dubbed them "wax cookies," and tossed them around. I didn't care, concentrating on Sweden. My friend Joe's mom made chicken teriyaki, the hit of the party. He urged me to try it, but I declined. I didn't, after all, have a crush on *him*. Love is a curious thing.

Among my favorite authors is Madhur Jaffrey, the cook and actress. Reading her books is to slip into a taste dream. Here is her heroic description of Lebanese tabouli:

> I saw a mound of it on her dining table and could not even begin to guess what it was. It looked speckled— brown, green, and red—was meant to be eaten with scoops of lettuce, and it was a sort of salad but not quite. I fell in love with its grainy texture and tart taste, then have continued to make it ever since.

And in writing of a kind of Indian trail mix, she exults:

> A glorious, spicy, complex ancestor of granola, cheewra combines cashews, peanuts, split peas, puffed rice, sesame seeds, and raisins with spices like cloves and cinnamon."*

One wants to reach into a bowl and devour immediately. Also, it's nice to know one can substitute Rice Krispies for the puffed rice.

I always winced when friends suggested I make them

*Madhur Jaffrey. *World-of-the-East Vegetarian Cooking* (New York: Alfred A. Knopf, 1955).

"curry." (In England, they might ask for "a curry," at least allowing that there's more than one kind.) Truth is, there's no such thing as a generic "curry." What you can have is curried eggplant, called baingan bartha, curried potatoes, called dum aloos, curried peas and tomato with fresh cheese, called muttar paneer, and several other hundred combinations and varieties. The spices used are coriander, cumin, turmeric, black mustard seed, and cayenne. But there is also asafetida, amchoor, anise, ajwain, and those are only the *A*'s. And never can we forget splendid saffron, precious commodity, rare flavor. On many a restless night, I heat milk with saffron and sugar to invite sleep.

For much of my life, I've been skinny. Weight was never a problem, although I wasn't crazy about my round Indian tummy as I squeezed into jeans. Then, for three years beginning in 1989, I was under a medication which had a side effect of weight gain. I had told my doctor that I'd rather be healthy than thin and he agreed. What I hadn't counted on was an accumulation of twenty pounds a year, which added sixty pounds to my body. It wasn't entirely the medicine. I didn't watch my diet—I indulged in cheese and sweets—and I had no athletic outlet to speak of. Still, the shock of going from a size six to ten to fourteen to X-Large confronted me in the mirror. I who had vowed I wouldn't end up a small round Indian woman wound up a large American. My inherited thighs and tummy took on a scope that resembled my grandmother's girth in her last sedentary years. Clothes were a problem, and suitcases of dresses and trousers were packed away. Encouraged by an Indian friend in California, I began to wear salwar kameeze, a

North Indian dress consisting of a long tunic over pantaloons. My father remarked I looked good in them. In India, then, I could hide my poundage. I didn't attempt a sari, however.

As I often did in my life when faced with a problem, I looked for a role model, and found Oprah. In her, I saw an intelligence and honesty about weight, and a determination to shed the fat. Her way was exercise and healthy eating. Her nemesis was French fries and chips; mine was Indian snacks. No more samosas, bhajis, bhel pooris. No more ghee, halvahs, ladoos. But of course, easier said than done. Out of anxiety, and of boredom, I reach for snacks. For five years now, I have shed and gained the same twenty pounds. I have tried calisthenics, aerobics, Aquacize, steps, weights. Now I am walking for exercise. I make no promises.

My attitude toward food has varied; unlike my teenage years when I used to throw away sandwiches from home at lunchtime, and my early twenties when I'd eat a few stalks of broccoli for dinner, my thirties find me in love with food. I love its texture, its smell, its taste. I like to spend a day making chocolate ganache and giving it away. I like roasting peppers for spaghetti sauce, chopping garlic for enchiladas. I like eating at home and in restaurants. I read food columns and reviews. When I was young, we could order a plain cheese pizza if we went out. Now, in Little India, Edison, New Jersey, an Italian cook sells masala pizza, extra hot. My brother makes pineapple curry. I experiment with tofu marinades. In twenty years, the vegetarian food choices have opened up. In Northern California, restaurants offer as many meatless dishes as meat, if meat is offered at all. We've gone a long way from boiled veggies over Minute Rice.

Perhaps I am filling up gaps in my life with food, gaps like a partner, or a house, or a dog. Maybe I like it for the same reason I like to go to a play or ballet, for entertainment, variety. Like it I do. Nguyen Qui Duc, the author of *Where the Ashes Are: The Odyssey of a Vietnamese Family*, writes in an essay:

> I had been fat as a young boy, but after I arrived in America the year I turned sixteen, I became more rotund. For years, American food had seeped into me, and I'd grown and grown, and it seemed Viet Nam was slipping further and further away.*

My Indian memories are dim. I evoke them with food and the memory of food: plunging my hand into a bin of rice grains to test the mangoes that have been buried there to ripen; competing with monkeys for chikku fruit; stopping at the roadside where a man will slice off the top of a green coconut with a machete so we can drink the milk. Those are remembrances. I left India long before the MacMahal Burger and MTV.

And perhaps to make up for the loss of India, I eat. Perhaps to hold on to it, I eat Indian food, so America can't claim me, despite my U.S. citizenship. By consuming its food, I can invent an India that won't reject me for my American accent, my foreign outlook, my leaving thirty years ago. My taste buds aren't traitorous; my loyalty lies within my tongue.

*Nguyen Qui Doc. "A Taste of Home," in *Under Western Eyes: Personal Essays from Asian America,* ed. Garrett Hongo (New York: Anchor Books/ Doubleday, 1995).

Boil water with milk. Add Assam tea leaves, making sure the pot does not foam over. When you can smell a fragrance of wood and earth and tea, strain into a cup. Stir in freshly ground cardamom. Sit near a window and listen to the sounds of tabla, of Sufi qawwalis. Imagine you are in Kashmir, listening to the rain; imagine you are an Urdu poet. In the cup, everything.

WHAT COLOR IS JESUS?

James McBride

Just before I quit my last job in Washington, I drove down into Virginia to see my stepfather's grave for the first time. He was buried in a little country graveyard in Henrico County, near Richmond, about a hundred yards from the schoolhouse where he learned to read. It's one of those old "colored" graveyards, a lonely, remote backwoods place where the wind blows through the trees and the graves are marked by lopsided tombstones. It was so remote I couldn't find it by myself. I had to get my aunt Maggie to show me where it was. We drove down a dirt road and then parked and walked down a little dusty path the rest of the way. Once we found his grave, I stood over it for a long time.

I was fourteen when my stepfather died. One minute he was there, the next—boom—gone. A stroke. Back then I thought a stroke was something you got from the sun. I didn't know it could kill you. His funeral was the first I had ever attended. I didn't know they opened coffins at funerals. When the funeral director, a woman with white gloves, unlatched the coffin, I was horrified. I couldn't believe she was going to open it up. I begged her in my mind not to open it up—please—but she did, and there he was. The whole place broke up. Even the funeral director cried. I thought I would lose my mind.

Afterward, they took him out of the church, put him in a car, and flew him down to Virginia. My mother and older brother and little sister went, but I'd seen enough. I didn't want to see him anymore. As a kid growing up in New York, I'd been embarrassed by him because he wasn't like the other guys' fathers, who drove hot rods, flew model airplanes with their sons, and talked about the Mets and civil rights. My father was solitary, gruff, busy. He worked as a furnace fireman for the New York City Housing Authority for thirty-six years, fixing oil burners and shoveling coal into big furnaces that heated the housing projects where my family lived. He drove a Pontiac, a solid, clean, quiet car. He liked to dress dapper and drink Rheingold beer and play pool with his brother Walter and their old-timey friends who wore fedoras and smoked filterless Pall Malls and called liquor "likka" and called me "boy." They were weathered Southern black men, quiet and humorous and never bitter about white people, which was out of my line completely. I was a modern-day black man who didn't like the white man too much, even if the white man was my mother.

My mother was born Jewish in Poland, the eldest daughter

of an Orthodox rabbi. She married my natural father, a black man, in 1941. He died in 1957, at forty-eight, while she was pregnant with me. She married my stepfather, Hunter L. Jordan, Sr., when I was about a year old. He raised me and my seven brothers and sisters as his own—we considered him to be our father—and he and my mother added four more kids to the bunch to make it an even twelve.

My parents were unique. As unique as any parents I have known, which I suppose makes their children unique. However, being unique can spin you off in strange directions. For years I searched for a kind of peace. I vacillated between being the black part of me that I accept and the white part of me that I could not accept. Part writer, part musician, part black man, part white man. Running, running, always running. Even professionally I sprinted, from jazz musician to reporter and back again. Bounding from one life to the other—the safety and prestige of a journalism job to the poverty and fulfillment of the musician's life.

Standing over my stepfather's grave, thinking about quitting my gig to move back to New York to be a musician and freelance writer, I was nervous. He would never approve of this jive. He would say: "You got a good job and you quit that? For what? To play jazz? To write? Write what? You need a job." Those were almost the exact words my mother always used.

My aunt Maggie, who's about seventy-two, was standing there as I waged this war in my mind. She came up behind me and said, "He was a good man. I know y'all miss him so much."

"Yep," I said, but as we walked up the dusty little path to my car to go to the florist to get flowers, I was thinking, "Man, I'm sure glad he's not here to see me now."

I'm a black man and I've been running all my life. Sometimes I feel like my soul just wants to jump out of my skin and run off, things get that mixed up. But it doesn't matter, because what's inside is there to stay no matter how fast you sprint. Being mixed feels like that tingly feeling you have in your nose when you have to sneeze—you're hanging on there waiting for it to happen, but it never does. You feel completely misunderstood by the rest of the world, which is probably how any sixteen-year-old feels, except that if you're brown-skinned like me, the feeling lasts for the rest of your life. "Don't you sometime feel like just beating up the white man?" a white guy at work once asked me. I hate it when people see my brown skin and assume that all I care about is gospel music and fried chicken and beating up the white man. I could care less. I'm too busy trying to live.

Once a mulatto, always a mulatto, is what I say, and you have to be happy with what you have, though in this world some places are more conducive to the survival of a black white man like me than others. Europe is okay, Philly works, and in New York you can at least run and hide and get lost in the sauce; but Washington is a town split straight down the middle—between white and black, haves and have-nots, light-skinned and dark-skinned—and full of jive-talkers of both colors. The blacks are embittered and expect you to love Marion Barry unconditionally. The whites expect you to be either grateful for their liberal sensibilities or a raging militant. There's no middle ground. No place for a guy like me to stand. Your politics is in the color of your face, and nothing else counts in Washington, which is why I had to get out of there.

All of my brothers and sisters—six boys, five girls, wildly

successful by conventional standards (doctors, teachers, professors, musicians)—have had to learn to plow the middle ground. Music is my escape, because when I pick up the saxophone and play, the horn doesn't care what color I am. Whatever's inside comes out, and I feel free.

My family was big, private, close, poor, fun, and always slightly confused. We were fueled by the race question and also befuddled by it. Everyone sought their own private means of escape. When he was little, my older brother Richie, a better sax player than I and the guy from whom I took all my cues, decided he was neither black nor white, but green, like the comic book character the Hulk. His imagination went wild with it, and he would sometimes lie on our bed facedown and make me bounce on him until he turned green.

"Do I look green yet?" he'd ask.

"Naw . . ."

"Jump some more."

I'd bounce some more.

"How about now?"

"Well, a little bit."

"RRRrrrrr . . . I'm the Hulk!" And he'd rise to attack me like a zombie.

Richard had a lot of heart. One morning in Sunday school, he raised his hand and asked our Sunday school teacher, Reverend Owens, "Is Jesus white?"

Reverend Owens said no.

"Then why is he white in this picture?" and he held up our Sunday school Bible.

Reverend Owens said, "Well, Jesus is all colors."

"Then why is he white? This looks like a white man to me." Richie held up the picture high so everyone in the class could see it. "Don't he look white to you?" he asked. Nobody said anything.

Reverend Owens was a nice man and also a barber who tore my head up about once a month. But he wasn't that sharp. I could read better than he could, and I was only twelve.

So he kind of stood there, wiping his face with his hand-kerchief and making the same noise he made when he preached. "Well . . . ahhh . . . well . . . ahh . . ."

I was embarrassed. The rest of the kids stared at Richie like he was crazy. "Richie, forget it," I mumbled.

"Naw. If they put Jesus in this picture here, and he ain't white, and he ain't black, they should make him gray. Jesus should be gray."

Richie stopped going to Sunday school after that, although he never stopped believing in God. My mother tried to make him go back, but he wouldn't.

When we were little, we used to make fun of our mother singing in church. My mother can't sing a lick. She makes a shrill kind of sound, a cross between a fire engine and Curly of the Three Stooges. Every Sunday morning, she'd stand in church, as she does today, the only white person there, and the whole congregation going, "Leaannnnning, ohhh, leaan-ing on the crossss, ohhhhh Laaawwwd!" and her going, "Leeeeeaaannnning, ohhhh, clank! bang! @*%$@*!," rattling happily along like an old Maytag washer. She wasn't born with the gift for gospel music, I suppose.

My mother, Ruth McBride Jordan, who today lives near Trenton, is the best movie I've ever seen. She's seventy-six, pretty, about five three, bowlegged, with curly dark hair and pretty dark eyes. She and my father and stepfather raised twelve children and sent them to college and graduate school, and at age sixty-five she obtained her own college degree in social welfare from Temple University. She's a whirlwind, so it's better to test the wind before you fly the kite. When I began writing my book about her, she said, "Ask me anything. I'll help you as much as I can." Then I asked her a few questions and she snapped: "Don't be so nosy. Don't tell all your business. If you work too much, your mind will be like a brick. My pot's burning on the stove. I gotta go."

When we were growing up, she never discussed race. When we asked whether we were black or white, she'd say, "You're a human being. Educate your mind!" She insisted on excellent grades and privacy. She didn't encourage us to mingle with others of any color too much. We were taught to mind our own business, and the less people knew about us, the better.

When we'd ask if she was white, she'd say, "I'm light-skinned," and change the subject. But we knew she was white, and I was embarrassed by her. I was ten years old when Martin Luther King, Jr., was killed, and I feared for her life because it seemed like all of New York was going to burn. She worked as a night clerk-typist at a Manhattan bank and got home every night about 2 A.M. My father would often be unavailable, and one of the older kids would meet her at the bus stop while the rest of us lay awake, waiting for the sound of the door to open. Black militants scared me. So did the Ku Klux Klan. I thought either group might try to kill her.

I always knew my mother was different, knew my siblings and I were different. My mother hid the truth from her children as long as she could. I was a grown man before I knew where she was born.

She was born Ruchele Dwajra Sylska in a town called Dobryn, near Gdansk, Poland. Her father was an Orthodox rabbi who lived in Russia. He escaped the Red Army by sneaking over the border into Poland. He married my grandmother, Hudis, in what my mother says was an arranged marriage, emigrated to America in the early 1920s, changed his name, and sent for his family. My mother landed on Ellis Island like thousands of other European immigrants.

The family settled in Suffolk, Virginia, and operated a grocery store on the black side of town. Her father also ran a local synagogue. Theirs was the only store in town open on Sundays.

He was feared within the family, my mother says. His wife, who suffered from polio, was close to her three children—a son and two daughters—but could not keep the tyranny of the father from driving them off. The oldest child, my mother's brother, left home early, joined the army, and was killed in World War II. The remaining two girls worked from sunup to sundown in the store. "My only freedom was to go out and buy little romance novels," my mother recalls. "They cost a dime." In school, they called her "Jew-baby."

When she was seventeen, she went to New York to visit relatives for the summer and worked in a Bronx factory owned by her aunt. At the factory, there was a young black employee named Andrew McBride, from High Point, North Carolina. They struck up a friendship and a romance. "He was the first man who was ever kind to me," my mother says. "I didn't care what color he was."

Her father did, though. When she returned home to finish her senior year of high school, her father arranged for her to marry a Jewish man after graduation. She had other plans. The day after she graduated, she packed her bags and left. After floating between New York and Suffolk for a while, she finally decided to marry my father in New York City. Her father caught up to her at the bus station the last time she left home. He knew that she was in love with a black man. The year was 1941.

"If you leave now, don't ever come back," he said.

"I won't," she said.

She gave up Judaism, married Andrew McBride, and moved to a one-room flat in Harlem where she proceeded to have baby after baby. Her husband later became a minister, and together they started New Brown Memorial Baptist Church in Red Hook, Brooklyn, which still exists. The mixed marriage caused them a lot of trouble—they got chased up Eighth Avenue by a group of whites and endured blacks murmuring under their breath, and she was pushed around in the hallway of the Harlem building by a black woman one day. But she never went home. She tried to see her mother after she married, when she found out her mother was ill and dying. When she called, she was told the family had sat shiva for her, as if she had died. "You've been out; stay out," she was told. She always carried that guilt in her heart, that she left her mother with her cruel father and never saw her again.

In 1957, Andrew McBride, Sr., died of cancer. My mother was thirty-six at the time, distraught after visiting him in the hospital, where doctors stared and the nurses snickered. At the time, she was living in the Red Hook project in Brooklyn with seven small kids. She was pregnant with me. In desperation, she searched out her aunt, who was living in Manhattan. She went to her aunt's house and knocked on the door. Her aunt opened the door, then slammed it in her face.

She told me that story only once, a few years ago. It made me sick to hear it, and I said so.

"Leave them alone," she said, waving her hand. "You don't understand Orthodox Jews. I'm happy. I'm a Christian. I'm free. Listen to me: When I got home from your daddy's funeral, I opened our mailbox, and it was full of checks. People dropped off boxes of food—oranges, meat, chickens. Our friends, Daddy's relatives, the people from the church, the people you never go see, they gave us so much money. I'll never forget that for as long as I live. And don't you forget it, either."

A number of years ago, after I had bugged her for months about details of her early life, my mother sat down and drew me a map of where she had lived in Suffolk. She talked as she drew: "The highway goes here, and the jailhouse is down this road, and the slaughterhouse is over here. . . ."

I drove several hours straight, and was tired and hungry once I hit Suffolk, so I parked myself in a local McDonald's and unfolded the little map. I checked it, looked out the window, then checked it again, looked out the window again. I was sitting right were the store used to be.

I went outside and looked around. There was an old house behind the McDonald's. I knocked on the door, and an old black man answered.

"Excuse me . . ." and I told my story: Mother used to live here. Her father was a rabbi. Jews. A little store. He fingered his glasses and looked at me for a long time. Then he said, "C'mon in here."

He sat me down and brought me a soda. Then he asked me to tell my story one more time. So I did.

He nodded and listened closely. Then his face broke into a smile. "That means you the ol' rabbi's grandson?"

"Yep."

First he chuckled, then he laughed. Then he laughed some more. He tried to control his laughing, but he couldn't, so he stopped, took off his glasses, and wiped his eyes. I started to get angry, so he apologized. His name was Eddie Thompson. He was sixty-six. He had lived in that house all his life. It took him a minute to get himself together.

"I knew your mother," he said. "We used to call her Rachel."

I had never heard that name before. Her name is Ruth, but he knew her as Rachel, which was close to Ruchele, the Yiddish name her family called her.

"I knew that whole family," Thompson said. "The ol' rabbi, boy, he was something. Rachel was the nice one. She was kindhearted. Everybody liked her. She used to walk right up and down the road here with her mother. The mother used to limp. They would say hello to the people, y'know? Old man, though . . ." and he shrugged. "Well, personally, I never had no problem with him."

He talked for a long time, chuckling, disbelieving. "Rachel just left one day. I'm telling you she left, and we thought she was dead. That whole family is long gone. We didn't think we'd ever see none of them again till we got to the other side. And now you pop up. Lord knows it's a great day."

He asked if we could call her. I picked up the phone and dialed Philadelphia, got my mother on the line, and told her I had somebody who wanted to talk to her. I handed the phone to him.

"Rachel? Yeah. Rachel. This is Eddie Thompson. From down in Suffolk. Remember me? We used to live right be— yeaaaaah, that's right." Pause. "No, I was one of the little ones. Well, I'll be! The Lord touched me today.

"Rachel!? That ain't you crying now, is it? This is old Eddie Thompson. You remember me? Don't cry now."

I went and got some flowers for my stepfather's grave and laid them across it. My mother wanted me to make sure the new tombstone she got him was in place, and it was. It said OUR BELOVED DADDY, HUNTER L. JORDAN, AUGUST 11, 1900, TO MAY 14, 1972.

He was old when he died and a relatively old fifty-eight when he married my mother. They met in a courtyard of the Red Hook housing project where we lived, while she was selling church dinners on a Saturday to help make ends meet. He strolled by and bought some ribs, came back the next Saturday and bought some more. He ended up buying the whole nine yards—eight kids and a wife. He used to joke that he had enough for a baseball team.

I never heard him complain about it, and it never even occurred to me to ask him how he felt about white and black. He was quiet and busy. He dealt with solid things. Cars. Plumbing. Tricycles. Work. He used to joke about how he had run away from Richmond when he was a young man because Jim Crow was tough, but racism to him was a detail that you stepped over, like you'd step over a crack in the sidewalk. He worked in the stockyards in Chicago for a while, then in a barbershop in Detroit, where, among other things, he shined Henry Ford's shoes. He went to New York in the 1920s. He never told me those things; his brother Walter did. He didn't find those kinds of facts interesting. All he wanted to talk about was my grades.

He was strong for his age, full and robust, with brown eyes and handsome American Indian features. One night, he had a headache, and the next day he was in the hospital with a stroke. After a couple of weeks, he came home. Then two days later, he asked me to come out to the garage with him. I was one of the older kids living at home; most were away at college or already living on their own. He could barely walk and had difficulty speaking, but we went out there, and we got inside his Pontiac. "I was thinking of maybe driving home one more time," he said. He was talking about Henrico County, where we spent summer vacations.

He started the engine, then shut it off. He was too weak to drive. So he sat there, staring out the windshield, looking at the garage wall, his hand on the steering wheel. He was wearing his old-timey cap and his peacoat, though it was May and warm outside. Sitting there, staring straight ahead, he started talking, and I listened closely because he never gave speeches.

He said he had some money saved up and a little land in Virginia, but it wasn't enough. He was worried about my mother and his children. He said I should always mind her and look out for my younger brothers and sisters, because we were special. "Special people," he said, "And just so special to me." It was the only time I ever heard him refer to race, however vaguely, but it didn't matter because right then I knew he was going to die, and I had to blink back my tears. Two days later, he was gone.

Standing over his grave—it seemed so lonely and cold, with the wind blowing through the trees—part of me wanted to throw myself on the ground to cover and warm him. We arranged the flowers. Plastic ones, because, as Aunt Maggie said, they lasted longer. I took one last look and thought, Maybe he would understand me now. Maybe not. I turned and left.

I suppose I didn't look too happy, because as I started up

the little road toward my car, Aunt Maggie put her arm in mine. I'd known her since I was a boy, just like I'd known these woods as a boy when he took us down here, but I'd blanked her and these woods out of my mind over the years, just like you'd blank out the words of a book by covering them with a piece of paper. She didn't judge me, which is what I always appreciated most about our friends and relatives over the years, the white and the black. They never judged, just accepted us as we were. Maybe that's what a black white man has to do. Maybe a black white man will never be content. Maybe a black white man will never fit. But a black white man can't judge anybody.

I remember when I was ten years old, when I pondered my own race and asked my mother, as she was attempting to fix our dinner table that had deteriorated to three-legged status, whether I was white or black. She paused a moment, then responded thoughtfully: "Pliers."

"Huh?"

"Hand me the pliers out of the kitchen drawer."

I handed her the pliers and she promptly went to work on the kitchen table, hammering the legs and tops until dents and gouges appeared on all sides. When the table finally stood shakily on all fours, she set the pliers down, stood up and said, "Pliers can fix anything."

"What about me being black?" I asked.

"What about it?" she said. "Forget about black. You are a human being."

"But what do I check on the form at school that says White, Black, or Other?"

"Don't check nothing. Get a hundred on your school tests and they won't care what color you are."

"But they do care."

"I don't," she said, and off she went.

Perturbed, I picked up the pliers and sought out my father, hammering at the fuel pump of his 1969 Pontiac. "Am I black or white?" I asked.

"Where'd you get my pliers?" he asked.

"I got 'em from Ma."

"I been looking for 'em all day." He took them and immediately put them to work.

"Am I black or white, Daddy?"

He grabbed a hose in his hand and said, "Hold this." I held it. He went inside the car and cranked the engine. Fuel shot out of the line and spilled all over me. "You all right?" he asked. I shook my head. He took me inside, cleaned me up, put the hose in the car, and took me out for ice cream. I forgot about my color for a while.

But the question plagued me for many years, even after my father's death, and I never did find out the answer because neither he nor my mother ever gave any. I was effectively on my own. I searched for years to find the truth, to find myself as a black white man. I went to Africa, got VD, came home with no answers. I went to Europe, sipped café and smoked in Paris for months, came home empty. Last year, while working on my '53 Chevy at my home in Nyack, while my four-year-old son rolled around in the leaves and ate mud, it hit me. I asked him to hand me the pliers, and as he did so, he asked me, "What color is Grandma?"

"She's white," I said.

"Why isn't she like me?"

"She is like you, she's just whiter."

"Why is she whiter?"

"I don't know. God made her that way."

"Why?"

"I don't know. Would you like her better if she looked more like you?"

"No. I like her the way she is."

It occurred to me then that I was not put on this earth to become a leader of mixed-race people, wielding my race like a baseball bat, determined to force white people to accept me as I am. I realized then that I did not want to be known as Mr. Mulatto, whose children try to be every race in the world, proudly proclaiming Indian blood, African blood, Jewish blood, singing Peter, Paul, and Mary songs at phony private schools where yuppie parents arrive each morning hopping out of Chevy Suburban tanks with bumper stickers that read "Question Authority." I want the same thing every parent wants—a good home for my wife and children, good schools, peace and quiet, a good set of wrenches, and a son big enough to hand them to me. And when he gets big enough to have his own tools and work on his own car, maybe he will understand that you can't change someone's opinion about you no matter how many boxes you check, no matter how many focus groups you join, no matter how much legislation you pass, no matter how much consciousness raising you do. It's a real simple answer. Give 'em God. Give 'em pliers. Give 'em math. Give 'em discipline. Give 'em love, and let the chips fall where they may. Pontificating about it is okay. Passing laws is important, but I never once in my life woke up not knowing whether I should eat matzo ball or fried chicken. I never once felt I'd be able to play the sax better if my mom had been black, or that I'd have been better at math if my father were Jewish. I like me, and I like me because my parents liked me.

POSTCARDS FROM "HOME"

Lori Tsang

I'm goin' up north where they say money grows on trees,
I don't give a doggone if my black soul leaves.
—Cow Cow Davenport, "I'm Goin' Up North"

My aunt Bessie claims that my father had to marry a Jamaican woman because no Chinese in New York would let their daughters marry a man from our family.* It had something to do with a great-uncle who had ten wives. "Three or

---

*The anecdotal materials in this essay are not intended to be a part of a definitive "family history." On the contrary, they are presented here as examples of the kind of fantastical stories that result from gossip and speculation filtered through the hopes and dreams, pain, disappointment, and frustration of many people spread across generations and continents—people who survived the experience of war and displacement, who in the aftermath struggled to gain a foothold in a new country, or to rebuild a war-torn nation.

four might be okay," she told me, "but ten is just too greedy." And even worse, he left nine of them in China and never went back.

But the myriad uncles and aunties who are the children of those various wives somehow ended up in New York, like my dad. They're about the same age he is, but one generation older. Auntie So-and-So, the third daughter of the second wife(?). Uncle What's-His-Name, the eldest son of the fifth wife(?). Whatever. My memories of them are pretty vague.

I was born in Waterbury, Connecticut. Aunt Bessie thinks her brother moved there to get away from all the family intrigue. We saw these relatives only once a year, at Thanksgiving. When I was twelve, we moved to Indiana, and then we never saw them. Maybe my father's cousin Russell, the son of the tenth wife, resolved the marriage dilemma by marrying a white Jewish woman. But that's another story. For whatever reason, Uncle Winston (the third son of the fourth wife? fourth son of the third wife?) married a woman from Jamaica, my aunt Nina. Aunt Nina's brother, Zeke, married my mom's older sister, Aunt Lucy. That's how my dad met my mom.

What I know of my family history is a jigsaw puzzle with most of the pieces missing. And there are no corner pieces, no straight edges, to mark the borders. No one talked much about our family when I was growing up. I didn't find this strange. I didn't know anything else. It didn't occur to me until I was an adult that other families talked more. Then I met my aunt Bessie.

History is created from stories conceived at the crossroads of myth and memory. Stories people tell to situate themselves in the world, to make sense out of their lives. Aunt Bessie was the only one I knew who really talked very much about our family. Stories that got passed down to her got passed on to me.

The last time I saw Aunt Bessie, I was wearing thermal underwear, a cotton turtleneck and two sweaters under my down jacket, three pairs of pants, two pairs of socks, and white Nike high-tops. It's January in Nanjing, China. Nanjing is too far south for the government to heat the buildings in winter, and too far north to be warm enough wearing anything less than half your wardrobe. January is no time for a spoiled American Chinese to be visiting Nanjing, but my father's sister is dying, and I have to say goodbye.

I've been coming to the hospital at 3 P.M. every day for the past week. Aunt Bessie is so weak, she shouldn't speak. I can't ask for advice, answers to unanswered questions. It's up to me to do the talking. Every day, I rack my mind for stories, memories. I make things up. As if my words could be invisible cords binding her to this world. But there are no words strong enough to keep her here. No words large enough to fill the absence between us. She's already finished saying everything she needed to say to me, and I've said everything I can say to her. Now she's just waiting for me to go back to the States so she can die. She wants to be able to tell the doctors to stop the daily blood transfusions. The blood is too scarce, and can be used to help someone who will live.

Making my way back from the hospital through the busy streets, I become part of China: the young parents carrying bundled-up babies on the back of their bicycles; the old men wearing blue Mao-style suits under their padded jackets; the giggling schoolgirls walking together arm in arm. Buried under all these layers of clothing, I look just like everybody else. But I'm not. Tomorrow, I'll be on a plane home. I wonder if I'll ever return.

As Aunt Bessie lies in that hospital bed dying of intestinal cancer, I feel my link with China slipping away. And suddenly, I find myself running back to the hospital, dodging bicycles and street vendors, running back up the five flights of stairs. But when I open the door to her room, she simply tells me to go home. And I do. I don't belong here. It's her own children who will feed her, bathe her, ease her passing into the next world. Her husband. And in the end, I think it was not really me but my father, her brother, that she wanted.

How do I explain why it was me who journeyed to the other side of the earth to sit in the hospital with Aunt Bessie for an hour each afternoon of that cold, gray week in January, and not my father? My father and Aunt Bessie grew up in both China and "America." But ultimately, my father decided to stay in the United States, and Aunt Bessie went back to China. Desire is born of separation, and my father and Aunt Bessie spent most of their lives in a constant state of separation: first from their father, who lived in "America"; then from their mother, who lived in Hong Kong; and finally, from each other. Idealized from a distance, Aunt Bessie was the embodiment of nostalgia, a conflation of memory and desire—the perfect smart, beautiful little sister. But in reality, she was a disappointment—a stubborn, willful girl-child who was always doing the wrong thing. When Aunt Bessie decided to go back to China, she knew the United States was engaged in a war between "black" and "white." She knew that to stay in the United States meant being trapped forever in the cross fire of that war. But my father decided to stay, to try to be "American." Did he ever regret that decision? Did he feel betrayed when Aunt Bessie left? In any event, I inherited a legacy of desire that drew me to his sister's bedside during the waning moments of her life—a desire for "home," a place where I could simply be a Chinese among other Chinese. But I also knew that Aunt Bessie had an "American" part of her that missed being in the United States.

My father and Aunt Bessie were both born in New York. But my grandmother didn't like living in a foreign country with a language she didn't understand and not as many female relatives around for company, so she took her children and went back to China. When the Japanese started bombing Guangdong Province, she sent my father back to New York. He was fourteen. My father worked hard and saved up enough money for his sister to come. But they didn't get along well.

I guess Aunt Bessie was considered to be quite scandalous as a young woman. When she was in college, she fell love with my uncle Ken and went traveling around the country with him. According to Aunt Bessie, my father became very upset. Here she was, a young, unmarried girl traveling around with a man. Ten years older. And Uncle Ken wasn't even from the same village as our family!

But I wonder if their different experiences and reactions to racism also contributed to the tension between them. During her travels, Aunt Bessie learned some things about the precarious roles forced on Asians living in the States: Honorary Whites. House Niggers. Model Minority. Aunt Bessie tells me they were traveling somewhere in the South, maybe Arkansas or Mississippi, and when they got on the bus, of course they decided they should sit in the back with the other colored people. Well, then, the white bus driver came and told them to sit in front with the white people.

The writer David Mura has a similar story about his father. He says there's a price for sitting in the front of the bus. The price is that you must try to be as much like the white people as possible. And you must deny any association with the people in the back of the bus.

But Aunt Bessie and Uncle Ken had no choice. They weren't told, "Here, you can sit with us on the following conditions." They were simply told to sit in the front. Race is the myth upon which the reality of racism is predicated, the wild card the racist always keeps hidden up his sleeve. The racist has the power to determine whether the card will be a diamond or a spade, whether a Chinese is black or white.

When I was in Shanghai, I went for an evening stroll in a park with Aunt Bessie's youngest son, my cousin Tung-tung. In the nineteenth century, the European colonial powers forced foreign trade onto China's weak and corrupt government. They occupied Shanghai and divided the city into foreign concessions. "There used to be a sign here that said NO DOGS OR CHINESE ALLOWED," Tung-tung told me. Now, Chinese are still treated like dogs. We're "allowed," but only if we "behave," like well-trained house pets, not like "those other people." That's the price for sitting in front with the white folks.

My friend Akinde claims there's a Yoruba saying, "The dog of the king thinks he's king of the dogs." Is that us? It's no mere coincidence that the myth of the "Model Minority" originated around the same time the black power movement was gaining momentum. Folks think we living up in the Big House with Massa. Forget men who got blown up tunneling through mountains to lay railroad track. Men who buried their pride under the stench of white men's laundry. Contract laborers who made the "middle passage" to the Caribbean after Great Britain's Emancipation Act of 1833, packed into the hold of ships like cargo. Women who went nearly blind bending over sweatshop sewing machines. And the lynchings—yes, the lynchings. Forget all that. We just some yellow, slanty-eyed house Negroes. Trying to pass.

But we're still in the NO PASSING zone. And Aunt Bessie and Uncle Ken were nobody's dogs. Eventually, they got off the bus. Got on a boat and went back to China.

I think Aunt Bessie's decision to go back to China was the major point of contention between her and my father. After the Communists took over, he decided to stay in the United States. But after the Liberation, Aunt Bessie decided to go back to help build the new China. She told me she married Uncle Ken because she knew he also wanted to use the education he got in the States to serve his country. But she never dreamed she would be separated from the New York side of the family—her father, her brother, all the aunties and uncles—for over thirty years. She thought she could go back and forth. But she was wrong. The United States cut off relations with China, and Aunt Bessie lived in China as a Chinese. The part of her that had learned to be "American" was out of place there.

But my father stayed. He got married to my mother, a Chinese Jamaican who didn't speak Chinese. He moved away from the other Chinese in New York to Connecticut, and had three children.

When my brother and sister and I were little, we knew nothing about Kwanzaa or Hanukkah. "Diversity" meant that some of our classmates were Catholic. "Multiculturalism" meant being the only Chinese family in a white neighborhood.

Everybody in our neighborhood was "ethnic": Irish, Italian, Polish, German, French, Russian. But our family were the only Chinese, and we were more different than anyone else.

Here we are at Christmastime, a family of five, living at 28 Devon Wood Drive, Waterbury, Connecticut. My brother and sister and I are sitting at the kitchen table, faces bowed over steaming mugs of cocoa too hot to hold with small hands freshly pulled out of wet mittens. The mugs are red and white Santa Claus heads, with rosy cheeks and blue eyes. Mom always has something warm waiting for us when we come in from the cold. Our mittens, hats, scarves, snowsuits, and boots lie in a soggy heap by the doorway. Any minute now, Dad will come home from work and add his black rubber boots to the pile. He'll be glad we shoveled the driveway so he can get the car into the garage.

Mom celebrated Christmas when she was growing up in Kingston, Jamaica. But Dad wasn't raised Christian. He converted when he was about twenty, thankful for having survived his stint in the U.S. Army during World War II. Because of this, I think my father took the personal and spiritual aspects of his religion very seriously. For the rest of us, it was more cultural and social—going to Sunday school after church, celebrating the holidays.

There was something magical about Mom and Dad making Christmas at home. How they managed to fit so much stuff into our stockings. Letting an old white guy in a gaudy red outfit get all the credit. Even after we figured it out, we pretended not to know. And they pretended they didn't know that we knew. But this was real: the house decorated with Christmas cards, red candles, and the nativity scene we kids made out of Lincoln Logs and Play-Doh; Mom in the kitchen, making butter cookies in perfect little Christmas tree shapes, chopping walnuts for the cranberry bread we'd have for breakfast Christmas morning; Dad taking us to pick the perfect tree.

Both of our parents were raised by extended families of aunts and uncles. Mom was orphaned when she was a child. Dad was separated from one or both of his parents during most of his childhood. Mom and Dad got together and created their own family. They made Christmas happen every year. It was part of their struggle to be "American," to make a home among strangers. I wonder if they ever got homesick. What does it mean to be homesick? Is it a longing for a place? Or your family. Your childhood.

Dad used to keep a picture of Aunt Bessie on the fireplace mantel. "My sister, Bessie, was so beautiful," he'd say. "You look so much like my sister." "Your aunt Bessie was so smart." For years, she was a constant presence in our home through this photograph. Then Nixon went to China, and people could go back and forth again. And after over thirty years, my father's wonderful younger sister came to stay with my parents for three months.

I had just moved to Washington, D.C. But my sister, Wendy, was still living at home. "All they did was argue," she tells me. "Aunt Bessie is always criticizing the United States: 'The Chinese way is better.' They argue about the guy who had ten wives. Dad thinks it was okay for a man to have a lot of wives because that way he could take care of girls from poor families who couldn't afford to provide for them. But Aunt Bessie argues that according to that rationale, a rich man could have a lot of wives, while a poor man wouldn't be able to have any. They argue because Aunt Bessie thinks Dad doesn't treat

Mom with enough respect. Then she tries to show Mom how to cook all of Dad's favorite Chinese dishes. This makes Mom really mad, so she complains to Dad, and he and Aunt Bessie argue some more."

Aunt Bessie and my mom must have had some good moments, though. There are pictures of them together where Aunt Bessie's wearing pastel-colored slacks and blouses instead of her gray and blue Chinese clothes. Mom tells me about hanging out with Aunt Bessie at Baskin-Robbins. Aunt Bessie said that two of the things she misses from the United States are banana splits and watching blond white men. But of course, she wouldn't want to marry one.

At the end of the summer, Aunt Bessie goes back to China, and my father, my sister and I, and our grandfather's ashes, all go back with her. During her visit, Aunt Bessie's been collecting things to take back to China. She goes to the drugstore and purchases half their inventory of knee-high stockings. Collects scraps of cloth—when she gets back to China, she'll use them to sew shoes for her grandchildren. To carry all her treasures, she buys four huge brightly colored duffel bags: red, yellow, blue, green. This makes my dad really angry. He doesn't want to haul these big bags all around China. "If you hate the United States so much," he shouts, "why are you taking half of it home with you?"

After all these years, they're still having the same argument. It's as if each one feels that the other one's choice somehow invalidates their own. My father went back to China only one more time after that, with my mom. He didn't really say much about that trip. I think it was too hard for him to go back and see how different it was from when he was a child.

But going back isn't that painful for me. Maybe because

I'm not really "going back." I don't have the memories. I know we don't belong in China anymore. But I'm already used to not belonging here. So for me, being in China, being with Aunt Bessie, helps satisfy some undefinable hunger. A sense of loss inherited from my parents.

On my mom's side, it's her youngest brother, my uncle Ronnie, who's the most interested in maintaining our family history. When my mom and dad and my sister Wendy and I go to visit him in Toronto, he pulls out all the old photo albums and a multipage chart tracing our family history back to the days of Genghis Khan. He says he got this information from another cousin. He's also found out that their grandfather got in trouble for rigging an election back in their village in China and this is why he came to Jamaica as a contract laborer.

When Dad got mad at Aunt Bessie for marrying somebody who wasn't from their village, she felt he was being hypocritical, because Mom isn't Cantonese either. Mom's family is Hakka—the people who wandered around for a while before kind of settling in Guangdong Province. Even after that, many of them traveled even farther, to other parts of Asia like the Philippines and Indonesia, or to the Caribbean, like my great-grandfather. Supposedly, the Cantonese used to look down on the Hakka, whose women ran around on big, loose feet and had supposedly even looser tongues. I don't know what happened to my mom. The only time you see her tongue flapping is maybe to lick an ice cream cone.

But I can tell from the look on her face she's happy to see her little brother, to eat Jamaican food again, to remember the old days in Jamaica. Mom's older brother, Uncle Stanley, lives in L.A. His oldest son, my cousin Randy, once told me that when his parents get homesick, they go to a reggae club. But the idea of Uncle Stanley and Aunt Elizabeth hanging out at reggae clubs is kind of weird, not just because they seem too old to be hanging out in clubs, but because I didn't think they even had reggae yet back when Uncle Stanley was still in Jamaica.

On our first night in Toronto, we have a Chinese dinner, but in the morning, Uncle Ronnie's wife, my aunt Joan, fixes a big Jamaican breakfast: salt fish and ackee that Aunt Joan got frozen from her sister who grows it in Florida; fried dumplings; "pear," which folks in the States call avocado; bun and cheese. After breakfast we go to a Chinese shopping center near their house in Scarborough. "Can we go to Chinatown?" my sister asks. "This *is* Chinatown," Uncle Ronnie tells her.

Later, we go to a bakery for patties, then to a carry-out for oxtail, curry goat, fricassee chicken, stew peas, and rice. They're both owned by Chinese Jamaicans. It's fun hanging out with my mom's side of the family, where it's normal to be Chinese and Jamaican at the same time. Our cousins, Ricky and Warren, are more Jamaican than we are. They play on a volleyball team called the Irie Chinee and listen to reggae tapes in the car. When the Jamaican soccer team scores a goal against the Canadian team on TV, they jump up and shout, "We scored a goal!"

Most people I know don't even know there are Chinese in Jamaica. The first time I told my friend Brandon that my mom's Jamaican, he thought it was just a joke. Even after I explained that my mom's Chinese Jamaican, not African Jamaican, he still didn't quite get it: "Your mother didn't look how I thought she would," he says. "How did you think she would look?" "Well, she's not very dark."

My friend Ethelbert asks me if I have any African heritage. He's editing an anthology of African American poetry, and he's trying to include me. It seems all my friends are going to be in this anthology, and I want to be, too. "You mean, genealogically?" I ask, and he says yes. I think about saying that, according to Ivan Van Sertima, the human race started in Africa, so everybody is African. But what comes out of my mouth is "Well, not that I know of."

But I first learned how to be "Asian American" from African Americans. After we moved to Indiana, we lived in another white neighborhood. The only black person in our neighborhood was this real light-skinned kid who was adopted by a Jewish couple who didn't know he was black when they adopted him. They didn't even tell him he was black until he was already pretty grown. The junior high school I went to was the only naturally integrated junior high school in northern Indianapolis. Not because of this one kid, but because there was a black neighborhood in that district. I used to ride my bike over there to see my friends Sherril and Elaine. There were no other Chinese, or even Asians, in our neighborhood. I remember another Chinese girl telling me that when her parents first moved to Indianapolis, they looked through the names in the phone book so they could find other Chinese. And in the summer, our whole family used to go to a special camp where Chinese families in the Midwest got together to be with other Chinese.

But race, like sex, was something my parents never discussed—as if it were something shameful. When two nonwhite Americans meet, each of us understands that we share the common experience of racial prejudice; it's our individual reactions to that experience that may be different: anger, self-pity, denial. Confusion. Probably, my parents didn't talk much about race because they didn't understand it. After all, who really does? The complex web of relationships among race, culture, and skin color remains just as elusive a reality as the relationships among sex, power, and love. Like water, it takes the shape of whatever contains it—whatever culture, social structure, political system. But like water, it slips through your fingers when you try to hold it. And maybe it was this, the unspoken, which remained elusive yet suspended in the silences, that drew me closer to my African American friends—the experience of being different from the majority of white people, the experience of racial prejudice.

I went to college at Indiana University in Bloomington, Indiana, just south of Martinsville, Indiana, which was supposed to be some kind of headquarters for the Ku Klux Klan. In college I hung out with four totally separate groups: some white, left-wing, Marxist-type students; some of the regular local white folks—carpenters, seamstresses, artists, and musicians; some Asian (not Asian American) graduate students; and some black (African American) law students. There was no overlap among these groups, except maybe me.

It was from my black law school friends that I began to learn about writers like James Baldwin, Toni Morrison, Amiri Baraka. Langston Hughes and Zora Neale Hurston, the Harlem Renaissance. I learned about images of African Americans in films, from *Birth of a Nation, Cabin in the Sky, Carmen Jones,* to *Bush Mama,* by Haile Gerima, with whom I studied film, later, at Howard University. Black actors and musicians: Billie Holiday, Lena Horne, Harry Belafonte, Paul Robeson, Miles Davis. People like W. E. B. Du Bois, Marcus Garvey, Stokely Carmichael, Eldridge Cleaver, Huey Newton. My exposure to African American history and culture made me understand the extent to which I had been viewing myself through the eyes and minds of white people. It made me understand that I needed to step back into my own skin to see the world through my own perspective. To find my own perspective.

But it's hard to be Chinese with no other Chinese around to be Chinese with. No community. When I moved to D.C., I noticed that there were a lot more Asian Americans than in Indiana. I discovered groups like the Organization of Pan-Asian American Women, the Organization of Chinese Americans, the Japanese American Citizens League. I began to hear about Asian American writers like Maxine Hong Kingston and Frank Chin. I met Asian Americans from California who had been involved with the Asian American student movements on the West Coast. I found out about Carlos Bulosan, a writer who was active in organizing migrant farm workers; Yuri Kochiyama, a Harlem activist who worked with Malcolm X; the I Wor Kuen, named after the people responsible for the so-called Boxer Rebellion in China, which, like the Young Lords and the Brown Berets, was modeled after the Black Panther Party and even had its own ten-point program. But a lot of these Asian Americans didn't understand midwestern Asian Americans who grew up without a community. And some of them didn't really understand the African American experience that was part of my socialization and that had become part of who I am. As an Asian American.

The Asian American community is something created through sheer willpower—the strength of our own desire. I'm hanging out with my friend Theo, when some visiting filmmakers from France ask us how we identify ourselves. "I'm

Chinese," I answer innocently. But Theo frowns and states, "I'm Asian American," claiming the history of Asians in America and asserting the correct pan-Asian solidarity in a very firm voice. But being "Asian American" isn't that easy. A lot of Koreans, Southeast Asians, and even Filipinos living in America don't call themselves Asian American. Some of them even accuse "Asian Americanism" of being some kind of Chinese/Japanese American hegemony.

Most of us Chinese American kids remember our parents telling us how the Chinese invented the printing press. This was supposed to make us feel better when the other kids made "slanty-eyed" faces at us and chanted "Ching-chong Chinaman" on the way home from school. But don't be talking that "we invented the printing press" stuff around any Koreans. It was only as an adult that I learned that the printing press was actually invented by Koreans during a period of time when the Chinese had conquered Korea and claimed it as part of China. If you're going to be "Asian American," you have to find out about other Asians' histories as well as your own.

The Asian American "movement" is at the same time both "nationalist" and contranationalist. We develop a heightened consciousness of the cultural heritage of our genealogical ancestors, but we also learn to traverse the borders of nationalism to create a new "Asian American" identity. Thus, we develop a heightened consciousness of the cultural and social constructedness of the concepts of "race" and "nationality." We learn to challenge acts of categorization as racist practice; we question the notion that such categories are mutually exclusive.

I learn how to be Chinese, Jamaican, Asian American, how to be black, by watching and listening to other people. Noticing things, remembering things. How to act, how to eat, what to eat, how to speak, what to say. It's a matter of ethnography. Mapping culture.

Having a late-night snack with friends, chewing on a chicken wing, munching some nachos, I find myself craving a steaming bowl of wonton mein. Morning finds me shoveling a bowl of rice, with scrambled eggs and kimchee, into my mouth. Stuff my non-Asian, non-Caribbean friends don't understand. There are moments when it suddenly strikes me how Chinese I am, how Asian American. But am I? What does it mean to be "Asian American?"

I surprise myself, doing things a certain way, as if I'd grown up doing them that way. But I haven't. I've learned it. I find myself thinking, "If I can learn how to be Chinese, I can learn anything." I collect experiences, chew them up and absorb them into the bloodstream. But what goes deeper than flesh, goes deeper into the marrow of the bone, is something more. More than a collection of acquired skills, habits, tastes. Community. Shared perspectives and experiences. Our assigned roles in this planet's history of colonialism and migration. Something in the silences between my parents and their parents, between my father and his sister, between me and my mother. The struggle to live outside your skin, beyond your own experience. The anger, shame, and embarrassment that separates one person from another, the struggle and celebration that draws us together. Where do you draw the borders of your community? How do you make a map of your own heart?

It's not just about "race." When Cornelius Eady teaches a poetry workshop in D.C. and tells us to write a poem about myth, I write about the time Malcolm X found out about Elijah Muhammad fooling around with his young secretaries. I start writing the poem in Malcolm's own voice. Putting myself in the place of a man whose faith had compelled him to block out all the hints and rumors, who finally forces himself to confront a painful truth, one that rocks the very foundation of his beliefs.

My friend Ernesto tells me I should write a cycle of poems about Malcolm. Captivated by Malcolm's pursuit of truth, his ongoing struggle to transform himself, I write some more poems. Detroit Red riding the rails up and down the East Coast selling reefers. Malcolm X driving around in a '56 Oldsmobile, "fishing" for converts to the Nation of Islam. Malik El Shabazz flying between Africa and Harlem, trying to build a bridge between Africa and African America, and to establish his own organization at home as well. The tension between his need to belong to a community and his urge to transcend racial categories to achieve his full potential. His search for identity, not only as a black man in America, but also as a spiritual being vulnerable to human emotion.

I ask my friend B.T. to compose music for a poetry and music performance and CD based on my Malcolm manuscript. "That's what I thought we should do when you first told me you were writing the poems," he says. B.T.'s a bass player from L.A. who came to D.C. over fifteen years ago, promising not to go back to L.A. until he had made it as a musician. Now he's touring around the country with a blues band. The last time he was back in town, we made pancakes and brown-'n'-serve sausages for supper, washed them down with Tsingtao beer, and stayed up half the night talking and listening to the blues. I beg him for stories about life on the road, longing to know what it's like, traveling around with a blues band, where music is your nationality and home is wherever your next gig is. "Being on tour isn't everything it's cracked up to be," he tells me.

I think about Aunt Bessie and Uncle Ken traveling around the South on a bus. My grandfather, who came to the United States under the Treaty Merchants Act and died penniless in a mental institution in Brooklyn. My father, who went back and forth, from New York to China back to New York, from Chinatown to Queens, to Connecticut and finally to Indiana. The Hakka, adventurers who wandered from place to place, scorned by other Chinese, like my great-grandfather who ran away to Jamaica. Blues musicians who migrated north and west from the (Mississippi) Delta along with other African Americans, searching for jobs, a record deal, freedom from Jim Crow. What's lost in that search for the Promised Land, the Gold Mountain? What endures?

B.T. writes my address in a little notebook, and even though he says he's not good at writing, I get three postcards. The first one's from Texas—it's one of those maps where the place it's from is really big and everything else is really small: "We went 2 a jam session in Houston. There was a Chinese guy playing the gtr & singing the blues. He was real cool." The second one's a photograph of Malcolm X: "I got this card in Albuquerque, N.M. It was calling your name. LORI. . . ." The last postcard pictures a sprawling metropolis—everything is brown, even the sky: L.A., City of Lost Angels. "I have returned to the place I called my own," he scrawls across the back, "and it is not."

FROM HERE TO POLAND

Nina Mehta

Once, quite a long time ago, there was a Danish side-board that crossed three oceans. It had been purchased in Frankfurt, Germany, when I was two years old and my sister had just been born. My parents must have been in love then, because they had defied both sets of parents to marry, parents who worried that their respective child would wind up in the other one's country and would then, therefore, be lost to them. What the parents may or may not have known at the time was that both sets would eventually be proven right, but also that their children had already been lost to them before they met each other in an art store on East 53rd Street in mid-Manhattan, staring at a darkened arrangement of thin, erratic flowers in a painting by Oskar Kokoschka.

From Frankfurt, where we lived less than a year, the long Danish sideboard was shipped on ahead to central Bombay, where it remained for seven years in the same prominent place, dusted and polished by careful servants who were all the more fastidious because they feared my American mother, and cooled by a large ceiling fan whose speed could at one time be accelerated and slowed only by climbing a tall ladder to tug at the dirty white string hanging from its belly. The sideboard stood implacably four stories up on Gamadia Road, between the dining area and the impossibly long living room, a false wall that escaped notice until it was sent across two oceans to New Jersey, to a town called New Providence, where it managed to sustain only a very short residence.

There, the sideboard was loaned a stretch of wall behind a beautiful secondhand baby grand that's now no longer in New Providence and that's hardly ever played. Some months passed and weekly piano lessons got under way, but eventually my parents decided to sell the sideboard because it was cumbersome and unnecessary and didn't go with the rest of the furniture. Though I had been a scowling, taciturn child who could not ask for anything directly, if at all, I suddenly couldn't help begging my parents not to sell the sideboard. I pleaded that the sideboard stay where it was, that it be rotated around to the other side of the piano, or that, as a last resort, it be given to me and moved upstairs to my bedroom. When no one else was in the house, during the hour I was supposed to be watching the music and not my fingers, I would drape myself over the edges of the sideboard and cry, always embarrassed afterward that I could feel such strong emotions about an adult piece of furniture, and embarrassed that I was not able to re-frain from asking my parents for a sideboard which I knew did not belong in my room.

Over the years since then, there have been a small number of people who've occupied my life in the same way that side-board did, over whom I've felt a halting, anxious sort of pro-prietary claim I couldn't often gauge, let alone explain, but for whom I could feel some simple feelings clearly and directly. One of these people has been my paternal grandmother, a woman with whom I'm unable to speak, though in recent years she has also become, perversely enough, as stolidly nonessential and baffling a presence as that futile length of fur-niture that disappeared when I was eleven.

My grandmother has always been an unremarkably ordi-nary part of the surroundings. She has a thick juglike physical solidity and seems the incarnation of dutiful familiarity, though I've never known whether her familiarity grew out of her sense of familial duty or whether my perception itself re-sulted from the inevitable familiarity with which I saw my grandmother. Hers is an unassuming, absent sort of presence, not a crucial one that focuses expectations, and she has no more sought me out or managed to affect how I see myself than a loaf of bread can bend a hologram. On many occasions, I've felt very close to her. Yet in the end, it's the rank impos-sibility of having a relationship with her, of having a rela-tionship that sits deeply on its haunches and that's at least somewhat mutually comprehensible, that makes me wonder whether our relationship has all along been doomed in ways I should have understood better. And yet it has been through various conversations with her that I have been able to per-ceive certain family relationships more clearly. And it is at least in part because of her that I have also realized how ambiguous some of my ties to my past really are.

My grandmother speaks Gujarati and grew up in Bombay and Jamnagar, a small city in the northwestern state of Gujarat, though in those years (and even into my father's youth) India was not yet an independent country and Jamnagar was a princely kingdom ruled by the wealthy family of one of my grandfather's childhood playmates. My grandmother speaks some Marathi and Hindi as well as Gujarati, but no English, and since all my life I have spoken only English, for nearly thirty-five years she and I have never talked to one another without the aid of intermediaries. This is an awkward way to converse with a grandparent, especially one I've seen as frequently as my grandmother, but for a long time I wasn't aware of it. On the contrary, what seemed presumptively normal and natural when I was young was the notion that events around me, however slight or large, took place in a few different Indian languages, and that like instruments they often had to be restrung in different alphabets and sounds. It seemed an ordinary matter of fact that conversations were complicated not just by who was present but by how they listened and what language they heard, and I got used to the idea that I was often privy to only part of a conversation, half an understanding. As a result, it came to seem inevitable that conversations either had to be accepted with all their ungainly, opaque areas, or else gradually deciphered.

When I was younger and lived in the Breach Candy section of central Bombay and my paternal grandparents lived in Sion, an area in the larger outlying city district, an established regimen of family gatherings ensured that there were always lots of grandchildren puckered around my grandparents. Because my mother was the only American in the family, and because she was the wife of the eldest living son, almost all the relatives were aware of her needs, or at least what they knew of her needs, and treated her carefully, with what I came to see as candid gestures of deference. Everyone spoke English. I was never taught Gujarati and picked up only what a child needed to know in order to get by with relatives who preferred Gujarati to English when my mother wasn't around. Occasionally, my grandmother would issue short, laconic commands to me in Gujarati or ask household-type questions in broken English. My austere, antique-looking grandfather would combine the English and the commands, telling me to bring his spittoon from wherever he had last left it, a task made necessary by his emphysema and which I found unbearable. During meals, my grandmother would nod her head approvingly, letting me know that it was good I sat on jute mats on the floor with my cousins and ate food without the aid of utensils, that no spoon was needed to lift food from my plate to my mouth.

My grandmother made it clear that if I stood in her doorway and stared at her long enough, I'd get hard candy suckers from the locked metal cabinet that stretched from floor to ceiling in the room by the verandah. She'd clap my back with her hand in a triangular wedge, saying something in Gujarati that wasn't important to understand, and give me ten paisa from the knot in her handkerchief so I could buy a black-and-white bull's-eye from a store that sold mounds of open-air powders, digestives, and candy. She moved with thick cautiousness, as if always aware that blood was coursing through her arms and legs, and when she walked, her keys jittered at her huge waist beneath her sari. Sometimes, after her rest, she'd call me for my afternoon bath, a bucket bath I couldn't refuse but never wanted because instead of wetting my body, she'd wet her hands and the soap, which always seemed a dubious way of working a lather and which usually left me feeling chastised.

My grandmother is now nearly eighty-five, though she's never been wholly certain when she was born. She lost her sight in one eye half a dozen years ago, and her hearing began to drift away slowly before that. She has had diabetes for most of my adult life, and she lost all her teeth, starting with the four middle ones on top, in the early 1960s, around the time my father married my mother against the wishes of both families, shortly before we moved to Bombay, and long after my father's father had given up on his ambition to become a cotton broker. My grandmother is now on her fifth set of teeth. They get replaced every seven or eight years by her Bombay dentist, who continues, inexplicably, to provide her with stark white dentures, making no allowance for her age and the state of the rest of her body. My grandmother, who is called *ba*—mother—by everyone in the family, as well as by people not in the family, now probably weighs about 170 pounds. And the name she answered to as a child is not the name she has had for the last seventy years since it was changed by her husband, as was a common custom, when they married. She was engaged without her knowledge at the age of fourteen, married at fifteen, and has now lived more than twenty years past her husband. And for many years, as my cousin Reema tells me, if there was a man in the house where she was living, she wouldn't remove her cotton sari when she went to bed, never mind that the man was usually just one of her sons or her son-in-law. This for the sake of decorum, which was also what caused her to feel uncomfortable when one of her sons helped her into or out of the wheelchair she sometimes used.

A few years ago, quite some time after my view of New Jersey as one of this country's malign territories had faded, I decided to move temporarily to Princeton from New York. At the time, my grandmother had relocated to New Jersey to live for a few years with her youngest son and daughter and their families. Eventually, she would go back to Bombay, where she had other sons and where her living conditions were more cramped, but where, she was unbudgeably certain, her health would be improved by Indian-manufactured pills and medicines and Indian humidity. But for some overlapping time, we were both lodged in the once dread state of New Jersey. And so I decided to spend some time with her. I decided to try to talk to her, since I had never attempted to do so seriously, since I felt I should make some kind of overture toward her before she died, and because my father had recently given me a sheet of paper that traced his family back patrilineally through sixteen generations and I had gotten curious. In the end, though, I never wound up learning much about my father's paternal ancestors, in part because my grandmother's memory only recognized a few generations and partly because all that began to seem remote and static once she started answering questions about her own life. Also, I asked questions because my grandmother seemed to like talking, because it enabled me to slip into an easy routine with her, and because she balked at my impolitic questions less than I sometimes balked at asking her to be a conduit to a past I had only suspicions about. And gradually, I also came to hope that talking deliberately and purposefully to my grandmother through family translators might give me a sharper, more angular perspective on her than what my relatives knew or imagined as a result of their more natural relationships with her. I thought I could interview my grandmother the way I sometimes interviewed authors for newspapers, and figured I could, if I were patient, slowly coax some understanding out of her. That these conversations dissolved into a morass of purposelessness now seems almost beside the point, however, since I did eventually realize a few things about my grandmother.

I'd detested New Jersey for a long time because moving to this country at the age of ten had been an angrily jolting experience and because it had unmoored me from everything I had known so comfortably and unquestioningly in Bombay. No longer was there anyone to play carom with, no getting bored watching milk get pasteurized in the kitchen with timers and cheesecloth and two-foot thermometers, no new habits that didn't automatically make me conscious of the differences between there and here. There were few friends here and none whose lives I properly understood, no thicket of relatives, no convulsively shifting relation between the sounds of outdoor noise and the time of day, no servants who weren't allowed to drink from the glasses we used at the table but who were much more central to me at the time than my parents, and no fans cutting apart the hot Bombay air after school as if this mechanical movement were the sole source of the motion needed to make afternoons disappear. Instead, there was, here, the straightforward sense of not belonging, of not having the right associations and memories, of not knowing when and how to do things in this grassy new suburban life. There was the vague sense of trespassing across the lives of strangers and in particular on the neighbor's lawn next door, which their youngest son soon enough forbade because he observed that I was a mulatto. There were some eventual friends, tentatively made and kept, there were all sorts of new electronic gadgets and ready-made clothes and a dozen television channels providing constant motion, and there was the unquestioned need to avoid certain groups of boys when I walked home from school through a wooded area because they liked to throw broken glass and rocks. Because I was regularly called nigger, spearchucker, jungle bunny, and kike, I tried to rid myself of the Indian-British accent others heard, at the same time wondering if the boys cursing me really thought I was black, later wondering where they had seen a black close up since there were none around, and wondering how they had heard I was Jewish and belonged to Temple Sinai in Summit. New Providence at that time was a racially conservative town, or at least a town with only three or four black families that never stayed long, and I never met anyone black in the ordinary course of things until I went off to college. But long before college, out of a lack of alternatives, I had begun considering what would be my near-decade in New Providence as a very lengthy cameo appearance.

During that cameo appearance, much time was spent in the unremarkable clutch of adolescence, worrying about the passing traumas that must have afflicted everyone around me as well, wondering why I had been born so dark, with dark hair covering a greater portion of my body than I thought natural, and withdrawing into books that provided some measure of escape but a still greater confirmation that strong emotions should be experienced privately, with a slow accumulation of words and sentences and, *in extremis,* an anonymous sort of empathy. Yet a few incidents from those cameo days still jut out with staunch familiarity, though probably less because of what happened than because my reaction descended so unusually into something like anguish. Once, a short while after I turned fourteen, I was walking across the parking lot of the New Providence Shopping Center with a friend, and a stone hit my back. It was nearing dusk at the time and we happened to be approaching an abandoned snow plow and I was suddenly crying—not because I had been hurt but because I wasn't alone, because Patti had seen this awful humiliation take place, because there was urine soaking my underpants, and because it had become so insurmountably, mortifyingly impossible to compose myself. The area where we were would later be dug up to build Burger Express, where I'd work at the counter as an "expediter" calling orders to people working the grill. But back then, when I finally stopped sweating and Patti stopped talking, I stood in the parking lot, distressed, trying to push the anger out of my head so I could decide whether to pick up the stones that had been thrown so no one would see them and wonder how they had gotten there.

That kind of confusion and anger about how I was seen as an adolescent has long since dissipated, but my relationship to my background became more ambiguous. The idea that my background, and my associations, like those stones in the parking lot, could be held and manipulated has remained compelling since then because it allows for the possibility of shifting theories about what things mean and what things can be made to mean. My connection to different parts of my past has grown stronger over the years, but it has also grown less real as it became more conscious and more deliberate. Names, I think, can also be fickle, serving as weights that hold our sense of ourselves against the flatness of some idea we may not yet have decided what to do with. Since I don't have a middle name, there was a time long ago when I took on phantom names as the need for different backgrounds and affiliations arose. My father's mother's first name was changed entirely when she married, and few people now know her original name. And my mother's father changed his surname when he finished law school in the mid-1920s. My mother's grandparents had come to Brooklyn from lower-middle-class Austrian, English, and Byelorussian stock, and her parents always spoke Yiddish when they wanted privacy, which, when I knew them, was when they played cards and ate pears while my sister and I sat transfixed in front of the television screen in their spare room. My grandfather was autocratic, very particular about his immediate environment and the beliefs of those who passed closely through his life, and somewhat racist in his later years. On most days, he smelled like witch hazel until lunchtime, since he brewed his own aftershave lotion, yet long before he discovered witch hazel, and shortly before my mother and her sister were born, he filled out the official paperwork and changed his last name from Levine to Leonard. He explained much later that there had been too many lawyers in the phone book named Levine, though the women around him always believed this to be an assimilationist's claim, an effort to create an edge of uncertainty between his name and his Jewishness.

There were other experiences when I was growing up like the one by the snow plow, but against them I'd stiffen just as quietly, letting new incidents push away older ones as if they had been paltry, diminuitive forces all along. My response to such besetting distress was consistent: I'd slip into a kind of détente and become impassive, and only later erratically argumentative. But even back then, when I tried to make sense of various conflicts, I generally believed that people's personalities were not very ambulatory, that they couldn't be hauled across great long distances, and that, unlike names, individuals could be altered only in bits and only under tremendous duress.

Instead, what I wanted was solemnly large ideas and throbbing, unifying principles to organize my life. I wanted to believe in something unimpeachable, maybe God, and to have certain faith that there was a kind of transparency all around me that required only unfailing belief to understand. In those years, the closest I ever got to anything spiritual was sitting by some creek and imagining for hours at a time that the entire planet was a falling particle in someone else's world and that what appeared to me to be tremendously long, sad afternoons were just instants to another person thinking inscrutable thoughts somewhere else. Or I'd imagine that the earth had been slid sideways inside a leaf and that stars were the pinpoint gaps and holes in a terrifically dense molecular leaf-world. I wanted my past to fit with my present and my life in New Jersey to make more sense to me. Short of that, I wanted a clean break. Eventually, I realized that the kind of dramatic anonymity I sought could also be had, if somewhat deficiently, from theories about evolution. Evolution required taking a long view toward the surrounding world and remaining impersonal. The only other experience at the time that might have passed for something reasonably religious was when I drew on my occasional talent for shutting my eyes and imagining I was heading across a sea to Poland. This went back to a mightily incorrect but firmly held belief I had when I was seven or eight that my entire class in Bombay International School had taken a long wooden boat ride across a dark, churning sea to the island of Poland, which was then located off the southern coast of India, where Sri Lanka, which was then Ceylon, now floats.

With time, this faint aptitude for religion eventually turned into a low-key, desultory interest in Orthodox Judaism, though always at a bookish remove since proper faith continued to escape me. I wished for strong, unambiguous commitments to organize my thoughts. In lieu of my need for clear working certainties, my mother has fluid, tunneling ideas about human nature and psychology; and in lieu of that, my father has an expansive knowledge of clinical pharmacology and an awareness of the effect drugs have on the nervous system and on the body's general functioning. And my grandmother has a Jain cosmology that explains everything to a certain degree of sufficiency.

Of everyone in my family, my paternal grandmother is curiously the most existential. Or at least the doctrines of her religion are, since her own life has been limited by broad, claustrophobic rules about how one should live in a social environment. Jainism came into its own in India in the sixth century B.C., at the same time as Buddhism. Both were reactions to the increasing ritualization of traditional Vedic Hinduism at the time, and to the stiffening of its social and religious hierarchy. There is no god (or pantheon of gods) in Jainism, no sovereign authority or omniscient anything that offers an explanation of the world or provides a sense of individual or communal purpose. Instead, Jainism is a sensationally individualistic religion centered around a number of logically related beliefs: that there are distinct, permanently autonomous souls in all things that are living; that reincarnation is the unmitigating way of the world; that one's life is the inevitable result of past deeds and karmic buildup; that actions beget consequences; that enlightenment exists and is self-generated; and that transcendence can be approached by following certain principles and by ridding oneself of the weight of attachment to worldly things. This attachment to kith, kin, material goods and ambitions, one's own desires and aversions, one's five senses, etc., is what condemns individuals to a bodily existence and what stalls salvation. In both lay and ascetic Jainism and among the various Jain branches of thought, knowledge can be pared down to recognizing the dichotomy between the soul and everything that's nonsoul and therefore imprisoning. And enlightenment is an ultimately individual task that benefits only oneself.

There is no sense of awe when my grandmother talks about religion, and her main affirmations are promissory ones of denial and forbearance: to not differentiate between souls, to try to do no violence to things that live, and to practice nonattachment to anything that touches her senses, including memories that might gladden her, relationships with her children and grandchildren that might bring her comfort, feelings of happiness or regret about things she has done or omitted to do over the years, and anything else that brushes against or depends on the stability of worldly phenomena. Because of the overarching Jain principle of noninjury to all life forms, she is of course vegetarian, but she also doesn't eat root vegetables since the part of the plant that's consumed is the seat of its life. So she eats no meat or fish, no eggs, no onions, garlic, potatoes, carrots, or anything that grows beneath the ground. And she eats after sunrise and before sundown every day to prevent microorganisms from entering her mouth and thereby expiring. Many of the laws that she observes, like the laws of kashrut, trace back to sensible dietary prohibitions from ancient times that have long since become part of an observant religious life. Years ago, when my grandmother was much healthier, she also underwent occasional fasts for eight days at a time.

My grandmother and I have little in common, but when we both lived temporarily in New Jersey, I'd drive up to Maplewood, where two sets of my aunts and uncles then lived, and ask my grandmother questions. I'd often ask about religion, since I wanted to know what the grandmother I felt oddly close to believed. I expected that because I didn't understand her beliefs all that well, I'd learn more about what she thought by entering this near-impenetrable thicket and trying to make sense of what I found. Perhaps I also thought that stray molecules containing some of her certainties, if not her beliefs, would fly off her body and settle comfortably on mine. In the end, though, what I was able to make of all these conversations was based almost entirely on the order I imposed on her comments from without, and on the complicated meanings I attached to her beliefs and descriptions of life, sometimes quite regardless of her own explanations.

Religiously, the person my grandmother gained the most sustenance from was a man who died in 1901 at the age of thirty-two. His name was Raichand Mehta, though he's now known by the honorific Srimad Rajachandra. And while he was no relation, he lived for a time in Rajkot, Gujarat, where my grandfather's family was from, and in the 1890s my grandfather's father knew him and considered him a great religious teacher. Rajachandra is seen as a modern saint by many Jains now, and there are a number of temples in Gujarat (and a few in this country) dedicated to his teachings. This eventual saint had been a gem merchant before he decided to pursue enlightenment full-time, and some twenty-five years after his death by self-starvation, it was his sister's husband who arranged my grandparents' marriage.

When my grandparents married, they were already related to one another by marriage since one of my grandfather's elder sisters had married my grandmother's brother. Before their own marriage, my grandparents lived in the household of their married siblings, though at that time purdah was observed in many north Indian communities, regardless of religion, and girls past childhood were kept separate and secluded from the men. So although my grandparents lived in the same house as young teenagers, they knew one another only by sight. Eventually, my grandmother's married sister decided that my grandparents should marry, but since it was inappropriate for a woman to suggest such a thing, the husband of Rajachandra's sister, who knew and was close to both families, arranged the match.

My grandmother didn't always get along with her mother-in-law, with whom she and my grandfather lived. But at least, she told a cousin who was translating for me one evening a few years ago, she had a home and a roof over her head and her husband's family didn't throw her out. My grandmother did the cooking for the entire household, except for two days every month when she wasn't permitted in the kitchen. During those years, my grandmother wasn't allowed to think of the house as her own. She was expected to cover her head with a portion of her sari when her mother-in-law was present, out of respect, and she wasn't allowed to invite relatives from her side of the family into the house since she herself was considered a visitor. If my grandmother wanted to go out, she had to request her mother-in-law's permission and then ask which sari she could wear. Then she'd touch her mother-in-law's feet as a sign of respect. On returning home, she'd again have to greet her mother-in-law by bowing and touching her feet.

My grandmother was also not allowed to speak of her six children as *her* children. If one of them got sick, she'd have to avoid the possessive pronoun and note, simply, that *this* boy needs medicine or *that* one needs food. Her mother-in-law sometimes said that just because a sack contains the grain, does that mean the sack owns the grain? In this way, my grandmother's five sons and daughter were not hers. They did not belong to her just as the grain did not belong to the sack.

My grandmother's mother-in-law lived for twenty-two years after my grandparents married, before breast cancer got the better of her. Her meanness was not especially more mean than most ordinary domestic behavior at the time, but her deep religiousness caused my grandmother to become more religious. My grandmother's devotion circuitously led her daughter, my aunt, to do the same, and as my aunt became more religious during the 1980s, she tried to bring her actions into greater consonance with the principles of noninjury, truth-telling, and nonattachment to worldly concerns. My aunt has never been as severe in her actions as my grandmother, but one expression of her concern for noninjury was that she stopped wearing silk saris since many hundreds of thousands of silkworms perish in the making of the silk she used to drape casually across her body. So the legacy that comes to me from one of my great-grandmothers, the one who sounds so bitter (but who is uniformly remembered by everyone besides my grandmother as pious and kind), is an utterly magnificent one: two drawers full of gloriously embroidered silk saris sewn with heavy gold thread. It's a legacy I should perhaps feel ambivalent about, but instead I am glad.

In the nearby Maplewood house of my other aunt, my grandmother's youngest son's wife, a photograph of Srimad Rajachandra used to always stand upright near an enormous religious book that my grandmother had been reading piece-meal for more than forty years. My grandmother prayed every day, and when she prayed the area around her bureau turned into a make-do shrine. Sometimes she intoned prayers and sometimes she chanted in a hoarse voice; all the while her hands made their habitual votive offerings. The photo, a black-and-white in an eight-by-ten frame, was occasionally garlanded with a string of marigolds. And it was garlanded on a Saturday morning a few years ago, an air-conditioned morning, when my mother and I walked into my grandmother's room as she was putting the lids back on various containers of vermilion and rice grain and whatever else she had been using in her puja. Her long gray hair still wet, my grandmother mo-tioned to us to come in and sit. Patiently, she finished what she was doing. Then she lifted the photo off the dresser, ran a calm hand over it as if feeling for a heat source, and said to us in English, "This, is, my-god. He, ba's-god. This is, god-photo."

A look of exasperation slid past my mother's face. All I could think about, though, was that through my great-grandfather I was connected to the person my grandmother referred to as God.

God was a stalk of a man seated in the basic lotus position, his thighs long and thin with not much flesh, his shoulders as compact as doorknobs, and his ribs so defined that his body looked as if it had been superimposed over its own X-ray. My grandmother's emaciated, X-rayed god looked like many thou-sands of Holocaust surivors, though seated very erectly. He was wholly anonymous in body, wholly ignorant of his body's meagerness, and unaware that what the camera was capturing looked like only the bony template of a man. For Jain ascetics (though Rajachandra had not been one) who want to go the distance, the ultimate way for the ready soul to be released from the cycle of births and deaths is by starving oneself to death, by denying the body's needs and controlling its myriad appetites, including that of survival. This is the height of self-consciousness. Such a transcendence, a pointedly self-conscious route to physical death, is considered different from suicide since the latter is seen as resulting from passion and self-violence and moral cowardice.

So when my grandmother held out her god-photo of the man with the emaciated body and glaring ribs, my mother withdrew her attention. She heard my grandmother's simple words, repeated loudly as if we were the ones who were partly deaf, she saw me watching my grandmother's photographic presentation of God, and she left the room. For my mother, this was a breakdown in conversation. When all understanding cocks back to one reigning idea, be it reincarnation or God or anything else, one large received idea that organizes behavior and funnels thinking through some single perspective, there is nothing left to say. But for my grandmother, praying to Rajachandra does not involve any beseeching or consolation, or a recognition of some untamable force at work in the universe. It's more a pledge to try to observe the principles of her religion, and her prayers are her way of offering daily respect to someone who accomplished this formidable feat. Her "god" was just a word that misfired.

But the kind of self-awareness that Jainism holds out to my grandmother does not work for me. I can't see such plain physical transcendence as the goal. And my grandmother's self-awareness isn't the sort that my mother has in mind. My grandmother thinks of shaving away the world, absenting herself from its material conditions and attachments. She lives by the positivistic assumption that there will be a reckoning for one's actions in the future (though with no sense of judgment), and she believes that we are the sum of our actions from many past lives and that no slates will ever be wiped clean once and for all. My mother, for her part, thinks about why people do and think what they do and what they think. Her understanding of relationships is lit by what she knows about psychology, about the fact that what motivates one person wouldn't be enough to motivate another, about irrational loyalties and mitigating circumstances. And by the mundane disappearance of time as one ages, the fear of leaving things unfinished, and the difficulty of having to make hard decisions and choose between commitments.

To my mother, it's the prominence of conversation that's important, whether of politics or literature or opera. It's the working out of ideas that's necessary, and the disparate meanings that grow from those ideas. These days, my mother regularly calls to tell me what she's been reading about Stalin's purges. Or to tell me about cyclones and murders in the news, or a lawsuit she and my father are engaged in over some property in Connecticut. Often, she calls to say that she's just finished a book and hasn't yet decided whether to start rereading nineteenth-century Russian writers. She's been putting off the Russians for a long while. Occasionally, she asks if I'm happy, but usually she conveys whatever information is lurking about, and then inquires, lately for the third or fourth time, what kind of music the man I've been seeing listens to, whether he thinks about me the way I think about him, and whether we are discussing Israeli politics yet. And just as it's always been possible to assemble my mother's questions into a point of view, and to know something about her slowly shifting priorities on the basis of her questions, so I used to think it ought to be possible to find a slim path to what my grandmother thinks—and through her, to how I relate to components of my past—through these discussions about religion.

Once, I drove to Maplewood because my father had decided to visit for the day. I thought I'd be able to ask my grandmother questions for hours, and I looked forward to having as a translator the person who could best guess what I wanted from these conversations. So my father drove down from Connecticut and I came from Princeton, and when we arrived I was told that my grandmother had taken a vow of silence for the day. Since she had settled on this the previous night, there was no talking her out of it or postponing her silence by a day. My grandmother, it was explained, wanted to retreat into her prayers and religious thoughts, and focus on what was important. This process, as I dismayingly saw it, included affirming her nonattachment to conversation. Disappointed, I talked for some time to my aunt as she worked all the burners on the stove top and both ovens, then went upstairs. My grandmother had just turned off her portable tape recorder and was laying it on a side table near her teeth. I sat cross-legged on the bed next to her, my father a few feet away on a chair. Pretty soon, my grandmother handed my father one of her prayer books. She looked at him expectantly, then gestured that she wanted him to read by lifting her hand, palm up, a few inches from the book toward my father's chest. My father's usual nonchalance gave way to sedentary reluctance, but my grandmother kept up her gesturing. Finally, after glancing at me, my father took out his glasses, coughed a bit, and began to make his slow way through chants he once knew by heart and used to recite every day as a child in Rajkot.

But my father's Gujarati had long since become an old man, stumbling and hesitating over words that once must have been as ready as the saliva that slicked them and separated one sound from another. Yet even after fifty years, there were many phrases familiar to his mind, if no longer so recognizable on paper. I marveled that my father, a boundless, unquestioning atheist, was reading these prayers at all, that he hadn't refused the task and called for one of his relatives to do it instead. As I listened to his half-foreign voice, and watched him rub an earlobe and shift position for better concentration the way so many Indian men seem to do, I began to hear my grandmother correct him. Her cloudy eyes were closed, his open. But his pronunciation of her prayers was wrong, and his speech much too jerky, and so she periodically slipped out of her vow of silence in order to correct what needed correcting.

My grandmother's commitments to Jainism are fluid, and my mother is perhaps right when she says that her pujas and daily rituals are the background noise against which her deep affection for her family seems all the more devotional. My grandmother is bent on doing what she thinks is right, and proper, for her family, and it's always been the function we serve for one another that's important, never the motivation. Yet from my grandmother's conversation and disparate memories, I can siphon out nothing that expands my basic self-understanding, or that intelligently complicates, or even simplifies, my relationship with her. And I cannot help doubting that I affect her life in any intimate way. Of course, it may just be the way of things that influence runs downward through generations and not the other way. For my grandmother, asking about my life or trying to understand some aspect of my life may be like walking backwards, or trying to understand *why* a ventriloquist would throw his voice from one side of a room to the other. My grandmother mainly wants to know that her twelve grandchildren and seven greatgrandchildren are healthy and plump, comfortably married if they're old enough, and that there is no grief harming their lives.

Sometimes my grandmother calls me her daughter. Referring to me as her daughter, or calling her first greatgranddaughter her "sixth daughter," may be just her way of speaking, her way of sweeping affection into as direct a statement as possible, or her way of claiming as much of her family as possible in defiance of her long-dead mother-in-law. It's hard to know, and my grandmother has no explanation to give since not all my questions even make sense to her. On the other hand, a sculptor friend of mine who has lately been thinking about having a child says she cannot figure out whether love is automatic, or even whether there's any automatic adhesive between people in the same family. "You have a child who has a child," she says, "and where's the connection?" My friend and I don't agree on this since I see irrepressible, if often inchoate, bonds everywhere I turn, but the fact that my grandmother sometimes refers to me as her daughter still doesn't mean very much to me. The connection we have exists and is real, but it has never really developed. Whatever bond exists between my grandmother and me, I expect it probably has more to do with the sheer physicality of her presence than anything else.

Sometimes more than being alone I like to sit in a room

with familiar people who are speaking a language I don't know, and be ignored. I'm content reading a book by Ivan Gold or stories by Isak Dinesen or a yet-unpublished novel I'm supposed to review, or sitting at a table plucking the stems off blueberries, while around me Gujarati words and sentences slip off the walls. Sometimes I can catch small words or latch on to a stream of English passing through a conversation, but it doesn't matter. I like listening to the inflection of my relatives' voices, waiting for the point in sentences where one person pauses in expectation that someone else will interrupt. And I like that most of the time no one bothers to explain these conversations to me because they've deemed it unnecessary to include me in a discussion that will only distract me from my book, or the berries. I suppose what I also like is that no one is deferring to me or making allowances, talking in a language that is somewhat slightly less natural in order to include me as a listener. Maybe, also, I know that the content of the conversation is likely to be less riveting than what's in my book. But I feel reassured, maybe mistakenly, in the presumption that people who understand what things mean in other languages and who care for me are guarding the conversation floating around, the same way I feel secure that when my radio is off the voices inside still continue their long conversations. But of course I also know that any conversation would be translated for me, if I asked.

The Maplewood conversations always followed the same general plot. My grandmother would put in her hearing aid, remove the cork coaster covering her water glass, take a long, noisy sip, and then sit up in bed and look not at me but at my aunt or uncle, waiting for one of them to translate the question I was about to ask. My grandmother used to look at me only when her answer was being translated into English, and I was never sure whether this was to see my reaction or to determine whether a follow-up question was coming, though I suspect now that it was the latter.

My aunt and uncle didn't always seem interested in my grandmother's answers. Sometimes they seemed to prefer speculating about what she might say, and they'd wait for her answers to see whose predictions were closer. Occasionally, my uncle simply answered the question himself, bypassing his mother-in-law altogether. Only after many weekends had passed, with them translating and untranslating conversations and exchanging what was being said, did it occur to me that I had been foolish to think that because of my questions my aunt and uncle were getting a qualitatively different account of my grandmother's life, or at least a fuller and more candid one, than what they already knew. I was extracting new and unexpected information from my grandmother because I was asking questions that hadn't been asked, either because they were too personal or too remote or otherwise inappropriate, but I was the only one clearly pleased with this information, and it was a yawning, disquieting realization that this was still all I knew of my grandmother. And that the answers I was getting didn't reveal much about what my grandmother thought. And were perhaps no different than what they would have been had it been someone else plying her with fresh curiosity. And I realized, too, that I would need to manipulate these stories and pieces of information into something that would do whatever work I had been expecting them to do. These conversations with my grandmother were a long-winded performance I had somewhat disingenuously organized for myself, and everyone involved was trying hard to get the details right.

Eventually, I suppose, I got what I wanted, though at the time I had no idea what that was. During many of our conversations my grandmother spoke in parables, compressing logic in half, segueing from fact to homily and from homily to non sequitur, establishing a view of the world that was clear and expansively disciplined but inevitably alien to me. Sometimes I just sat in her room, in whichever house she happened to be staying, and marveled that we were related to one another at all.

One afternoon, she told me about something she had figured out. At some point, she had had a decent sum of money. She gave it to two people and lived on the interest they passed on to her. But after a while, when one of them stopped sending her the interest, she wrote to one of her sons in Bombay and urged him to get the money back from the man. My uncle tried and couldn't get it back. Eventually, the man wrote to my grandmother and told her that he was poor and had nothing left so the money could not be returned. At some later date, she went to the village of Vavania, where there's a Jain religious center, and when the people there began talking about money, she realized that the money she had wanted back was money she owed the man from a previous life. And if she wanted to get the money back so badly, she would be born in her next life as a dog because dogs take and take from the person who cares for them. And since she didn't want to be born as a dog, she stopped thinking about the money.

Had my mother heard this, she would surely have dismissed the story as a skinny, ranting bit of reasoning, but she would have objected to the comment about dogs since she absolutely does not believe that dogs take and take without giving something back. Both my parents would have had

head-shaking responses to many of the things my grandmother said, and while my own responses weren't always far
from that, I can't help thinking that my grandmother simply
deals in large-scale metaphors of causation, although for her
everything tacks back to some very distant past that can't be
accessed.

A long time after hearing this story, after I had given up
trying to understand how my grandmother thought, I realized
that she had in fact been answering my questions as straight-
forwardly as possible, and that she had done so with no embarrassment and much more frankly than any other of my
relatives or I would have done. My grandmother treated all
information equally, without distinguishing between the
questions asked: no information she conveyed seemed more
significant to her than other information. Moreover, I realized
that my grandmother had been talking mainly because I had
been asking her questions. The conversations and memories
didn't hold much meaning for her, even though she sometimes
cried when she answered my questions. In fact, the main rele-
vance her memories now had seemed to be that they enabled
her to answer my questions.

And yet I got something of value from these conversations.
We're born to particular parents and into particular families,
my grandmother would often say through my aunt or uncle,
because in our last life or four lives ago or a hundred lives ago,
we had something to do with each other. Sometimes I'd ask
my grandmother variations of earlier questions to make sure I
hadn't misunderstood her, so another time she said that, yes,
she knew she had had relations with people in her family in
previous lives, though she didn't know what they were. She
then explained that there was something Bharati *faiba* had to

give to me and something I had to give to my aunt, something she and my cousin Rhushabh had to give one another, and so forth in a long process of reciprocal exchange that was true for all the myriad relationships we had. Because we had something we needed to give one another, we were born related.

Only once did my grandmother ask me a question. It was simple: "Will you be born in another life?" I hesitated opaquely when I heard the question, surprised by what was being asked and not really wanting to say no to the grandmother with whom I wished I had more in common, and the only reply I managed to get out was that I didn't know about being born again, but that I sometimes felt drawn to people I didn't know for no particular reason. "Sometimes," my grandmother replied to Indu *fua*, my uncle sitting on the floor next to me, who would die the following year of a massive heart attack, "you meet someone and he doesn't know you and yet he takes a dislike to you. Or there are two brothers with the same circumstances and backgrounds and one becomes successful and the other fails miserably. You say it is luck. It is really just the result of your deeds from previous lives."

My grandmother is very adept at throwing everything back into the confusion of previous lives, answering every dilemma by shuttling back in time, smelting chronology, and so forth. And this I find terribly consoling, as well as anathema to everything I know and believe. When I was younger and my past in Bombay was a whole lot closer, I wrote letter after letter to a number of friends whose lives are now beyond the farthest reaches of what I know about them, but whose correspondence meant something important to me for a long while. These days, I'm used to writing reviews of books and articles for anonymous readers, and a book I'm doing research for involves conducting a couple hundred interviews with Orthodox Jews and Indians. So I spend a lot of time with people whose associations with certain aspects of my past are, in many ways, stronger than my own. Compared to them, I am equipped with few unimpeachable beliefs. And compared to them, my commitment to components of my own history is fairly weak. But maybe the ruminative, vicarious relation I now have with my background is the only one that's possible, the only one that makes sense, just as the simplest, most unembellished relationship I can have with my paternal grandmother is the only one that's not impossible. Though in the end, it's still hard to be sure.

TECHNICOLOR

Rubén Martínez

For my father—

FADE IN.

INTERIOR DAY, MOJAVE DESERT.

OVER THE SHOULDER SHOT: WRITER, a Latino in his mid-thirties, dressed rather shabbily, sits at a poorly put together Ikea desk that wobbles with each letter typed into a PowerBook 540c, which looks like it's suffered one too many punches from writer's block–inspired fists. Writer stares intensely at the screen, as if closely examining his face in a mirror.

CLOSE UP on COMPUTER SCREEN, where we see these very words appearing.

SLOWLY PULL BACK, revealing the rest of the cluttered desk: Camel Filter cigs, a pile of audio cassettes, a navy-blue bandanna, a stack of unpaid bills, scattered books (Baldwin's *Another Country,* Steinbeck's *The Grapes of Wrath,* Fante's *Ask the Dust,* a Whitman collection, a Bible in Spanish, a title on Santería, etc.), a beautiful nineteenth-century gold-leaf Virgin of Guadalupe statuette sitting just before the window.

CAMERA GOES THROUGH WINDOW and out into the desert, a tremendous ascending crane shot that floats over the few isolated homes and the expanse of sand, creosote, and cacti. Now and again a human appears below us — a middle-aged white lady hanging laundry on the line, a black gardener raking a sandy carport, a Mexican kid slamming a porch door, a Vietnamese woman cussing out her towheaded Marine Corps husband as he gets into a red '68 Mustang . . .

I've always spent more time at movie houses or huddled up next to my TV and VCR than with my nose between the pages of a book. Truth be told, I read only books directly related to my research and a handful of literary faves. But sit down to read a new novel or the latest six-hundred-page biography on the *Times*'s best-seller list? Nah—who has the time in the Age of MTV? Me, I want to see colors rippling across a wide screen! I want to hear the characters' voices not with my mind's ear but with my real ear! And I want a soundtrack of violins and trumpets composed by a nonagenarian Russian émigré. I want crane shots and spaghetti-western super-closeups of eyes and crow's-feet crinkling. I want Bergman (Ingrid), Mitchum, Hayworth, and Poitier forever teamed up with Curtis, want them sneering-panting-whistling, and a single, soft-focused tear tracking down every one of their cheeks—

I grew up in Hollywood. Literally. ABC Studios was just across the Shakespeare Bridge from us in a neighborhood we always called Silver Lake but that the yuppies have recently rechristened Franklin Hills. The imposing set for D. W. Griffith's *Intolerance* once stood about a mile away from my elementary school. In nearby Edendale, now called Echo Park, Mack Sennett filmed the comedic greats of early cinema, including Hal Roach and Laurel and Hardy. (Echo Park, with its elegant Victorians and quaint courtyard bungalows, has been a Hollywood favorite over the decades; much of *Chinatown* was shot there, as well as *L.A. Confidential.*) My alma mater, John Marshall High, has a New England Gothic façade that has served as the quintessential American high school for dozens of TV shows and movies; John Travolta and Olivia Newton-John bobby-soxed on my football field when I was a freshman.

And, as if to live up to these origins in my adult life, I have, for the past several years, worked for the local PBS outlet at KCET Studios, a couple of blocks away from the Jewish Community Center that I, a Latino Catholic, once frequented because most of my friends were Jewish.

The house my father grew up in (and where my parents, and occasionally I, live now) is nestled in the hills of Silver Lake, about two miles from Franklin Hills. "Mixville," the ranch owned by early western hero Tom Mix, was once only a block away from my family's house, a real-life rendition of what my father saw at Saturday matinees.

Pop was quite the Cowboys-and-Indians kid, in spite of the fact that he was born to Mexican parents whose blood was much more Indian than Spanish. In the radio days he regularly listened to *The Lone Ranger,* whose by all accounts clever Indian sidekick was inexplicably named Tonto (which means "stupid" in Spanish). In the golden California afternoons of his youth, my father gathered with the other kids in Silver Lake—from Italian, German, Irish, and, up until Pearl Harbor, Japanese families—and the unlucky draw became the Indian to be chased down and shot dead with cap pistols.

My father wasn't the only Indian who loved Cowboys. Throughout what we used to call the "Third World" just about everybody was weaned on westerns in which the Indians were bad and the Cowboys good and the Indians always outnumbered the Cowboys but the Cowboys were better shooters and there the Indian (actually a Cowboy stuntman) goes down, clutching at his chest, a puff of dust as his body hits dirt, and the Cowboy and the Cowgirl hug and steal a kiss behind his hat and the violins come up and the credits roll. We all loved the Cowboys.

Over the years, Hollywood's given me great and terrible things—a culture as tangible as the mix of race and ethnicity I grew up around—and somewhere between my "reel" and "real" lives lie my deepest beliefs and my greatest fears, my nightmares and my dreams. As a kid and now an adult with a perpetual identity crisis, Hollywood has been a constant mirror for me, and what I've screened has resulted in validation and self-loathing, vindication and betrayal (I of it, and it of me). I was raised in a swirl of cultures that at times melded seamlessly and at others clashed violently—a contradiction that exists at the very heart of Hollywood, the tension between its most noble and most debased instincts.

For starters, I think I'd hate white people if it wasn't for Hollywood. This is not to say that I haven't hated some white people, and sure, the entire race, on occasion. But how can you hate someone you're on such intimate terms with—on screen and off? At my elementary school, I was the only Latino until the third grade. In addition to two Iranian brothers who were often mistaken for Latins, the extent of our integration was one black girl and a smattering of Japanese and Chinese. The vast majority of students were Anglo or Jewish.

My English was somewhat lacking when I began kindergarten. For kids of immigrants, there weren't exactly a lot of cultural choices back in the days before bilingual education and "multiculturalism." You either "assimilated" or you fought the dominant culture to the death. In my junior high school, a much more mixed environment, I came across Latino kids who embarked upon the latter course: *cholos* who followed in the footsteps of older siblings or parents and wore the uniform of an ethnic rebel (dickies, hairnets) and lived a life at odds not just with white society but also Mother Mexico. I always envied them; however troubled their lives, their style, when compared to white kids in Hush Puppies, was way *cool* (a look that would have to wait nearly fifty years before Luis Valdez made the film version of *Zoot Suit* to get the flashy Hollywood treatment it deserved).

I, on the other hand, did everything I could to assimilate, or, in the more modern lingo, "acculturate." My father was crucial in this regard. He, too, had eschewed the *cholo* way of life. That his parents had made enough money to move into a middle-class neighborhood is not an unimportant detail here. By living among the Other, it was much easier to become conversant in their language and perspective. In America, acculturation is usually as much an economic rite of passage as it is a cultural one.

My father entered the American mainstream with a Graphic Arts International Union card and a cultural sensibility honed as much by Hollywood as by my grandparents' Old World family values. His teachers might have taught him to read and write English, but it was John Wayne, Audie Murphy, and Gary Cooper that taught him how to play American. He fulfilled his Hollywood dreams, to a degree, by working at a print shop that held lucrative contracts with several movie studios. Thus, instead of a typical Mexican household decorated with Catholic icons and gaudy, oversized family portraits, we had the movie posters my father had done the color-separation work for hanging on the walls.

I experienced "race" (Latinos are not officially a race, though this country has a long history of racializing them, especially the Mexicans) pretty much the way that I imagine my father did when he was growing up, since he, too, was often the odd one among his classmates. I had to endure the occasional wetback jokes (Who's the president of Mexico? Manual Labor), but I stubbornly remained an assimilationist. I came to speak an accentless English, just like my father. In fact, I was so good at listening to and mimicking the language that I became something of the Rich Little of my class. By junior high school I was imitating John Wayne and Richard Nixon about as good as a kid with Mexican looks can.

Hollywood helped, and hindered, me all along the way. In my youth, Hollywood was hitting the peak of the first phase of its race vetting. I'll never forget when the film version of *West Side Story* aired on network TV for the first time in the late sixties, around the time that *Guess Who's Coming to Dinner* was probably still in the movie houses. That first screening is etched into memory as much for how fascinated I was by the movie as for what happened the day after.

Of course I fell in love with Natalie Wood's Maria, which placed me firmly in white-kid Tony's shoes. Although I'd had minor brushes with racism before, I arrived at school the next day not thinking of having to fight the Jets—hell, I *was* a Jet and a white girl named Wendy was, in fantasy, my Natalie Wood. Only in hindsight can I see the irony of a brown kid who thought he was white and desired a white classmate standing in for a white woman playing a Puerto Rican.

That morning at Franklin Elementary, all the kids arrived snapping their fingers, whistling, and talking darkly of a "rumble" after school. I walked out of Mrs. Goodman's class after the afternoon bell rang and heard a prepubescent voice screech: "SHARK!" I looked around, but of course everyone was looking at me. There wasn't any physical harm to the game (some Jewish kids, probably second-generation red-diaper babies, played the liberals and saved my skin), but I can point to the experience as the moment in which a schizophrenic consciousness began to grow in me.

On one hand, just about everyone I saw on TV and in the movies was white, except for a handful of minor roles for blacks, Asians, and Mexicans ("Latinos," from Central or South America—like my mom, who was born in El Salvador—simply didn't exist back then, except, of course, Carmen Miranda). Without dwelling on the contradictions, I viewed things from a white perspective. My father helped me in this regard, since he supplied me with a healthy dose of westerns and WW II hero-flicks at home on the tube and at revival houses.

Despite the fact that he was one of my father's favorites, I never much cared for John Wayne. In John Ford's *The Searchers,* a film I saw several times as a kid, he portrayed the brutal Ethan, who almost kills Natalie Wood because she'd "turned Indian" after she was kidnapped as a child by a renegade tribe. In *The Searchers* I sympathized with Wood and her half-breed half-brother, played by a bronzed, stunningly good-looking Jeffrey Hunter. In *West Side Story* I'd been a Jet; in *The Searchers* I leaned Indian.

But there were other great actors of mid-century American cinema that I adored and that, unlike Wayne, often played thoughtful, complex characters. Jimmy Stewart humanized his heroes with psychological depth and downright vulnerability—I remember him crying in some western I saw on TV one day I stayed home from school (I often acted like my minor colds were full-blown pneumonias just so that I could watch movies all day on the tube). Jack Lemmon's nervous comedy was thoroughly modern, and it seemed to capture some of the anxiety my young parents were going through in the early sixties. And Jerry Lewis—the French are so right about him—made us all feel at home with the absurdity of things American.

Let's just say that in some "raceless" way, I did learn a lot about life through the characters and stories. But there was something Faustian about my love affair with Hollywood's whiteness. Sooner or later, the Mexican character appeared on the screen, almost always a stereotype, a jester whose jokes are at his own expense. This was always most obvious in the western genre.

I bought the video of John Ford's *Three Godfathers* the other day to screen again the image of myself that I saw in my youth. The film is a simple, sentimental Christ-child parable with Ford's brilliant eye giving us plenty of wide shots of characters nearly lost in the pastel immensity of southwestern desert space. Mexican film legend Pedro Armendáriz plays John Wayne's sidekick. I don't know if Ford prodded Armendáriz to play a howling caricature of a Mexican or if Armendáriz found the stereotype of his character through the Method, but his ethnicity becomes the comic foil for the film.

As a kid, I laughed at Armendáriz's antics (howling like a cantina character, over-emoting everything), and I laugh today. I laugh at myself. It is a strange experience: you are disembodied as you laugh at the image that represents you on the screen. Your consciousness splits and, in a desperate attempt to survive the humiliation, identifies with the subjectivity of the culture that made the film, no longer with the objectified body that once belonged to you. Lose your body a few hundred times as a kid and a reservoir of pain and rage starts to build up inside you.

The ramifications of all this became apparent in the transition between my reel and real lives. My heroes were white, just as my father's heroes had been. But I wasn't allowed to "pass" like Anthony Quinn and play an exotic ethnic role (Zorba, let's say) more palatable to mainstream American culture. That culture, I would slowly discover, wanted me to play a "dirty" outsider: if not the greaser, the Latin Lover; if not the Latin Lover, the revolutionary, or, these days, the narco-terrorist. (I was recently detained at Los Angeles International Airport because I fit the description of a drug dealer: "Tall Hispanic in a dark suit.")

My first experiences of being relegated to the outsider role resulted from my early romantic failures. In the tenth grade, I had a terrible crush on a blond-haired, blue-eyed girl named Gloria. She had braces. Her best friend, Kitty, was the object of desire of every straight boy at Marshall High. Gloria wasn't exactly homely, but she didn't hold a match next to Kitty's smoldering, Brigitte Bardot–like sensuality. A common thing in school society: the hottest kids always have an entourage of less handsome kids floating about them, whose job it is to hold a mirror up to the prince or princess.

Like Gloria to Kitty, I was an underling to one Michael Delaney, who was quite short but had remarkable green eyes and a "cute" (as the girls said) freckled face beneath a mop of jet-black hair. A curious thing about Michael. He was Irish-Mexican. Clearly, his looks leaned towards his Irish father. But Michael's mom had bequeathed him quite a bit of the maternal culture. It was Michael who first taught me to play Mexican romantic ballads on the guitar. I was taking lessons at the time, but I was intent on becoming a bluegrass legend, true to the "western" part of my upbringing.

Michael was from a poorer neighborhood where more Mexicans lived, and he sometimes lapsed into *pocho*-speak (a slang combining English and Spanish), which was a revelation to me, since I'd grown up in a family where we were intravenously fed *The Brady Bunch* and *The Partridge Family* on the tube.

At any rate, Michael fell for Kitty, and I for Gloria. He was french-kissing Kitty in the hallway within a matter of days. I, on the other hand, held marathon telephone sessions with Gloria, playing the "friend," since I'd never had a girlfriend— never even kissed a girl before—and I was terrified of rejection. Michael soon advised me to take the plunge or else risk being stuck in the platonic forever. So one night after school, he and I walked to our favorite phone booths down at the Mayfair Market (which stood on a lot that had once been home to Disney Studios). He dropped in the dime to call Kitty, and I, heart pounding, dialed Gloria's number to ask her to go steady.

Amazingly, I'd never considered the possibility that a white girl like Gloria wouldn't date a Mexican. Kitty could date Michael Delaney; he was only half Mexican and of course he didn't play up his Mexican half around her. (He saved that part of himself for me.) Me, I couldn't play down my Mexican-ness. I wore it on my brown (not tan, not copper, but brown) skin.

Through my first sixteen years, I'd done everything I could to become white, from plucking a five-string banjo to buying Beach Boys albums. I went to the beach quite often—always to the "white" beach at Santa Monica, staying away from the pier, where the Mexicans, who were usually too poor to have bathing trunks and swam in their shorts and sometimes even their underwear, hung out. But after a long day in the sun I'd come home and notice my skin, which was no longer just brown, but verging on *chocolate.* I clearly remember one time standing in the shower with a bar of Irish Spring soap, scrubbing as hard as I could, raking nails across skin, hoping to soften the darkness.

Gloria never came out and said she'd never date a Mexican; indeed, the thought may never even have crossed her mind. And yet, I hadn't stopped to notice that there wasn't a single interracial couple on the entire campus, except for a few Anglo-Asian pairings (always white boy and Asian girl; never the other way around). Actually, it didn't dawn on me that the race issue even existed until long after the sting of Gloria's rejection had faded. It was the twelfth grade and I had another crush, on a girl whose name I can't remember, but I'll call her Cybill, because I swear she was the Cybill Shepherd of John Marshall High with her silky blond hair, perfect teeth, and magnificent body. I waited the entire year to get the nerve to speak to her. It was at the last dance of the spring, and even then I waited till a couple of minutes before midnight before finally walking up to her. I crossed the gymnasium in slow motion, my body feeling strangely light; she stood on the other side of the mid-court line, bathed in pulsating disco oranges and reds, surrounded by her entourage of girls with glasses and tiny breasts. I don't think she saw me until I was a yard away from her, from where I asked her to dance. She stared at me expressionless for a moment, and then, loud enough for her lackeys to hear (loud enough to bounce her voice off the gymnasium walls, it seemed to me at the time) she said, "With *you?*" To this day, I cannot ask a girl who is not my date to dance.

I looked around me at the dance floor with new eyes: Mexicans danced with Mexicans, blacks with blacks, whites with whites. Who the hell did I think I was? Still, it would take a while for the gringo-hater in me to bust out.

> **mestizo** (mĕ stē′ zō) *n., pl.* **mestizos** or **mestizoes.** A person of mixed racial ancestry, especially of mixed European and Native American ancestry.

It was only a matter of time before I turned away from my whiteness and became the ethnic rebel. It seemed like it happened overnight, but it was the result of years of pent-up rage in me. No matter how hard I tried to live out my "colorless" fantasies, deep inside, in some corner of my psyche where it is difficult for the pain to find words, much less ideas, I always sensed my outsider status and yearned to fit in, completely, somewhere.

History helped me. A civil war broke out in my mother's El

Salvador, a cause that I became quite involved in (just short of running arms). In my early twenties, I traveled incessantly through Mexico and Central America. I relearned Spanish (came to speak it without an accent as a matter of fact—damned if I was going to be the outsider among my "own people"), penned anti-gringo manifestoes, betrayed Whitman for Roque Dalton (the great Salvadoran revolutionary poet), and, of course, started dating Latinas. After so many years trying to play the Cowboy, I wholeheartedly took the role of the Indian.

And Hollywood, bless its liberal soul, was right there for me. Oliver Stone romanced the revolution with *Salvador,* Gene Hackman discovered the terrible truth in Nicaragua, and even Jack Lemmon had a run-in with the fascists in South America.

Yeah, sure, all the movies told the story through gringo eyes, but at least the story was being told—*my* story.

My story?

The irony of the first twenty-five years of my life was that at first I, a kid born to a Mexican father and a Salvadoran mother, was convinced I was white and that later I, the erstwhile white kid, renounced gringo-ness to become Latino. Both were fantasies, beautiful lies, Hollywood constructs.

The truth was that I was always both, that dreaded ambiguity—and how Hollywood hates ambiguity! For to say that I am both is not a simple thing. What is American in me, what is Latino? Let's try the American: my Jewishness, my blackness, my Asian-ness, my Scandinavian-ness, my immigrant-ness. And how about the Latino: Indian-ness, Iberian-ness, creole-ness, African-ness. Many Chicanos, a community with which I have a hate-love relationship, describe their identity crisis as a simple north-south paradigm, gringo and Mexican,

English and Spanish, rich and poor. As if Chicano would be Chicano (or white, white, or Asian, Asian) in America without the cultural rock at the center of it all: the black. Practically every Chicano aesthetic (oldies, lowriders, graffiti) is the result of at least a collaboration with, if not a downright plagiary of, African American culture. But don't expect to hear that in Chicano Studies courses or, for that matter, in Western Civ. The irony is that Americans (and here I speak of all the races and ethnicities) have always prided themselves on their exceptionalism. Here was a country without Old World or Third World nationalism ("Patriotism is the last refuge of a scoundrel"). But what is segregation if not an internal form of nationalism?

Some years ago, at a point where I was beginning to tire of the binary notion of cultural identity, I wrote a poem that included the line "I am much more than two," aping, of course, our bawdy bard, Whitman ("I am large, I contain multitudes"). And thus began what I see as the third phase of my cultural maturation, in which I'm exploring the interconnectedness of it all.

Looking back on my youth today, things don't look as white as I once believed them to be, the color lines not as fast. The Virgin of Guadalupe was always there, right alongside my *Brady Bunch* visions. For Latinos, this is certainly not a new state of affairs. Mestizo is just another word for mixed—very mixed—race. Perhaps the one thing the Cowboys and the Indians (gringos and Mexicans) have in common is their denial of the complexity of their identities. It strikes me that the story of America's past and present segregation is all the more ironic, and tragic, for the way that the colors really do bleed into one another (I mixed that metaphor on purpose), and have done so all along.

It certainly was so in the Martínez household. My parents were quite the partiers when they were young. Dancing cha-cha-cha and cumbia at our house were many of my mother's friends, mostly women from El Salvador, who'd married, almost all of them, American Anglo men. The women would chatter in Spanish and the men would joke about those crazy Latinas, like *I Love Lucy* with the gender roles reversed, even as their hips struggled with the tropical rhythms. The men's superficial banter, a mild and mostly benign form of racism, masked the complex process that was occurring. What of the children of these marriages? What of my own mother and father, the Salvadoran and the Mexican American, and the negotiation of their influences on their kids?

There is something innately comic about communication between two cultures that see each other as exotic, a humor that has both its light and its dark side. We laugh at how difficult the simplest things become, even as it is obvious that there is a power struggle occurring. Ideally, the power is divided equally and both sides become the richer for it. But often cultural influences can be democratically sorted out—we can dance to each other's musics, eat each other's foods—without a negotiation of any power beyond the aesthetic realm. This is why African American culture is undeniably America's most powerful while African Americans themselves don't have political or economic power proportionate to their numbers. It's called racism.

And so I can celebrate what I feel to be my cultural success. I've taken the far-flung pieces of myself and fashioned an identity beyond that ridiculous, fraying old border between the United States and Mexico, that line so important to the nativists. I am not the "melting pot," nor do I feel myself to be the "chunky stew" (the in-vogue term which hints, however slightly, at segregation). I am both Cowboy and Indian.

But my "success" is still marked by anxiety, a white noise that disturbs whatever raceless utopia I might imagine. I feel an uneasy tension between all the colors, hating and loving them all, perceiving and speaking from one and many perspectives simultaneously. The key word here is "tension": nothing, as yet, has been resolved. My body is both real and unreal, its color both confining and liberating.

The Hollywood kid in me still yearns for the happy ending. And there are clear signs that some fundamental things are changing. My family was quite the anomaly when I was growing up in Silver Lake: middle-class Mexicans weren't very common back then. Over the years, my neighborhood has grown increasingly mixed. The new immigrants move in alongside the old; Mexico and Central America move into black, white, and Asian enclaves. I don't have to leave Silver Lake to visit Mexico, El Salvador, China, or Vietnam. They have come to Silver Lake.

It is a demographic change taking place all over the United States, in every major city and even in the formerly all-white or black-white rural towns. Last spring I undertook a journey across the United States, my first cross-country trip, to research the phenomenon of Mexican migration and its impact on both the "native" and the "foreign" culture. The trip was my first foray into the "heartland" of America. As I drove through the plains of East Texas on I-30 toward Texarkana, an old fear rose up in me. Would I be welcome in Mayberry, or would the good ol' boys see me as some kind of furriner?

My cultural survival strategy in Texas, Arkansas, Kentucky, North Carolina, Illinois, Missouri, and Wisconsin was the same as it had been all these years: when in Rome, *talk* like the Romans. Language is a powerful thing, something I learned intuitively early on. With accents gleaned from the likes of John Wayne, James Dean (*Giant*), and even Billy Bob Thornton, I got along well enough. But in doing so, wasn't I just denying my body once again, silently laughing at my inner Pedro Armendáriz?

At times, I felt, or imagined that I felt, that old joy of being colorless again (being a journalist with a sophisticated-looking broadcast-quality tape recorder and microphone also helps soften the color separation, since my relationship to the media—which are, of course, mostly white—comes before the color of my skin). And then I'd be back, smack in the middle of America's segregation-integration wars. In Texas, some poor white guys straight out of the pen complained about the "niggers." A black street-maintenance worker in Arkansas protested the "sneakiness" of latter-day white racism. And the Mexicans, who are all over the map on matters of race (and who, I suppose, saw me as one of their own), spoke schizophrenically of desiring white girls and hating white bosses and sympathizing with blacks and thinking blacks are just a bunch of welfare freeloaders.

In the end, my journey showed me that playing the Cowboy wasn't enough, that the Indian was just as important. Mestizo, that culture chameleon born centuries before Boy George, is the essence of my role. Among the Dominicans of Washington, D.C., the Nigerians of New York, and the very particular kind of Americans that are the descendants of Scandinavians in the upper Midwest, I discovered parts of myself that were both new and old. The mestizo in me needs to embrace—appropriate, I mean—every influence it encounters, not to recall that I was conquered but that I *survived*. The Indian wears a Cowboy hat, but is no less the Indian for that fact; the Indian is ever becoming. It's probably the greatest lesson my father ever taught me—even if I had to laugh at Pedro Armendáriz to get it.

A postscript from my American tour: In Norwalk, Wisconsin, a tiny town where everyone is employed by the local meat-packing plant, Mexican immigrants now make up half the population. At first, tensions dominated the relations between the Mexicans and the Mennonite, Amish, and Plain Christian stock. But in the matter of a few years, dozens of Mexican men became romantically involved with local white girls. The white girls began liking *norteña* music, the Mexican boys walked down Main Street with heavy metal buzzing in their Walkman earphones. Recently, a bunch of sandy-haired, golden-skinned babies have been born, speaking a Spanglish patois—a new kind of Chicano. Because everybody is poor in Norwalk (except for the white owner of the meat-packing plant, an important detail), race is somewhat less of an issue in terms of power, though gender (machismo and its discontents) is a battlefield.

This is the future. America is becoming a mestizo nation.

Today, I live in the Mojave Desert. It's a long story, one that I won't tell here. Suffice to say that it's a place where mostly poor people of every color come, to forget, in some way or another, where they came from. Kind of like immigrants. Me, I remember where I came from all too well out here. In the black, brown, yellow, and white faces, I see Silver

Lake and El Salvador and Mexico. And more than ever before, I feel at home. For that's the redemption for someone who's played the role of the outsider for so many years: if you're an exile long enough, eventually you'll be at home wherever you are.

INTERIOR NIGHT, MOJAVE DESERT.

Writer again at the wobbly desk. Snow-capped desert peaks in the distance.

MONTAGE SEQUENCE:

Writer as a tot posing for the camera, sitting astride a pony, dressed in cowboy hat, cow-print vest, and chaps.

Writer at about nine years, sitting before the tube, giggling (with what the Buddhists call the "laughter of recognition") at one of Ricky's Spanish-language tantrums.

Thirteen-year-old writer playing "Dueling Banjos" on an authentic five-string banjo (not long after seeing *Deliverance,* one of the first "adult" movies he ever saw).

Junior high school writer imitating John Wayne's voice to a crowd of white classmates who burst into laughter (it is unclear whether they are laughing *with* him or *at* him).

Writer in high school, awkwardly attempting a Mexican ballad on guitar, Irish-Mexican friend helping him finger the chords.

Writer dancing, in a wet dream, with Cybill Shepherd.

Writer, twentysomething, declaiming anti-gringo verse before an audience of enraptured Salvadoran revolutionaries and weepy gringo liberals.

Writer, thirtysomething, walking the teeming streets of Mexico City, an Indian among Indians, remembering his father's and his grandfather's footsteps.

RAPID CUTS:

Writer stealing kisses from white, black, yellow, brown women and men.

WE FREEZE on the last kiss, with a white man. Brown and white—you may imagine Pedro Armendáriz and John Wayne—separate and, at arm's length, regard each other with looks that reveal myriad emotions: desire, loathing, tenderness, shock, etc.

WE SLOWLY DISSOLVE back to the desk and a CLOSEUP of the computer screen again. These words appear:

I am in between, and beyond, colors.

FADE TO BLACK.

AN ETHNIC TRUMP

Gish Jen

That my son, Luke, age four, goes to Chinese-culture school seems inevitable to most people, even though his father is of Irish descent. For certain ethnicities trump others; Chinese, for example, trumps Irish. This has something to do with the relative distance of certain cultures from mainstream American culture, but it also has to do with race. For as we all know, it is not only certain ethnicities that trump others but certain colors: black trumps white, for example, always and forever; a mulatto is not a kind of white person, but a kind of black person.

And so it is, too, that my son is considered a kind of Asian person whose manifest destiny is to embrace Asian things.

The Chinese language. Chinese food. Chinese New Year. No one cares whether he speaks Gaelic or wears green on Saint Patrick's Day. For though Luke's skin is fair, and his features mixed, people see his straight black hair and "know" who he is.

But is this how we should define ourselves, by other people's perceptions? My husband, Dave, and I had originally hoped for Luke to grow up embracing his whole complex ethnic heritage. We had hoped to pass on to him values and habits of mind that had actually survived in both of us.

Then one day, Luke combed his black hair and said he was turning it yellow. Another day, a fellow mother reported that her son had invited all blond-haired children like himself to his birthday party. And yet another day, Luke was happily scooting around the Cambridge Common playground when a pair of older boys, apparently brothers, blocked his way. "You're Chinese!" they shouted, leaning on the hood of Luke's scooter car. "You are! You're Chinese!" So brazen were these kids that even when I, an adult, intervened, they continued to shout. Luke answered, "No, I'm not!"—to no avail; it was not clear if the boys even heard him. Then the boys' mother called to them from some distance away, outside the fence, and though her voice was no louder than Luke's, they left obediently.

Behind them opened a great, rippling quiet, like the wash of a battleship.

Luke and I immediately went over things he could say if anything like that ever happened again. I told him that he was 100 percent American, even though I knew from my own childhood in Yonkers that these words would be met only with derision. It was a sorry chore. Since then, I have not asked him about the incident, hoping he has forgotten about it, and wishing that I could, too. For I wish I could forget the sight of those kids' fingers on the hood of Luke's little car. I wish I could forget their loud attack, but also Luke's soft defense: No, I'm not.

Chinese-culture school. After dozens of phone calls, I was elated to discover the Greater Boston Chinese Cultural Association nearby in West Newton. The school takes children at three, has a wonderful sense of community, and is housed in a center paid for, in part, by great karaoke fund-raising events. (Never mind what the Japanese meant to the Chinese in the old world. In this world, people donate at least two hundred dollars each for a chance at the mike, and the singing goes on all night.) There are even vendors who bring home-style Chinese food to sell after class—stuff you can't get in a restaurant. Dave and I couldn't wait for the second class, and a chance to buy more bao for our freezer.

But in the car on the way to the second class, Luke announced that he didn't want to go to Chinese school anymore. He said that the teacher talked mostly about ducks and bears and that he wasn't interested in ducks and bears. And I knew this was true. I knew that Luke was interested only in whales and ships. And what's more, I knew we wouldn't push him to take swimming lessons if he didn't want to, or music. Chinese school was a wonderful thing, but there was a way in which we were accepting it as somehow nonoptional. Was that right? Hadn't we always said that we didn't want our son to see himself as more essentially Chinese than Irish?

Yet we didn't want him to deny his Chinese heritage, either. And if there were going to be incidents on the playground, we wanted him to know what Chinese meant. So when Luke said again that he didn't really want to go to Chinese school, I said, "Oh, really?" Later on, we could try to teach him to define himself irrespective of race. For now, though, he was going to Chinese school. I exchanged glances with Dave. And then together, in a most carefully casual manner, we squinted at the road and kept going.

ABOUT THE AUTHORS

Julia Álvarez is originally from the Dominican Republic, but emigrated to the United States with her parents at the age of ten. She is the author of three novels, *How the García Girls Lost Their Accents, In the Time of the Butterflies,* and *¡Yo!,* and two books of poems, *Homecoming* and *Their Other Side.* She teaches literature and creative writing at Middlebury College.

Meri Nana-Ama Danquah, a native of Ghana, is the author of the memoir *Willow Weep for Me: A Black Woman's Journey Through Depression.* Her home is in Los Angeles.

Roxane Farmanfarmaian is the author of *Blood and Oil: Memoirs of a Persian Prince.* She was born in Salt Lake City, Utah, and grew up in Holland. She lived in Iran during the Khomeini revolution, during which time she founded *The Iranian,* an independent weekly news magazine. She has written for the *New York Times, Time* magazine, the *Christian Science Monitor, USA Today,* the London *Times,* and *Mirabella.* She lives in West Marlin, California, and is currently West Coast editor of *Publishers Weekly.*

Indira Ganesan was born in Srirangam, India. She was educated at Vassar College and the University of Iowa, and now teaches in the English department at South Hampton College. She is the author of two novels, *The Journey,* for which she was a finalist in *Granta's* Best Young American Novelists, and *Inheritance.*

Malcolm Gladwell was born in England and raised in Canada. He is a 1984 graduate in history from the University of Toronto. He spent nine years with the *Washington Post* as a business and science writer and finally as the paper's New York bureau chief. He has been a staff writer for the *New Yorker* since 1996 and is currently at work on his first book, titled *The Tipping Point.* He lives in Manhattan.

Francisco Goldman's short fiction and journalism have been published in many magazines, including *Harper's, Esquire,* the *New York Times Magazine,* and other publications. He is the author of *The Long Night of White Chickens* and *The Ordinary Seaman.* His home is in New York and Mexico.

Garrett Hongo is a poet born in Hawai'i, and raised there and in Los Angeles. He is currently a professor at the University of Oregon at Eugene, where he lives with his family. He has written two volumes of poetry, *Yellow Light* and *The River of Heaven,* and is the author of the memoir *Volcano.* He is also editor of *The Open Boat: Poems from Asian America* and *Under Western Eyes: Personal Essays From Asian America.*

Gish Jen's work has appeared in numerous magazines, including the *Atlantic Monthly* and the *New Yorker,* and in over fifty anthologies, including *Best American Short Stories 1988* and *1996.* She is the author of two novels, *Typical American* and *Mona in the Promised Land.* Jen graduated from Harvard and has taught at Tufts, at the University of Massachusetts, and in Jonan, China. She and her husband and her four-year-old son live in Cambridge, Massachusetts.

lê thi diem thúy was born in South Vietnam. She and her father left Vietnam in 1978, by boat, eventually settling in Southern California. The rest of her family followed a few years later. Lê is a writer and a solo performance artist, and her first book, *The Gangsters We Are All Looking For*, is forthcoming from Knopf.

Rubén Martínez is an Emmy Award–winning journalist, poet, and performer. He is an editor for the Pacific News Service and a guest commentator on National Public Radio's *All Things Considered*. His work has appeared in the *New York Times,* the *Los Angeles Times,* the *Village Voice,* the *Nation, LA Weekly,* and *SPIN,* among other publications. Martínez is a professor of journalism at Claremont McKenna College, and he teaches in the Chicano studies department of the University of California at Santa Barbara. He is the author of *The Other Side: Notes from the New L.A., Mexico City and Beyond* and is currently at work on his second book, about the changing landscape of U.S./Mexican border cultures.

James McBride is a writer, composer, and saxophonist. He is the author of *The Color of Water: A Black Man's Tribute to His White Mother* and an upcoming biography of Quincy Jones. He is married, with two children, and lives in South Nyack, New York.

Nina Mehta is a free-lance book critic and journalist in New York. She spent her childhood in Bombay and has lived since then in New Jersey, Connecticut, and New York. She is currently writing a book about modern arranged marriage in Western countries.

Bharati Mukherjee was born in Calcutta. She became an American citizen in 1988 and is now a professor of English at the University of California at Berkeley. Mukherjee is the author of six novels, *The Tiger's Daughter, Wife, Darkness, Jasmine, The Holder of the World,* and *Leave It to Me,* and a book of short stories, *The Middleman and Other Stories* (which won the National Book Critics Circle Award in 1989).

David Mura is a poet, creative nonfiction writer, critic, playwright, and performance artist. A Sansei, or third-generation Japanese American, Mura has written two memoirs: *Turning Japanese: Memoirs of a Sansei,* which won a 1991 Josephine Miles Book Award from the Oakland PEN and was listed in the *New York Times* Notable Books of the Year; and *Where the Body Meets Memory: An Odyssey of Race, Sexuality, and Identity.*

Lisa See is the author of *On Gold Mountain* and a novel, *The Flower Net.* She has been the West Coast correspondent for *Publishers Weekly* and lives in California.

Danzy Senna has worked as a journalist for *Newsweek* and *SPIN* magazines. She is the author of a novel, *Caucasia.* She currently lives in New York.

Lori Tsang was raised by a Chinese Jamaican mother and an American Chinese father in Connecticut and Indiana, and currently lives in Washington, D.C. She has appeared at the Nuyorican Poets' Café, the Whitney Museum, the Library of Congress, and various other poetry/performance series and venues. Her chapbook, *Circumnavigation,* is in its third printing, and her poems have been published in *dISorient, The Drumming Between Us, Controlled Burn, WordWrite,* the *Journal of Asian American Renaissance,* and the *Asian Pacific American Journal.*

Philippe Wamba is currently working on his first book, a memoir on relations between Africans and African Americans, due to be published in 1999 by Dutton. He lives in Manhattan.